AF521660

SAMSON

By the same author

Adam
The Man Who Did
Gurkhas

SAMSON

David Bolt

St. Martin's Press • New York

St. Martin's Press, Inc., 175 Fifth Avenue, New York, N.Y. 10010.
Manufactured in the United States of America

Library of Congress Cataloging in Publication Data

Bolt, David Langstone, 1927-
Samson.

1. Samson, Judge of Israel–Fiction. I. Title.
PZ4.B693Sam 1980 [PR6003.0473] 823'.914 80-14715
ISBN 0-312-69848-8

Designed by Manuela Paul

For Sally

who walked with me
in the Vale of Sorek

Samson ben Manoah

c.1105 B.C.–c.1065 B.C.

SAMSON

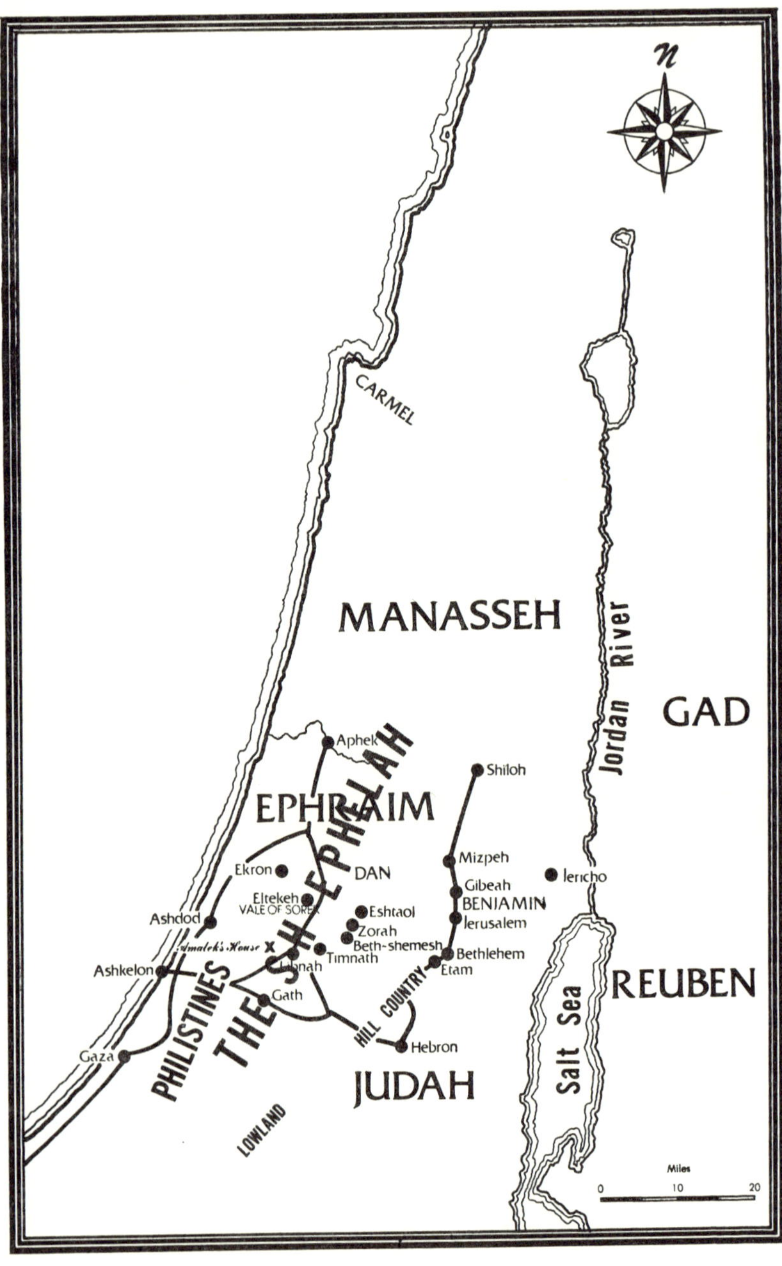

n
CARMEL
MANASSEH
Jordan River
GAD
Aphek
THE SHEPHELAH
Shiloh
EPHRAIM
Mizpeh
Ekron
DAN
Gibeah
Jericho
Eltekeh
VALE OF SOREK
BENJAMIN
Ashdod
Eshtaol
Jerusalem
Zorah
Amalek's House
Beth-shemesh
Timnath
Bethlehem
Ashkelon
Libnah
Etam
REUBEN
PHILISTINES
Gath
HILL COUNTRY
Salt Sea
Hebron
Gaza
JUDAH
LOWLAND
Miles
0
10
20

1

IN THE NOON FACE of the sun god Shemesh, a carrion eagle hung on the numb air, over against the shadowed ridges of the Judaean mountains. It tilted to a slow descent of the invisible bypaths of the sky, high over the dusty evergreen oaks and barren stonecrops of the foothills called *Shephelah,* the country below. It planed down to race its own shadow arrowing black on white across the flat rooftops of Zorah, and soared like a slingshot to hover again, scanning the broken ground below the refuse heaps at the edge of the village, where there was something recognizably the remains of a man. But it would not alight because of the child.

He stood at the edge of the cattle track, still clutching in his fist the metal icon he had come down the hillside to retrieve: a boy still as a tree, more dwarf oak than sapling, grown wild in the hills and burned all summer browns. A scrap of blue linen, armless and girdled with hemp, was his only garment. A twist of the same cloth sheafed the thickness of his hair behind solid shoulders. He was planted on one leg, stork-fashion, the bare foot curled about his shin in an agony of indecision. The dead man lay in a cleft between rocks, as if felled by an unimaginable blow that had left little more than a heap, nowhere resembling the natural order of flesh and bone; but he seemed to be face down. So the boy was not yet sure who he was. It was the flies that had brought him to the place.

The boy was of the religious order of Nazirites, and forbidden to approach a dead body. He lowered his foot and listened, turning his head but not his eyes, his ears cocked like a cub's. They told him that the other children were still at their game, up beside the ash heaps; no one had followed him down. The sun was like a hand pressing on his head.

He was aware of the eagle; aware of fat-tailed sheep just moving among scrub on the far side of the valley, which were his father's; a few lop-eared goats kept back from the flocks for the villager larder, listless in the heat. Nothing else moved under the sky.

And then the eagle's shadow was gone. He saw the gods in the same moment; almost before he turned his head.

They were coming out of the tree shadows on his left hand, two gods and a third behind them. The boy urinated down his leg. He slid his foot sideways and went like a crab, but they caught him easily, three giants of burning brass, plumed like no eagles he had ever seen, their shields like millstones, their spears taller than trees; his arm paralyzed in their grasp still clutching the precious icon.

"How came this man by his death?"

Even if he had known, he could not have freed his tongue; but he had the wit not to look up. Everyone knows if you look on the face of a god you are good as dead. He concentrated on their legs, which were bronze plated with greaves, kilted with a milky weave that hung to a point between the knees, heavy with metal strips sewn crosswise in front, where a man is most vulnerable, so perhaps a god also; which also bordered the skirt. It was their breast armor that had caught the sun. They had daggers attached to their upper arms; which the boy knew were daggers; though he had never seen a dagger before.

"Where is your village?"

His head was jerked back by a fistful of hair and his neckbone cracked audibly. Through a haze of pain his eyes focused on faces beardless as his own; yet men's faces, the three all turned in question toward him, carved of the light sandstone, straight of nose and brow under the fantastic red and white plumage of their helmets, all alike and not like men at all. They spoke among themselves in an unearthly tongue like shallow water over rocks; but he understood the words, and that they had lost their way. He tried to speak, and they waited.

"My *arm!*"

They were surprised into mirth. "The cub has a tongue!" But they released his arm, with the icon. "Come, cub, waggle your tongue while you can. The Lord Athol is coming, and he is not patient like us. He will cut your tongue out, and your bowels too, and throw you on the garbage with your friend if you don't answer quick. How do they call you?"

The boy stammered it: "Samson."

"Shemeson," the man translated: "son of Shemesh."

They drew aside and he passed between them, a thin cornstalk of a man, pale-skinned and beardless like the gods, the baldness of his skull relieved by a white band embroidered with silver. His robe was of cotton so fine it was almost transparent, his sandals the soft yellow leather of the camel. But it was the young girl beside him who held the boy's eyes. Even his awe of the gods was forgotten. Like the man she wore a fine headband, but of gold, encircling short hair the weave and color of ripe barley. The yellow of her cloak rippled with every motion like sunlit waters, gathered in a jeweled sash. She wore gems in fiery clusters on her delicate fingers and thumbs, like a king's daughter. She in turn was gazing at him intently, a frown spoiling the tranquillity of her brow.

"Do not be afraid," the cornstalk man said. His face was human and not unkind, in spite of the gods' warning. "None shall harm you, little son of Shemesh."

With the ebbing of fear the boy sensed mockery, and bridled. "I am son of Manoah."

"Samson ben Manoah. You are from Beth-shemesh?" The man lifted a long finger toward the valley. He said to the princess, "We passed it just now by the way: where I pointed out the great temple to their sun god. No doubt the child is named in his honor." And to the boy again: "You are young to be abroad by yourself. These are wild parts." He glanced meaningfully at the flies. "What are you doing here?"

"It is my village."

But you could not see the houses for the oaks, and the rise of the terraces; only the black tent by itself above the olive groves, which was where the hermit Uzziel lived. It was a moment before the man understood. He asked the name of the village, and the boy told him, Zorah. He had to say it twice. It was evident that the wise man, who spoke the tongue of the gods and understood all about the temple of Beth-shemesh, knew nothing of Zorah. "Your people are not of the Canaanites?"

Samson shook his head, watching the princess take a small sachet on a chain about her neck and crush it under her crinkled nose; doubtless against the insistent smell of the corpse; but she was looking at the boy, and he lowered his head like a dog, still watching her through his lashes.

The man persisted. "Amorites? We did not look to find Amorites this far in from the sea coast." The princess replaced the sachet and yawned, turning her head to lisp something in their own tongue, to which the man replied privately, "Nevertheless, a ruler should learn something of the peoples he rules."

"Nobody rules *us,*" the boy said. "Except our god Yahweh."

They swung to stare at him in astonishment: his small face clouded with bewilderment and a fearful anger. The man's hand was like a yellow spider on his shoulder. "What tribe is this, that has no ruler?"

"Dan. My people are of Dan."

"Danites?" The man withdrew his hand. He searched his mind. "Hebrews, then."

But he used the word *Habiru,* which to plainsmen means any barbarians, and it ran through the little group like a wind through standing corn. The princess said it again—Habiru—turning round and walking up to Samson to examine him like some rare animal. Her shimmering cloak was so close he put out a finger involuntarily to touch it, and the next instant the sharp edge of a hand bloodied his face and sent him backside into the dust.

"Would you lay hands on the Lord Athol, cub!"

They twisted his arm until he was sure it would come away from his body, wrenching him over with casual cruelty to kneel before the supposed princess, his face in the dirt with a foot on his neck; more surprised than hurt. It was at Athol's lisped command that he was let up, wiping the blood and earth from his nose to see that the marvelous creature, for all the delicacy of feature, was indeed male.

"I like him," Athol announced. "See how black his eyes–and the brutish, scowling face he has! If I did not like you, little Hebrew, I would have your hand cut off, for touching me. Know that my father is *Ser* in Gaza: what you ignorant folk call king. If only you were more wholesome, I would take you back with me to warm my bed." He seemed to consider it. "A perfumed bath would get rid of the goat smell, I dare say." The old man said something in an undertone, remonstrating, and he shrugged. "But not now. We have to be back before nightfall, and there's no room for you. My tutor has a nervous disposition; and the others are waiting."

He put his jeweled fingers behind the boy's suddenly rigid neck and let them rest there, fingering the wild tresses of hair. "I will see you again, little Hebrew."

It was one of the gods who broke the silence. "What of the dead one?"

"It is not important."

Abruptly Athol turned away, the cornstalk man and the gods following. They went the way they had come, under the trees, without looking back, leaving the boy alone with the corpse. Presently there came the whinny of horses, and the grinding of chariot wheels on the unseen road.

Only then did the boy move. He shook himself like a swimmer emerging from the water, and rubbed his neck violently where the jeweled fingers had rested, as if it had been nettles. Temper erupted in him; he tore at grass tufts to wipe his hand clean and bruised it against a stone twice as big as his head, immovably embedded; and thwarted, turned his childish rage absurdly on the stone itself, calling aloud on his god like a man, for the first time in his life. It was more like a demon than a god that entered him, threatening to burst out of his chest; and then incredibly the stone came free. He lifted it, staggering, and swung himself madly round to launch it bounding mightily down the empty hillside. In his imagination it smashed the delicate skull of Prince Athol like an eggshell, and sent the yolk of his royal brains flying satisfactorily outward into the grass.

It was only when Samson saw the size of the hole from which the stone had been torn that he realized what he had done.

□

From the dim, fly-pestered oven of his doorway, the man Manoah had watched the children marking out their lines on the iron ground, his huge frame squat as a bear in its cave, and as amiable. He had himself fetched a goatskin from inside, there being neither wife nor servant available to fetch it for him, and had forgotten the necessary cushions; so there was nothing but the linen of his chalouk between his buttock and the scratchy hide. He sat cross-legged, talking to his god as a man will who has no friends.

"A husband who has no wife."

He ripped a sliver of wood from the rotting doorpost.

"A master who has no servant."

He began to pick his teeth morosely through the thicket of his beard, warming to the riddle. From where he sat he could see most of the village–there was not much of it: the houses scattered about the descending, cultivated terraces, haphazard among the vineyards and groves, their whitewash flaking in the sun, like building blocks thrown down from the destruction of the Tower of Babel. Little Zorah, and its sister village of Eshtaol, all that remained of the once great tribe of Dan of which he was chief.

"A chief who has no tribe."

The children were at the bottom end of the village, too far to discern, but a boy in him remembered the ritual: thirty open strides from marker stick to first line, a cubit between lines–a short cubit, measured with the child's forearm, the tallest child present. It had nearly always been Manoah. But he would no more have run off to play with the village children without first seeking leave of his parents than sit down to eat with unwashed hands.

"A father who has no son."

This was a monstrous thing to say, though it suited the riddle; and he shifted uneasily.

"Aye, well, you know he's more yours than mine, though it's my roof he sleeps under."

The hovel at his back was generations old: built by some long-dead Canaanite of the local stone, much patched and propped by Hebrew hands like all the houses; you could tell where the stones were not squared off like the Canaanite stone, only crammed into the gaps and botched with puddled clay. Manoah had done his best to see that the village buildings were kept in good repair, relentless with backsliders; but the tribe were too close to their tents to be much hand at masonry, even to this day. Nevertheless, it was a good house, with three rooms and proper stone steps outside up to the roof. Tents were for nomads nowadays, for shepherds in the hills and time of war. Only Uzziel the hermit–priest still kept to his tent above the village in Zorah.

If they had gone down two terraces lower they might have had shade of the first oaks for their play; but in the way of children and lunatics, never felt the heat. Now they squatted still as hares on the hillside. Their discarded kirtles mottled the ground with unseasonal colors, blue and orange, yellow and red, reminding Manoah of wildflowers when they are cut down and raked into heaps. A boy stood up in turn, kilted his tunic, and weighed a stone in his palm. It was evidently the crucial throw. Visible tension drew them back like bowstrings, every face toward the marker. A white butterfly zigzagged among them undisturbed. The stone caught the sun in flight, and sent up a puff of dust a hairsbreadth from the marking stick. Instantly the spell was loosed in a volley of cheering, the children on their feet like warriors into battle, their dancing shadows long and menacing.

"Warriors!" Manoah spat the wormwood of it between his feet in disgust. The last of the Danite warriors–children, and the shadows of children. Eighteen towns had Dan for an inheritance, from the Shephelah hills to the seacoast; until the Amorites with their bloody raids drove them back to the two towns only: Zorah and Eshtaol, on their twin hills insignificant as the breasts of a half-grown daughter. Somewhere in between, if a man went down into the empty plain to look

for them, he could still find under the cattle and sheep dung traces of the altars and hearths of the great camp of Mahanneh-dan, where the tribe had forgathered for the last time; and mourn.

Manoah's father was buried down there, with all the noisy ceremonial befitting a tribal chief; but it was not his father he mourned. The days of the great clan chiefs were over and gone.

"A strong arm, Lord." Manoah slapped his own with no pride. "A strong right arm and strong sons; that's all the law there is among your people now. It's all the young ones know."

It was from Mahanneh-dan, from this same high valley, that the tribe had sent out their five spies, up the Vale of Sorek into the mountains northward to seek out a new homeland.

It had been spring then, the new grasses blowing down the hillsides alive with the flowering of tulips and anemones, iris and cyclamen, and the many-colored standards and pennons of the clans fluttering bravely against the green hills, scattered among the multitude of tents–the six hundred fighting men, and twice their number of women, children, men too old to bear arms; there the great square tent of the congregation; and there the saffron robe of the young Levite priest, grandson of Moses himself, standing alone among the hurrying soldiers like one crocus among blown leaves; the glitter and flash of spearheads, the lowing, jostling cattle, the movement of sheep in their penned hurdles, the few camels, the ox wagons standing by under the blue sky–Manoah saw it all.

He saw the morning watch running, the day the spies returned down the mountain road with the first shafts of the sun, travel-stained with their long journey down the length of Israel from the unknown northlands; watched the men of Dan spill out of their tents like bees from a shaken hive swarming to hear tell of the new homeland, undefended and for the taking; heard the thrilling battle cry swell up from the valley to threaten the hills.

But it was only the children at play.

The carrion eagle was over the refuse heaps again,

searching as usual for a morsel overlooked by the hyenas during the night.

And then it came upon Manoah again with no warning, the dark of soul like a cold cloud across the sun: the familiar and terrible sense of having awakened in Zorah in the morning to find the tribe gone with the dew; to be left among the few, the old and the stubborn who stayed behind, clinging to their crops and hovels like jetsam on the shore when the tide has gone out: the Godforsaken Remnant of Dan, lapped by the incoming breakers of the Amorites and Canaanites then; and now threatened by the great wave of the Philistines from the sea itself.

Manoah reached blindly for the doorpost and pulled himself to his feet by main strength from a palsy of horror, shaking himself out of it like a wet dog. He called out once—*"Sharah!"*—and it was the boy's voice. All his strength was in the one hand holding the world still, his face pressed to the knuckles. The back of his hand tasted salty. *A wandering Aramaean was my father. And he went down into Egypt. . . .*

"My Lord?"

And sojourned there few in number, and became a great nation, mighty and populous. . . .

"Manoah is sick?"

"And the Egyptians evil entreated us," Manoah said aloud: "And afflicted us, and laid upon us hard bondage." He opened his eyes and Sharah was there, his wife with her arms to the elbows in flour.

She said, "And when we cried. . . . "

"And when we cried unto Yahweh Adonai, God of our fathers, he heard our voice. . . . " Manoah found her hand tentative on his arm, and crushed it in his own. Of course, she knew the prayer of the first fruits as well as he did himself. He let her hand go. "Aye, so he did, Sharah; he did once. But this is not Egypt."

"You have had the dream again," she said.

He nodded, not contradicting her, because although it was not a dream, he did not know what else it was. She had come in soundless haste from the back of the house in nothing but her old household shift, still kilted from her chores. But he felt better. His steadying gaze took in the altered landscape of her features: the remembered contours of her fine bones (for she was a Benjaminite) gentled to fullness, the slender stalk ripened to the bound sheaf, familiar to him as the Land itself. The innocence of her exposed flesh–standing there like a plump child, half-naked in her kilted shift–made him feel randy and ashamed, even now.

"I grow old, Sharah. You are right: an old man dreaming dreams."

She scoffed at this. "Two score years come next Passover. And the last hardly gone."

It was still far from young. But he had not meant *old* like Moses or Abraham; he had meant old out of his time, like a fly in winter. It was not something you could explain to a woman, and he dismissed her instead, with a small cuff to show it was not in displeasure. The children were shouting again, and he told her to fetch his son.

"It is too hot for him to be in the open."

Sharah had half gone, and turned. "Samson?"

"Who else?" He was going to say *in the name of Yahweh how many sons have I?* One. He thought she had gone to veil herself before going to fetch him; but she was still there.

She said, "You are not angry with him?"

"No."

"I said he could go."

Manoah paused in the act of fastening his sandal. "Aye, well, send Tamam if you like."

"Tamam is down at the well."

"She will be there all day gossiping," Manoah said, exasperated. "You are too easy on the girl, Sharah. In my father's day the pitchers were filled in the house before sun up, or there would be a whipping. You treat her more like a daughter than a slave."

And he said, "Why should I be angry with Samson?"

"I thought, if my lord sent to fetch the child, it must be in anger to chastise him," Sharah said.

Manoah was numbering the far children. He lost count, his shoulders stiffening in physical disbelief. God in Heaven. "*Adonai,* Lord"–he flung his palms to the sky in violent appeal–"Listen to her! Am I angry?" He beat the words into his skull with the heel of his hand. "Yes–I–am–angry. Be my witness! Have I once . . . since the day of his birth until now . . . lifted a hand to the child?"

Behind him Sharah said, "Neither in anger nor affection."

Manoah had his cloak in hand, and drew it close about him with dignity, isolating himself from the woman's temerity. He turned his face toward the olive grove. Herein is a new law which Moses never taught us, that the man shall grow tits and suckle his young. But he said it to himself, walking a little way up among the trees, peering to see if the olives were ready for the harvest, as he did every day. What manner of father took his son to his knee, except the lad was old enough for schooling? Sharah knew the custom as well as he; yet she let Samson run unshepherded among the village boys like any ordinary child. Manoah peered down the hill again. And the lads from Eshtaol. But even with the Eshtaolites, there were still too many by the ash heaps–from Beth-shemesh; they must have come over from Beth-shemesh.

"Canaanites!" Manoah roared.

Sharah had disappeared into the house, but he did not stop to look for her. He went down the hill like thunder, his sandals scattering the stones. The children turned their heads and scattered, some snatching up their kirtles to melt away into the trees. Manoah caught the nearest of those remaining by the thinness of his arm. "I'll have no Canaanites, no westerners in Zorah! Do you hear?"

"Yes sir."

"Where is Samson?

The boy looked about him, not knowing, and another pointed to the edge of the terrace where the track descended. "Sir, I saw him go down there."

Samson, who seldom walked when he could run and climbed like a goat, came now with dragging footsteps upstream through invisible waters. The blue of his tunic was lost behind an edge of rock, and so slow in reappearing that Manoah began to run. The boy lifted his head and saw him, and stopped.

He stood with his mouth open like an idiot. He has the sun sickness, Manoah thought: I warned Sharah. She never listens. He caught Samson as the boy half stumbled, mouthing words of which Manoah heard only *the dead man.* "There is no dead man, you have the sun dreams. What have you got in your hand?"

"Father there is a dead man in between the rocks, stinking."

"Show me."

Samson turned to point, and Manoah said, "Show me what you have in your hand."

It was an Astarte, a miniature figure of the local fertility goddess, fashioned obscenely out of the rare Philistine iron. Manoah held it like a turd in his fingers. "Do you know what this is?"

"It's my prize," Samson said, visibly more cheerful to remember it. "I won it, but the boy wouldn't give it to me. I wrestled him and beat him; but he threw it down the hill."

He held out his hand for the icon and Manoah drew his own hand back and hurled it almost as far as the lower tree line, silencing the boy's cry of vexation with one word:

"Filth!"

Samson had never seen his father so angry. He stepped back and nearly fell over.

"Anathema!" Manoah roared, his face black with rage. "An abomination, a blasphemy wrought by perverted, heathen hands–that's what it is! And you a Nazirite"–he lifted both hands together as if to crush Samson, but without touching him–"A Nazirite! Have you forgotten the vows we made for you?"

"I never touched it," Samson said, and shivered.

Manoah stared at him with mounting anger. All boys are liars, which is to say dreamers: but how can a boy say he has not touched a thing when his father takes it out of his hand? He said, quietening his voice with difficulty, "You are sick, child. Can you walk? Then go to your mother and lie indoors, out of the sun."

But Samson meant the corpse rotting between the rocks, and eventually Manoah understood this, and went on alone. He found the place as Samson had, by the massing of flies. Even before he turned the body he knew it was Heber the Hivite. Heber belonged to Nahor ben Beriah, a mean man, who had sent his servant down with the ox in the chill of morning in a rag of clothing and Manoah, preparing for the morning prayer on his rooftop, had tossed the man his own cloak against the cold. The cloak was still recognizable, the man barely so. The body looked as if it had been pierced through with blunt spears. So far as Manoah could make out, there was no mark on the ground but the usual tracks of men and cattle, though the path was too hard to be sure. In addition, the upper part of the remains was half-obliterated, as if by clubs.

Death, even violent death, was nothing uncommon in the Shephelah. Nevertheless, Manoah was troubled to find a man slain so close to Zorah, and in daylight. The silence made him uneasy. Lord, who would trouble to kill a poor Hivite–unless it was another, settling a personal score?

He had dispatched Samson to fetch the elders; knowing the whole village would come.

The young men came first, several bringing spears but most, Manoah noted in disgust, empty-handed, fierce in nothing but curiosity. When they saw it was a Hivite their interest waned. Manoah waved them aside, and they made a show of poking among the shrubs and boulders. Nothing else moved on the hillside under the sun. The women began to gather at a little distance, Samson there with Tamam, but Manoah disregarded them. The elders came last, led by old Eleazar, wheezing upon his staff and peering at Manoah with watery eyes for guidance. They saluted him and paused to consider the matter.

That it was murder was plain. Jethro, the father of six sons, was for sending the young men to search farther afield; but it was obvious the man had been dead for some hours: the cloak was dried stiff. Whoever attacked him could be over the hills and halfway to Jerusalem by now. "Unless," Eleazar suggested uncertainly, "he was from the villages."

This was serious: because if Heber had been slain by a Hebrew it was in breach of the Covenent of Joshua, and punishable by death.

Manoah was relieved half an hour later when a careful questioning of the men, then of the children who had been playing by the ash heaps, revealed nothing. Heber had no family or known attachments–he was thought to be a homosexual–and Manoah gave simple instructions for his burial, and the customary sacrifice of an unworked heifer, in token of the village's innocence. Mordecai, the youngest of the elders, showed little interest. He alone had come down without troubling to fetch his cloak, and stood like the boys in his brightly striped chalouk, scratching his pockmarked face and examining his fingernails. "I have ploughing to be done, if you have not." He grimaced when Manoah reminded him that they should have a priest; then gave a sharp laugh.

"A Levite?" he said incredulously. "Where shall we find a Levite?"

"There is Uzziel," Manoah said.

"That old fool? You would do better to make the sacrifice yourself."

It was not the first time Mordecai had spoken against him. Uzziel was said to be a hundred and fifteen years old, so feeble he scarcely set foot outside his black tent above the village since first they had pitched it there for him, three years before, when he came out of nowhere. The women took turns to tend to his meager needs, fearfully, because his mind wandered and they feared him mad. Few others visited him; Manoah himself no more than occasionally from a proper respect and duty. It was more stubbornness than reason that made him answer now: "Nevertheless, he is a Levite and a priest."

He turned his back to end the discussion and began to walk up the hill again, feeling suddenly stiff in his bones.

□

Although Uzziel's tent, like the village houses, was swept scrupulously clean, it had the smell of corruption about it, which emanated not from the man himself, as a casual visitor might suppose, but from the rotting scrolls of his library. The scraped, wafer-thin skins were stored carefully, along with his clay images and his threadbare robes, in the darkest corner of the tent; but the pots which once housed them had crumbled away years since in his travels; the air and the morning dews had done their work. It was a smell Uzziel himself was conscious of, but without offense to him. More offensive were the crude perfumes that preceded the village women when they came to bring his food and to clean: the cheap imitation nard made from some local plant;

cassia, and the heavy balm which lingered hours after they had left, though he had them leave the tent open at both ends. He preferred the honest smell of sweat; even the body's own decay. He neither complained nor commented, and kept its importance to himself. For smell was important to him.

It was the smell of the sea that had brought him down three years before to the Remnant of Dan: not the flat, unleavened smell of the Salt Sea but the remembered wind-blown spume of the Great Sea itself, beating in on the endless sand dunes. It had been many years since he had seen it. He had meant to die by the sea. But when he found himself on the edge of the wheatfields in Canaanite country, those with him from Ephraim had turned back. He could not go on alone, and so turned aside into Zorah by what an unthinking man would call chance. And in Zorah he heard of the boy Nazirite; and had stayed.

Manoah found him reclining as usual on his blankets, his emaciated frame curled like the old fox he resembled, peering at the tent door with his head to one side, for he relied more on sound than sight nowadays. "Manoah?"

"*Shalom alekh hem*," Manoah greeted him formally, and told him what had occurred, down to the condition of the body. "I'd not have known him but for the cloak. It was a man called—"

"Heber, Nahor's slave."

"Aye." Manoah's eyes widened. "How did you know?"

"A bird of the air," was the unhelpful answer. Uzziel appeared to be nodding off. "Ask a man *what* he knows, Manoah, never ask *how;* or no one will tell you anything." He opened one eye like an owl to inquire what arrangements Manoah had made.

Manoah told him, controlling his irritation, and the hermit nodded his approval; but at the suggestion that he should officiate as priest at the sacrifice, put up his hand, palm outward, like a man shielding himself from the heat of a fire. "Do not ask this, Manoah. I am not your priest; nor anyone's priest now. No more sacrifices."

His eyes turned inward, gone traveling somewhere in his mind. Then he said, "It is the law that a death before noon must be reported by sundown."

"It is Philistine law," Manoah said hotly. "We have no such law."

"As you say. But not all are as single-minded as you, Manoah. There are those who say any law is better than none." Uzziel's squint was sly. "I did not say I was among their number. The child Samson: he did not approach the body?"

"No."

"But you touched it."

"I, and I alone. And the slaves who took it down for burial."

"Come to me after three days and I will give you the water of purification."

"You will do this," Manoah said. "And yet you'll not come down for the sacrifice of the heifer."

Uzziel might have been asleep; even dead. His head had fallen altogether to one side, his mouth an open hole. But he sucked in his bald gums and sneezed. "Your village butcher will do it well enough." The change in Manoah's breathing lifted his head. "Does that offend you?"

"Aye it does. We're not talking of butchering for a feast. We are talking of atonement for one man's blood spilled by another."

"We are?" Uzziel's head drooped, but he went on talking to himself as if he had forgotten. "A man who speaks without knowledge is like . . . What is he like, Manoah? I forget. I forget so much these days."

"An ass that brays," Manoah said. "What does that mean?"

"It means you have examined every witness already except the one witness who can tell you the truth."

"What witness is that?"

"The ox," Uzziel said wearily. "The ox."

They were interrupted by the arrival of a group of villagers. They had found the ox, Nahor's stud, in among the sheep, spectacularly bloodied on hoof and horn. Plainly Heber had been gored and trampled to death by his own charge. The ox would now be stoned to death for the murder and there was an end to it.

When they had gone Manoah said, "You *knew.*"

He stopped himself in time from asking how. But Uzziel

might not have heard. "Poor Nahor. First he loses a slave, then the prize stud he was so proud of. And the heifer besides, for the sacrifice. Now tell me what you climbed the hill to say to me."

Manoah was startled. "Answer me this–

"A husband who has no wife.

"A master who has no servant.

"A chief who has no tribe.

"A father who has no son."

The hermit settled back to consider it, thoroughly awake now. His love of riddles was well known. He said after a moment, "Adam. Am I right?"

"Aye," Manoah lied, relieved. He already regretted the impulse that had loosed his tongue. "Adam."

"The first man, before Eve was made. . . . a husband with no wife. Master of all living creatures, but none servant to him. Chief, he was chief of the twelve tribes to come . . . father of every child yet to be conceived." Uzziel looked pleased with himself. "Have you told anyone else this riddle?"

"No."

"Why do you think you have no son?"

Manoah had seated himself on the ground opposite Uzziel, and unclenched his hands in defeat. "I have been thinking of nothing else all day since morning. God forgive me, Uzziel, I have been wishing for a son like other men's sons. A boy as I was. That's all we ever wanted–a boy child. We never asked for more. Who am I?–or Sharah, who is she? We are simple folk, we have no knowledge of these things."

And he said gloomily, "You think the time has come? For me to tell him?"

The old priest nodded.

"Sharah thinks so too," Manoah said. "She doesn't say so, but it's in her eyes, all the time. I have no peace of her. And now this death on our hands. Thank God it was only"– He was going to say *a slave,* but remembering Uzziel's unexplained familiarity with Heber, changed it to–"the ox."

"How much does the boy know?"

"Nothing. The Nazirite vows we took for him, that's all."

"He knows more," Uzziel said gently. "The elders know. They have sons. Have you forgotten how cruel children can be?"

"He can look after himself."

"It is time you took him from his mother."

"He's over young for schooling."

"He is bright."

"Aye." Manoah hesitated, for this was the moment he had been most dreading. "I've been thinking all along how I should teach him . . . well, I've told him stories of course, as my father told me. But I'm not one for the reading and writing. . . ."

"Send him to me, if you wish."

It was what Manoah had wanted the priest to say, and had hoped he would not.

At the tent door he said, "Aye, I'll do that."

□

Samson moved along the side of the tent as his father came out. When Manoah had gone, he slipped inside. Uzziel listened to his story as Manoah had not, and said, "It was the ox," and the boy nodded.

"I knew it was. When I saw the signs on the ground, I knew."

But he had said nothing; knowing it, and then not sure when they began to go about searching for the murderer. He had liked the idea of a murder better.

Samson found a figure among the old man's treasures, something like the icon Manoah had taken from him, but crudely made. It was not particularly male or female.

Uzziel said, "Tell me again of the gods."

Samson told him, hugging his knees on the tent floor. He showed the mark where the god's hand had struck him, guiding the old man's fingers to it; when he had gone to touch the supposed princess. The priest heard him out with no comment, even when Samson described the gods as men of iron with eagles' heads that touched the sky; for so they must have appeared to the child. "Nobody rules *us,*" he repeated when Samson had finished; and chuckled. "To say that to a god requires unusual courage."

He motioned the boy closer and took his arm. "It is good to be courageous. But courage without caution is like running in the dark. You must take care. It might have gone ill with you if the Egyptian had not been there. His name is Ptullis. He was brought back from the last battle, it is said, to be slave companion to the present king, the Ser; then he became tutor to his son, the boy Athol. Men of iron they are, Samson, but not gods: they are the sea peoples, who came to the Land in ships from across the Great Sea: the Philistines." And he said, more to himself, "Philistines in the Shephelah! It is the beginning of the end." He asked Samson if he had told his father, and the boy shook his head.

"It is better so. I will speak to your father presently. It shall be our secret until then."

It was not the first secret between the old man and the boy, and would not be the last.

But the icon, which Samson had retrieved from the lower terraces a second time, the boy showed to none but the slave girl, Tamam. She came to call him, and he brought it out from under his blue tunic, and she laughed and thrust out her slim belly in imitation of the little iron girl herself; then caught him by the wrist and hurried him down to the house. He had forgotten to tell Uzziel about the stone. He told Tamam. She slid her hand warm into his own, her violet eyes amazed, but he sensed that she did not believe him.

There was a stranger at the house, a man from Ephraim with a bundle, seeking the village headman. Manoah came out to meet him, and he threw the bundle down, and it unrolled in the sight of all who had gathered to hear what he had to say. Tamam's hand flew to her mouth and she jumped backward, so that the boy collided with her. Over her barring arm he looked with fascination at the thing at Manoah's feet.

It was part of the leg of a young female, severed below the knee.

2

EVEN OLD UZZIEL left his tent and came down to the edge of the terraces to witness the war gathering, leaning upon Samson's shoulder. For two days the men of Zorah and Eshtaol had been busy in the plain below, setting up and patching the light, goat's hair tents they would carry with them, many of them rotting from disuse; mending the ox carts, honing their few swords and spears, penning the selected sheep and goats which would be their rations on hoof. The women were busied also, roasting wheat in great quantities, which would keep fresh to eat with the meat, or ground for pottage; making cakes of dried figs, sewing together the green and white cloths to make the ancient battle pennons of Dan, which had begun to burgeon everywhere like spring flowers. The children were left to their own devices, and Samson had gone as usual to Uzziel's tent, and fetched the old man down to see.

"Look, Grandfather. We are going to fight the Philistines!"

Uzziel, looking down on the few ragged lines that marched and countermarched to Manoah's enthusiastic orders, was glad they were not. He let his hand fall on the lad's unruly head and said gently, "Not today. Your father marches north."

"Where?" Samson lifted his head.

"To a place on the Ephraim border. A town on a hill called Mizpeh."

Not everyone, Uzziel was aware, was as enthusiastic as Manoah. They had come, because the summons was from Yahweh as sure as if God had spoken himself: the twelfth part of that mercilessly disembodied corpse to each of the twelve tribes. But they had taken their time, half mindful of the ungathered olives, the coming watermelon crops. It was hardly the great camp of Mahanneh-dan he and the lad looked on now; only a handful of villagers with not enough spears to go round.

"Mahanneh-dan," Samson breathed, as if Uzziel had spoken aloud. He was dancing about under the hermit's hand, rebellious at his own insignificance, too small to march with the men. "It is just as my father said it was. When I am grown I shall lead the men. I shall be chief, as my father is now."

"Let us hope you lead them wisely, then. And now you can lead me back to my tent."

"I shall lead them in *war.*"

So speak the young, knowing nothing of war but the brave stories. Uzziel let Samson take his frail weight again up the hill. "The men are not going to war, child. Your young minstrel . . . what is his name? the hunchback . . . He has made a song about it."

"Baasha. He makes songs about everything. I will ask Baasha then."

Uzziel paused for breath. "Better you ask me. I will tell you they go to punish some wicked men who have broken the holy law. You must help your mother while they are away. And you are to come to me for your schooling."

"Did the wicked men kill the woman?"

"Eh? Oh, yes, child; and more. They threatened the life of a Levite priest."

"Did anyone ever threaten your life, Grandfather?"

Uzziel's frown became a wry smile. "You are thinking that's not such a terrible thing. But this was no ordinary Levite. He is Custodian of the sacred shrine of Mount Ephraim, no less: not a man to be trifled with. Come now."

They moved on, and Samson said, "They must have been very angry with her."

"Angry?"

"They must have truly hated her."

"Perhaps."

Samson glanced up expectantly, knowing it was Uzziel's way of disagreeing. He never contradicted you, as Manoah did, but always delayed his reply, as if it was worth thinking about. Uzziel said now, "Consider, does the wolf hate the lamb he pulls down from the flock? Or does he know nothing but his own appetite. A man without the law is like the beast of the wilderness. To such a one love is hunger, and hatred thirst."

"Is that why they chopped her in pieces?"

"Ah, no . . . " Uzziel lost his footing, and Samson dived to support him. The boy's strength was as alarming as his curiosity. Uzziel said carefully, "You remember how it was with Abraham? When he was to have sacrificed his son Isaac, and Yahweh sent him in his stead a ram, caught in a thicket. Think of this woman as the ram . . . better, a *lamb.* For when the Levite found her there murdered already he made of her a votive offering; that is a sacrifice sealed in blood, to bind the tribes to a vow of vengeance." A frown creased the boy's forehead, as well it might, and Uzziel said, "Remember what I tell you. You don't understand now. One day you will."

"I do," Samson said.

At the tent door he said, "Was the woman the Levite's wife?"

"In a manner of speaking. Go now. Tamam is calling you."

To Samson, retracing his steps down the terraces again, running free of the restraint of the hermit's hand, the ways of grown men remained a mystery. If someone chopped Tamam in pieces he knew what he would do: as soon as he was big enough he would seek them out and chop *them* in pieces. By himself–who else would be so concerned? The woman was only a woman, after all; and only the Levite's wife *in a manner of speaking.* Nahor's ox had been a valuable stud.

He wondered what all the fuss was about.

□

"We are not going to *war.*" Manoah told his wife. He had come up from the camp for the last night before they moved off. He had seen little of Sharah since the summons came. Now, on his rooftop in the evening cool, he allowed himself to relax for the first time. Sharah, never one for idle hands, had fetched up her sewing things to attend to a rent in Manoah's heavy traveling cloak, but set it aside in the failing light to be finished in the morning, saying nothing at all, and her silence made him uneasy; so he said they were not going to war; and she raised her eyes for the first time to ask why the clans had been gathered up and down Israel, if not for war.

"A show of force, woman," Manoah reassured her. "Once they see us camped on their borders they'll not argue. All we want is those sons of Beliel who attacked the priest. Don't frct yourself; we'll be back before you know it. Mizpeh's no distance."

"They are saying it was our own people."

"It's the truth." Manoah's beard rose like the hackles of a dog. "These were Hebrews, can you believe?" He was shamed even to say it. "Picked up their filthy habits from their neighbors, no doubt, along with their Baals and their sacred groves. And to think the Levite'd not turn aside into Jerusalem as his servant lad wanted–it was getting dark, d'you see, and not safe with just the three of them on the road. It was to be among his own people that he made them go another two or three miles, for all that it's an evil road to travel except in caravan by day, never mind by night. I'd have done the same myself."

Sharah never doubted it. It was easy to picture: the three of them coming at last into the blessed light of the market square, safe inside the town gates with a silent prayer of thanksgiving for deliverance: the Levite on his ass and the lad leading another with their provisions, the Levite's woman following with a last look over her shoulder; unloading the beasts under one of the cheerful torches that blazed on the walls, and waiting expectantly for the offer of hospitality from the townspeople that never came. Manoah would have been incensed. To leave a stranger standing in the street was shameful enough; but the man by his dress was a holy priest, and moreover could be seen to carry provisions for his party and his animals, and no burden to the poorest host. Sharah said, "The woman was from Judah," and Manoah nodded.

"Aye, Bethlehem."

"Why should the Levite travel so far to find a woman?"

Manoah shrugged, thinking of the morrow. "Happens he fancied her. You know what they say about the women of Bethlehem-judah."

Sharah did not, and Manoah didn't enlighten her. Who knows why the Levite took a country girl from Bethlehem? He had; that was enough; the way the messenger told it. And not only *took* her; he had settled her in his own house in Mount Ephraim with servants to wait on her and more good things than she could have dreamed of; and she rewarded him by playing the whore among his neighbors. Amazement was duly expressed at the chit's ingratitude; though Manoah's private guess was that she had got above herself, as women will, and tried to incite him to marriage. The Levite, who seemed a reasonable man, instead of having her put to death as he was entitled, merely beat her to show he minded; whereupon she had upped and returned to her father's house. Not surprisingly, the father was ill pleased to see her, and when some four months later, as soon as the harvest festival was over, the Levite came down to reclaim her, it was to a warmer welcome than true son-in-law ever had; so warm indeed that it was only the approach of the Sabbath on the fifth day, when travel would be unlawful, that enabled him to make his excuses and extricate himself for the return journey, and then not before mid-afternoon; so that it was well into the dark before he reached that infamous town where none gave him shelter.

Sharah had heard that they were taken in, after all.

"Aye," Manoah agreed: "But t'was none of the townsmen. A sojourner; an old man from Mount Ephraim like the Levite, a widower who lodged there with his daughter for the harvest season, when he came to work in the fields; he it was who took pity on the stranger and took them in; no man of the town."

That too, Sharah could picture: a poor house, such as a casual laborer might rent for a few shekels, one of a discolored row, halfway down a narrow alley; but with a stout wooden door to the street, and they would all have felt easier when the pin was dropped into place behind them. The asses installed below, the heat of their body smells rising comfortingly to the dwelling floor above. The old man entertained them royally, as if to atone for the churlishness of his neighbors, washing the Levite's feet with his own hands, and lavish with whatever victuals were in the house, which would likely have been no more than barley bread and dried fish, and the rough wine of the region; but nonetheless welcome for that. They were still at it when there came the hammering at the door below, which shook the house.

The old man was first down. There were a dozen of them, maybe more, for the street was ill-lit: foul-mouthed and bloodshot with wine, their garments in loutish disarray. The old man, having called through the timbers to no avail, went out to reason with them. But it was not him they wanted, nor his homely daughter. *The man that came into your house,* they said. And they made plain in word and gesture what they meant to do with him.

Sharah shivered. She said, "And the Levite offered them his woman, in his stead."

"Aye. It was the only thing that saved him."

"And they took her."

"Praise God they did."

"And in the morning, when he opened the door, she was there dead."

"Aye, poor soul." Manoah did not like her tone. "Woman, it could have been the Levite himself! Then you'd have had war right enough."

Sharah had no answer to this, acknowledging the truth of it with her bowed head; closing her eyes privately to shut out the other pictures: how the night must have passed for the country girl from Bethlehem-judah, at the mercy of a dozen drunken and vicious men, or maybe more, with none to hear her cries, or none to heed. Manoah was looking down on the camp fires in the vale below the village, clearly visible from the rooftop. Baasha the psalmist was down there with his lyre among the camp guards, taking his share of their meal for an impromptu song. His voice carried clearly in the stillness. Both of them listened.

Out of Ephraim has Yahweh spoken!
From the mountain his voice has called his people.
Hear, O Israel, and be not afraid.

Let them tremble that fear not the Lord,
That have despised his holy covenant.
They shall be as chaff,
And as straw before the wind of his vengeance.
Rise up, O Dan, against Gibeah. . . .

"Gibeah!"

Sharah half rose. "That was the town? Gibeah?"

Her face was ashen. Manoah stared at her.

Her eyes met his, searching for a denial. "On the borders of Ephraim, you said."

"So it is."

"But not on the Ephraim side. *Gibeah is in Benjamin.*"

So that was it. Because she was herself born a Benjaminite. Manoah's face hardened.

She saw it, and said quickly, "You don't understand. Manoah–you must not go tomorrow."

"*Must* not?"

He was at the top of the steps when she caught at his chalouk. "Where are you going now?"

"To sleep in the camp," he told her. "Aye, and to call the others to do the same, lest there be other wives with kin where we're going." Sharah flinched visibly at the cruelty, but without letting go. He tugged his chalouk free and went four steps down; and then, seeing her stiff in distress against the reddening sky, he added more kindly: "*Yahweh* has sent for us. Do you know what that means, Sharah? To hold back would be a worse crime than that done in Gibeah. If they were Danites we should still go up."

She did not answer, and he said losing patience, "Woman, we've no quarrel with *Benjamin!*–a few maggots in the grain don't spoil the sack."

"You don't know these people as I do. A ravenous wolf, devouring his prey in the morning, and at night dividing the spoils–that was how Jacob spoke of his son Benjamin, the father of the tribe."

"Wolves, is it?" Manoah said, and chuckled. "Aye, well, Dan is a lion's whelp. It was Moses himself said that."

"I will bring your cloak down to the camp in the morning," Sharah said.

□

In Manoah's absence it fell to old Eleazar, as senior of the elders remaining, to take charge of the summer ploughing in of weeds and the preparation of the olive presses; but he was suffering from one of his frequent stomach upsets, and once the ceremonial tapping of the olive trees was done, and he had formally pronounced the fruit ripe for the first harvest, he let them get on with it. The main crop would not be for three or four months, after the first rains, but there was still overmuch work for their numbers. They went to Uzziel in his tent.

"How are they managing in Eshtaol?" he said.

They sent to enquire and came back. "They cannot spare anyone. They have brought in men themselves from Beth-shemesh and Timnath, for a tithe of oil and some sheep." It was what Uzziel would have done himself. They shifted their feet.

"You know what Manoah's like. He will find the footprints of the Canaanites in the village. He will smell them on the air."

"Well, and if he does," the old man told them, "they will smell no worse than the olives rotting under the trees."

The Hebrew women kept to their quarters when the Canaanites were about the place, and went veiled to and from the well. But Tamam the slave girl was not a Hebrew. Samson had gone over the valley south to Etam, with loaves, a full skin of wine and cheeses for the shepherds, and on the second day, when he had not returned, Tamam went to fetch him wearing a new purple-red shawl. He heard the tinkling of the little ornamental chains she wore about her ankles, like distant sheep bells, and came running from among the shepherds' tents to greet her—"Tami! Tami! How pretty you are! What news of my father?"—before she had breath to unleash the scolding she had rehearsed all the way up the hills. He heard her out with great meekness, fingering her shawl until she snatched it away, his tousled head bowed in the sunshine. It was a shame they wouldn't cut his hair tidy, like the other boys; it was like a girl's hair. Not that you could ever mistake him for a girl. She relented, and told him there was no news of the Danite men. He overwhelmed her at once with his own tidings: there had been wolves in the sheep pen during the night; the dogs had gone mad with barking and they had piled the fires high; but in the morning there were three sheep dead and seven astray. He had found one himself, following the bleating, and brought it back–"Like this, look!"–on his shoulders. "That's how they carry them. It doesn't hurt them. Sometimes they tie one leg to their tail; so they can't wander too far."

Tamam guessed it was a lamb, since he could hardly have managed a grown sheep by himself; and the wolves were more likely jackals or foxes; but she kept her doubts to herself. To question his story would be to invite a sulk, and the dark withdrawal he had inherited from his father: he had many of Manoah's mannerisms. She liked better his harmless, boastful chatter, and the companionship of his stocky little figure picking the easiest way down for her. He asked her where she got the shawl and she told him, from one of the Canaanites.

"A peddler came with the workmen: you should have seen the things he had loaded his ass with! Cloths, perfumes, some jewels even: and shoes–several of our men traded for shoes. He is coming back soon."

There was almost no shade on the pathway, only a few carob trees they passed between, and Tamam found herself wishing she had rested at the shepherds' tents to refresh herself. There might have been water there; there would certainly be wine; but she did not like to take wine in front of the boy, who was forbidden it, even well watered down, the way children drank it. It was a nuisance, especially in the summer, when wine was easier to come by than water. But even Manoah never drank wine when Samson was there; though he made up for it when he wasn't.

"You got the shawl from the peddler man?" Samson asked. "It matches your eyes." He pulled down a couple of long leathery pods from the carob and broke one open to suck the honeylike pith. He handed her the other.

"Not from the peddler," Tamam told him. The carob pith only made her more thirsty. "There was a man in charge of the workmen: he gave it to me."

"What did you give him in exchange?"

She told him he asked too many questions. "Hurry up! I am dying of thirst." She made a hood of her shawl against the sun.

"Is it a secret, Tami?" Samson peered round searchingly

and up into her face as they walked, going crablike to watch her, teasing. "I like secrets. I have a secret."

"If it's a secret well," Tamam said, turning away and giggling despite herself, "it would be cruel not to show me." There was no well. Even the rock pools had dried up months ago.

"But it is!" He was astonished at her cleverness. "Not a *well.* But the coldest, sweetest water you ever tasted."

He was so much in earnest that the girl stopped, half believing him. The path twisted sharply downward over boulders rounding two thorn trees, narrowing between rock cliffs to give passage to no more than one at a time, and no water anywhere. Almost, she expected him to strike the rock with his hand, like old Moses in the story she had heard Manoah telling the child; to see the water come gushing out. She liked the stories of their wild, mountain god almost as much as Samson did, and often sat quiet behind the curtain of the women's quarter to listen.

"Up here," Samson said.

He had bounded onto a high boulder as if to climb the smooth rock face like a fly, and even as she watched him, vanished from sight. It was not until Tamam had kicked off her sandals and clambered up after him that she saw the cleft in the rock face: a gap big enough for a body to pass through, invisible from the track below. Samson's hand pulled her inside the cave mouth. His voice was eerily amplified.

"Take care, Tami. You have to jump *down* . . . that's right! That's why the sheep couldn't get out again."

At first she could see nothing; only feel the sudden chill like dew on her skin. She shivered, and drew her shawl close, making out the high, vaulted roof of a great cavern, whose floor sloped downward away from the small light of the entrance. There was a great pile of rocks that blocked her further view; but Samson led her confidently round it. The floor was clammy under her bare feet, slippery with condensation. She clung to the small firm hand that led her. Something rushed past her head, and her shriek went out to the walls and came back with the boy's delighted laughter, and the leathery beating of wings.

"Bats!" he shouted, as if that would calm her. "They are

unclean; but they won't touch you if you keep still. The floor is made of their droppings. They've been here since Noah, I expect. Do you think a lion once lived here?"

She said, "Noah?" not liking to think of lions in the dark, but he had gone on, where the floor rose like a little bridge over blackness, and reached back for her hand. "There are holes here. I don't know how far down they go. I dropped some stones in, but I couldn't hear them hit the bottom. Perhaps it's bottomless."

"What nonsense!" But she kept hold of him. He was standing higher, being farther back; but the want of light too, which opened her eyes like a cat's, tricked her into seeing him as a man for a moment: as the man he would be. At the back of the cave he had discovered a pool, in the hollow of a ledge in the rock. It was continually filled–she could make it out now–from twin rivulets that trickled down from somewhere above. The water was ice cold, and shrank her throat. He said, "You won't tell anyone, Tami. It's my secret."

"Now it's our secret, then."

"Uzziel says you should never tell a secret to a woman."

He bent over to drink in turn as he said it, and she pushed his head under. She couldn't hold him. He came up in a furious spray, soaking them both, and seized her wrists in such a grip that she cried out in alarm, really thinking he would hurt her.

"I'm sorry." He let go at once, puzzled. In daylight he was half-ashamed to be seen with his hand in hers. Only a child would do such a thing. He already considered it unmanly. He said, looking for her eyes, "What did you give the man, in exchange for the shawl?"

Tamam giggled, and ran a finger down his wet tunic between belly and thigh; not speaking until she felt the little swelling under the cloth; and the boy shrank back as if it didn't belong to him, half afraid.

"Come here," she said, "and I will show you."

She was twelve years old.

□

The first rains came at last, and vanished through the cracks in the iron ground, and the men of Dan had not returned. The first word came from a wandering band of coppersmiths returning from the mines on their way to the fleshpots of the coast. They had come in from the desert by way of Jericho, passing through the Hebrew encampments because there was no way round them so far as eye could see. They had been roughly challenged, but afterwards welcomed, in much demand for their craft, and detained several weeks. That there would be war was certain. The Hebrews had sent for their ark of Yahweh, and had it brought down by night from the shrine at Shiloh. Messengers had been dispatched throughout Benjamin to demand the heads of the men who had attacked the Levite, and returned empty-handed; in some instances actually beaten. The Hebrew federation had taken an oath, that no man return home until the matter was settled: which explained why none had brought news back to the villages. Lots had been drawn in the tabernacle of the ark, and it fell to Judah to lead the attack. So much they knew.

"At least it is Judah," Sharah said.

She had been more and more alone the last few months; but then she was by nature a solitary person. Her childhood companions had mocked her betrothal, pitying her exile to the little handful of Dan in Canaanitish country, and she had left them without affection. Looking back over the threshold of adolescence she had no difficulty in excusing their natural cruelty, for she had been a hardworking, obedient child (which was no doubt one reason Manoah's father chose her), with an incurious innocence that must have made her a dull playmate, shining in nothing but purity and nothing remarkable to look at. And Manoah himself, when he came to her village that first time, was a startlingly virile figure. Moreover his family was, by the standards of the time, well off.

Many girls when they are married at thirteen or fourteen leave their clan for another, and Sharah's small and private apprehension was brief. The valley of Sorek pleased her with its yellow wheatfields and wooded hills, and the distant hint of the sea. More important, she made the discovery for the first time in her life that somebody had need of her. The knowledge made her almost beautiful. Manoah's roughness, the brutal strength and weight and lust of the man did not trouble her. She had never imagined it could be otherwise. She went with him as naturally as the mortar to the pestle, delighting in her own usefulness. It was the happiest time of her life until, within the space of little more than a twelvemonth, she knew that she was barren.

It was then that she rebuilt about herself that hedge which had separated her spirit from the other women who might have been her companions. She was too much respected as Manoah's wife to be openly mocked; and indeed her cousins brought their children so frequently to her house that it was sometimes difficult to remember which was the mother. She was twenty-three, in her middle years. She had been nearly ten years without issue. Manoah was strict and intolerant, and sometimes cruel; but he was just. She thought Yahweh must be like Manoah. But when she implored her husband to give her a babe, instead of losing his temper he said seriously, as one speaks to a child: "It is Yahweh who has withheld the fruit of the womb from us, not I"—totally misunderstanding her.

"Take a mistress," she had begged him, though she trembled to say it. "Only let me have a child by her, on my knees. Wasn't your own forefather Dan born of a handmaid, when Rachel bore none of her own to Jacob?"

"I am not Jacob," Manoah retorted, not liking to be reminded of their bastard origin; which saying meant nothing to her at the time. Afterward she discovered that he blamed himself for their childless state, never allowing that Sharah could ever have incurred Yahweh's displeasure.

After that he was kind to her, which was hard to bear. His contempt and unfaithfulness she could have fiercely welcomed; glad, if the truth were known, for the chance to rail at the injustice of it. But there was nothing to rail at but herself, her smooth and useless body. For a while she came close to despising Manoah for an imagined weakness, for his want of anger. And then gradually she had grown dully to accept her own part as despised of God. She had even gone, one evening when Manoah was absent, to an Asherah of one of the Canaanites' sacred groves Manoah hated so much, and had stared at the obscure carvings on the upright stake; not daring to speak aloud, but concentrating with a fearful intensity on the sinister fertility goddess, terrifying herself with the conviction that Manoah's Yahweh *knew.* But nothing came of it.

If Yahweh knew, he surely forgave a woman's foolishness.

She was sitting at the edge of a goat track one day, long afterwards, on her way back from the lower vineyards before the heat of the day, the pruning knife still in her hand. She had taken the lesser path through the oaks to be by herself, but the women had for the most part already hurried on up to the village. So she sat alone, the tip of the shining copper blade pressed against the softness of her empty breast, teasing the linen strands of her shift there, thinking that if she were dead Manoah must then take another wife; wondering who. And turning her head on the thought in the direction of their house, she found herself looking into the eyes of a man who stood no more than three paces from her.

The shock of it paralyzed her an instant; the knife fell onto stones and slithered into a hollow. The next instant she had made the small, instinctive movement to veil her face, and started to her feet.

The brown of his cloak merged with the shade of the oaks' narrow, leathery leaves which made an irregular pattern across his cheek. She could feel the thudding of her heart. She thought: one of the wandering nomads. To her great alarm, he spoke to her.

"Why do you delay here? Why have you not gone home with the others?"

She averted her face. "It was warm, sir. I was tired."

"And you have no child to tend, in your house."

She started, and looked at him again, too confused to care if he thought her brazen. Was it a question? Some of the women took their children into the fields, but not all. How could a stranger know? The shadowy face told her nothing.

"I was watching you," he said. "As the women went up with their little ones. It is a hard thing to be barren, Sharah."

The use of her name frightened her again. She wished Manoah were here. She said uncertainly, "You seek my husband, sir?"

"Whom I seek is found. I am come to you, Sharah. I am come to tell you that you shall conceive, and bear a son."

"A son!"

"It is written. You must make ready and prepare yourself. From this day drink no more wine, nor strong drink.

Take care that you eat nothing unclean. Do you hear me?"

"I hear you," Sharah said. "I hear you say a son."

"Hear more. No razor must come to his head; he shall be a Nazirite, given to Yahweh from the womb. And he shall begin to deliver Israel out of the hands of the Philistines. Now take up your knife, and go tell your husband all you have heard."

She ran without looking back until she was clear of the oaks, and then of course, it was too late to see if he was still there.

No one else had seen him. She was afraid afterward that she had imagined it, suffered the sun sickness; perhaps the man was only in her head; but how could she have imagined the saying about the Philistines? She had never seen a Philistine. Manoah, however, never had a moment's doubt.

"A man of God."

She could hear Manoah saying it now, as he said everything to his son, with massive certainty; his great log of an arm heavy on the young Samson's shoulders, while she listened through the open doorway. "*A man of God*–those were your mother's very words. Shaking like a reed she was, I'd never seen her so pale. I had to catch hold of her or she'd have fallen. She had been with the harvesters, in the corn; still had her sickle in her hand, I remember. I was alarmed! I took her by the shoulders–gently, like this to calm her down–and that was what she came out with: a man of God. Out of a clear blue sky."

For a moment, Samson was interested. Sharah could not see his face, but she could tell from the hunching of the child's imprisoned shoulders that his imagination was at work. But he did not interrupt.

"I went down straightway," Manoah went on, "to find the man, this prophet, but there was no sign of him. I went down with the men and we searched high and low, but he was not there. I can see them now, shaking their silly heads and clicking their tongues. But I never doubted your mother's story. We made the necessary preparations for the child that was to come–*you,* that was!–though old Dorah the midwife didn't believe it."

"Then you saw the prophet again," Samson prompted.

Manoah nodded. "Not then; later we did. It was after

the latter rains, when the spring crops were ready for sowing. I prayed Yahweh, my son. Three days and nights I prayed on the rooftop here, prayed without eating and sleeping, ask your mother; prayed Yahweh to send the man again, to tell us what we should do. For by then there was no more doubting; your mother's time was getting close. And one day she was down in the valley, over by the watermelon fields, and she came running, big as she was, up the hill like before. And she said the man was there, the same man. So I went down with her, and there he was, waiting. And I said, 'Are you the man who spake to the woman here?' And he said, 'Aye, I am.' So I said, 'Tell me again, then.' "

Sharah had never known her husband defer to any man; never drop his voice or his eyes before a fellow being. But he had not said Tell me again; he had said *Now let your words come to pass,* which is the same and not the same, because he said it with a strange and wonderful humility; the way he spoke at his prayers and nowhere else. *How shall we order the child, and how shall we do unto him?*–asking; and Manoah never asked anybody anything, unless it was Uzziel. And the man repeated about the wine, and the strong drink.

There had been Nazirites from olden times, dedicated to Yahweh in thankfulness for some great blessing; but for a time, for a given period. It was written in the law of Moses as everyone knew, that they should abstain from wine and let the hair grow upon the head unshaven for the days of separation. There had even been a Nazirite in Eshtaol once, a notorious winebibber who had gone half mad from the lack of it until his time was fulfilled, when there was the greatest celebration the village could remember, and still talked of. But whoever heard of a Nazirite *from birth?*

It had little meaning for the child, however, squirming under Manoah's arm. To this day his locks were scarcely longer than those of his companions, and a child has no natural thirst for wine. It was the last part of the story Samson liked best: when the stranger had repeated the instructions he had given Sharah before, and made the expected gesture of leaving them. Manoah was so awed, he almost forgot his manners. But he pulled himself together and said hastily, "*Please* . . . let us detain you until we have prepared a kid for you. Sharah–"

"I sent your mother up to the house," Manoah recalled. "And had them fetch a kid, the youngest weaned, and they slaughtered it and brought it down. And the man said, *Though you detain me*–for he stayed there with me–*I will not eat of your bread.* He said if I wanted to offer a kid, it should be a burnt offering to Yahweh. So we set up the stones we had ready to make an oven and made an altar instead, and set the carcass on the fire. . . . "

"And the angel went up to Heaven in the smoke," Samson said.

It was the only time Sharah had ever seen her husband afraid. She had fetched the kid down herself; there was no one else with them. Only the stranger, watching from across the altar, through the flames that crackled merrily from the thornwood, dancing up with the sweet savor of roasting flesh; so their offering was accepted of Yahweh, and the stranger nodded gravely, as if to say, It is done.

It was then that there came the sudden rush of wind around the hill that sent the flame roaring like a lion over the grasses and she had cried out, for he must be burned. Manoah grabbed a handful of anything, grass and dust, and flung it on the flame to quench it; and it choked the fire into a great billowing of smoke that climbed into the sky, drawing their eyes upward with it. And when it had cleared, the stranger was no longer there.

"So we knew it was an angel," Manoah said.

It was a lie: he had thought it was Yahweh himself. He had fallen to the earth with a groan, pulling Sharah with him, and covered his head. "We are dead, Sharah." And she cried out, "No!" and he repeated it. "Because we have seen God." Even in her fright, this seemed ridiculous. "If Yahweh wanted to kill us, he'd not have received the burnt offering; nor would he have told us what we've heard today."

She raised her head, though in trepidation, and Manoah raised his. There was nothing to see but the blinding sun. Sharah felt the child stir within her, and said suddenly, "He must have a name," and Manoah said, "Shemesh," before he understood that she meant their unborn son; and they both began to laugh, Sharah half weeping and Manoah bellowing like a bull. "We have a child of the sun!"

So they named him, then, the dark child that was to be, Shemeson, the sun child: Samson the Nazirite.

□

He was beside his mother, treading the grapes in their own press, his dancing legs stained with the red juices, when the news came. The man was from the villages, known to Sharah only by sight. His grin was wolfish in the taut flesh of his face. The war with Benjamin was over.

"This day there is one tribe lacking in Israel."

Even the child was still, sensing the magnitude of the occasion without understanding it. Sharah's voice cracked. "All of them? *All?*"

The messenger shrugged off the irrelevance. "A few hundred Benjaminite survivors, and they've taken to the wilderness."

The first line of the attack at Gibeah, led by the men of Judah, had been cut down by Benjaminite slingers: a picked group, all left-handed with a javelin in the right, so there was no closing with them after the first volley. The second day the tribes fared no better, and it looked as if they would be utterly defeated despite their great superiority in numbers. They ran to the ark of Yahweh in some despair, with fasting and burnt offerings, to be told: *Tomorrow I will deliver them into your hands.* The Ephraimites led the tribes then, and they used an old strategy: an ambush party, lying in wait to the west of the town. The main attack was a feint, quickly falling back and drawing the Benjaminites out hotfoot in pursuit; when the ambush party fell on the undefended town and fired it. The smoke was the signal for those in the fields to turn again, and they caught the Benjaminites between the two, and slaughtered them wholesale along the northern road–the way the Levite had carried the dead girl. Some few Benjaminites had escaped through the lines, and taken refuge in the wild rock country.

Sharah asked the question: "Is Manoah safe?"

"He is safe, and will be returning, though there's many that won't."

Samson understood then that their army had won a

great victory for Yahweh, and his father would be coming home with glory, and gave a whoop of joy that died away when he saw his mother's face inexplicably streaked with tears. "What is it? Are you not happy? We've won! We've won!"

Sharah embraced him, wet and stained as he was, and said, "Sometimes a woman cries when she is most happy, my son."

But when the messenger had gone she was still weeping, and Samson heard her say, "There were my own kith and my kin." But she never explained it, and it made no sense, her kin being Dan the same as his, and the Danites had won.

3

THERE WAS A WARNING GONG in Eshtaol, a bar of bronze tethered high on the ruins of an ancient watchtower, on the highest point of the hill. The watchtowers in the vineyards were wooden, but this was of stone, much fallen away and unsafe. Manoah had made the place out of bounds to the children. It was one of Samson's first, tentative acts of rebellion against his father that he tried the entrance; half idly, for the door was well sealed, and there was no other visible means of ascent. But when he grew tall enough to reach the first gap in the stonework, he made his own, scaling the outside like an ant. His companions followed him, as they followed him in everything he did, to lie face down on the good part of the platform where they could not be seen from below, with the gong rope creaking above them like a soul in torment. Sometimes the tower was the prow of a tall Phoenician ship ploughing through the Great Sea; sometimes the outer wall of a besieged citadel, from which they rained down arrows and sling shot on the attackers–Benjaminites for a time after the war; and then, when Benjamin was reinstated in Israel, usually Amorites or Canaanites. But for Samson, they were always Philistines.

On a clear day the sea was plainly visible, and you could see the dust clouds moving ever so slowly across the coastal plain, which were the iron chariots of the Philistines on maneuvers, or it might be a hunting party, though Samson could not imagine what they would find to hunt in the open country, where there was nothing bigger than jackals, or the little brown foxes. Sometimes he thought he saw the god-king's son, the prince Athol–he had never forgotten the name–in the first chariot of all, his cloak flapping like a golden flag, the wind plucking at the cropped yellow hair but no wise disturbing the cold mask of his face. He had seen the bronze soldiers many times since, their foot patrols in the valleys, but he had not seen the old Egyptian or the young prince again.

What he knew of the Philistines he learned from Uzziel, since Manoah would not speak of them: it was not much. Like the northern Phoenicians they were great sea peoples, which meant they were mad, since nobody sane would venture away from land from free choice. He had seen himself what Yahweh could do to the Great Sea in one of his rages. Uzziel said they had first come to the Land in a time long past; they came as merchants, and founded their trading settlements there. Those who followed were of a different ilk.

These were said to have come in their fighting ships from somewhere called Atlantis, beyond the Isles of the Sea, rushing up against the coasts of Egypt like a tidal wave; but the Pharaoh old Rameses beat them off, and they scattered up the Canaan coast like locusts, establishing their city strongholds at Gaza, Ashkelon and Ashdod, and inland at Gath and Ekron–the five cities of the Philistine League with their *Seren* kings, "as they are to this day," Uzziel said, screwing up his eyes as if he could see them from his tent. "Why did Yahweh permit them to come?" Samson asked; because Manoah had often said Yahweh had given all the Land to Israel, right down to the seacoast; but for once Uzziel had no answer. Not all the Philistine soldiers were as Samson remembered them, Uzziel said. Those he had encountered that day on the hill were probably handpicked from the temple bodyguard at Gaza. Most of the rank and file were Canaanites, recruited locally, under Philistine captains. Some were Amorites. Some Hebrews.

"Hebrews!"

The hermit shrugged. "So it is said. Do not tell your father I tell you. He would have none of it."

Samson seldom told his father anything. They had never been intimate that he could remember. At the age when other boys left the harem and went to their fathers for instruction in the law, the *Torah,* he was packed off to Uzziel with no explanation. Not that the rejection was untempered with relief. Since the war, the gruff reserve which Manoah had maintained as clan chief had turned to a moroseness which made him unapproachable. He had suffered a minor wound, soon healed, but there were other wounds you could not point to, which broke open at a word: a festering ill-humor not even Sharah could placate. Sharah too was changed. Samson's gradual resentment manifested itself in a reflection of his father's own sullenness, which Manoah called slow-witted. Uzziel called it laziness, and tolerated it. He asked the boy one day, when he was slow to repeat a phrase of the law, what he was thinking of, and Samson said, "Tamam." He would never have said it to his father.

"They watch me," he told Tamam.

She was out milking the household goats, and he had risen early and come looking for her, before the house was awake. She had grown taller with the approach of womanhood–they were of a height now–her arms more rounded, and in every way more interesting. It was hard to think of her as the same skinny waif his father had fetched home one day from nowhere, who had coaxed and scolded him in her funny foreign accent almost before he had any memory at all. The morning mist filled the valley like a milky lake, and he stood shivering. Apart from a distant barking of dogs, they were alone in a new world. She said, "Shalom," without surprise, and went on with her deft manipulation of the dugs. The twin squirts alternatively frothed into the pan clasped between her knees, with a sound like sawing wood. "My father," he said, "and my mother. But especially my father."

"He watches me too," she said. "I had a whipping from him yesterday." And she eased her shoulders remembering it, but without interrupting the rhythm.

"I know." He had heard it through the house; everyone had. He asked curiously, "What did you do?"

"Ask your father. Since you're here, you may as well make yourself useful. There's another pan there."

He went obligingly and fetched it, and brought a second goat and tethered it alongside hers. She had on her old shawl as usual, much washed and faded to the mauve of hyacinths, as much a part of her as her misty black hair and her bangles. He said, "If my father saw me doing a woman's work, maybe he would beat me too."

"He would, if he knew."

"I'd not care if he did," Samson said.

She made a scornful face. "That's because you've never *been* whipped; you don't know how it hurts!" And then, glancing at him again, she thought he meant *I'd not care if he did know about us,* and was really alarmed. Whipping was one thing; she was used to whippings; but Manoah was capable of having her stoned, if he found out. She had seen a man stoned once: taken to a cliff twice his own height, and thrown over it onto his back which was supposed to stun him but didn't; and the first stone aimed at his heart, but that missed as well, and he died horribly. She could not tell from the boy's face what he meant, because his liquid eyes showed nothing but affection; and she carried the pan impatiently to the churn, slopping some. "It is well for you," she said. "He is afraid of you, that's why."

She surprised herself by saying it; but the boy much more. He blinked in astonishment. She told him cleverly, "That is why he watches you all the time."

"Afraid? Of me?"

"Of your god, then," Tamam said. "Manoah is afraid if he strikes you your god will come down and burn him to a cinder!" And she pointed jeeringly into the rising sun, the most effective way she knew of annoying Samson, Shemesh being her god not his–he hated the Canaanitish rendering of his name. "Shemesh-son," she said.

But he was lost in visible thought, a trick he had picked up from old Uzziel, too much interested to be provoked, only saying back, *"Tam'am,"* in Hebrew *the last straw,* which was the name Manoah had given her long ago for some forgotten misdemeanor. He had left off milking his goat which, turning its head to seek the cause, came upon his buttock as he knelt, and nipped it. The boy jumped like a frog, sending the milk pan flying. Tamam clung to her goat's neck, speechless with laughter, having with great presence of mind stuffed the end of her shawl into her mouth, not to wake the house. Samson turned his back on her and flung one arm about his own goat's neck, furiously imitating her, but not shaking; his body went rigid, braced like a young tree in a gale. She took the shawl from her mouth. The goat's legs splayed violently outward, threshing, its head strained to the limit of the tether, the eyes rolling. Tamam beat Samson with her fists. *"Stop it!* You are strangling her!"

He exploded into laughter. "Don't be silly! You can't strangle a *goat."* But he let go, and ruffled the silly creature's ears good-naturedly. Its flanks heaved.

"You nearly did," Tamam said. "Poor Leah!"

"You care more about poor Leah than me."

"She didn't hurt you," she said. "Did she? Show me."

She lifted his tunic, and he knocked her hand away. He was bruised all down one leg; she had not noticed before. She said, "Leah never did that."

"We were wrestling," he said; and became interested again. "It's gone blue, hasn't it. I must have been on some stones. You finish the milking, Tami; I am no good at it."

"You are no good at anything." She brushed him aside and had the milk squirting into the pan, but even she had difficulty. "There! You've upset Leah. Who were you wrestling with–some of the girls, was it?"

She was rewarded, at last, by a flush that darkened the boy's face. But it was quickly gone. "Manoah should have called you Deborah," he said: *"the bee.* Everything you say pricks and stings. No wonder my father beat you. I–" and stopped.

"Ah, you would like to beat me yourself. You are big enough now, you're thinking."

There was a cloud over the valley, pierced through with the sun's first rays, the fingers of Shemesh touching the earth to waken everything growing. Perhaps heralding the first rains.

Samson said, "But I love you, Tami. You know that."

She rose with the pan and passing him, kissed him on

the mouth, touched; and moved on. "I know. But don't get ideas. I belong to your father, remember."

"You belong to me."

"Sometimes," she agreed. "Now run along. They will soon be awake, and I've much to do."

"It was Jemuel I wrestled with."

She was leading the goats back to their shed. "Jemuel ben Jethro? I thought he was your friend."

"Yes, he is. I wouldn't wrestle with him otherwise." He was surprised that she didn't know this.

There were the six sons, brawny youths all of them, run wild after their father's death in the war. Jemuel was the youngest, but still a year older than Samson and taller by a head. There was a sister too, Abigail, a backward child who lived in their shadow. Tamam said, "Did you win?" lifting the milk churn on her head to go.

Samson shook his head. "I would have; but he pulled me by the hair."

If he took off the headband he wore, his richly curling hair was as long and black as hers now and much thicker; and the thought came to her that it must be a disadvantage to a boy. She was so used to it, she had forgotten. She gave him her secret smile, going by, and said more kindly, "Maybe, I will come to the cave later."

His *No* stopped her.

"That's what I came to tell you," he said. "I am to go with the others to bring the flocks in. My father said I could."

Tamam raised her eyebrows. "Well! You are growing up, aren't you. All those wolves and bears! Manoah must want to be rid of you. Make sure you keep close to the others, then. How long will you be away?"

"I don't know. Four or five days."

She could see he was thinking of the wolves and bears, not of her, from the way he grinned; and she walked on moodily.

Pondering on Tamam's curious saying, he wondered if there was any truth in it; if the Nazirite dedication to Yahweh included a measure of protection even from his own father.

Sharah had a surprise for him: a proper *Maddim* cloak

of woven goat's hair, stiff and new with a distinctive smell nothing like goats: more like the warm and musty smell of corn when it is stored. It billowed tentlike almost to his ankles, until she showed him how to gather it in with the leather girdle. This too was new, a full span in width with slotted pockets which would serve as purse and satchel. He explored every one with mounting excitement. He had never owned anything so splendid. Sharah gave one of her rare smiles to see him, catching her breath in the fierceness of his embrace. "You made it for me?–when? where?" He had not seen her working at it.

"The cloak I made," she told him, noting with her critical eye that if it was big on him, he would grow into it soon enough. "Tamam made the girdle. She pricked her fingers making it. Especially for you to go with the shepherds." So Tamam had known all the time.

He shuffled comically up the hill to show Uzziel. He wanted to show Tamam, but she had gone off somewhere and was not back when it was time for him to leave.

Though he had been often to the near folds with food and messages, he had never before ventured so far from the villages. He left with Jemuel and his brothers, striking westward up through the oak groves in a thin rain that hissed on the leaves and softened the contours of the hills in a gray mist. It stood in tiny pearls on his cloak and his eyelashes. Jemuel had sandals on his feet; Samson went barefoot. Among the groves they passed upright stakes, like limbless saplings, but the boy could see they were planted there in some sort of pattern. The brothers pressed on at a fierce pace, so there was no time to ask; but later, when they took their first rest in a high circle of cedars, it was close by another such stake, and Samson could see that it was carved into a semblance of human shape, and that there were the remains of fruit and ashes before it. It reminded him of the little iron maiden he had the day he met the Philistines, which Manoah had flung away so angrily. Jemuel caught him looking, and grinned. "We are not in Zorah now," he said. "This is an Asherah–*you* know. The grove is sacred to Astarte. No, don't touch it: you don't want to upset *her.*"

He said it half mockingly, but his voice dropped in the

silence of the place as all their voices did, and before they moved on the boy noticed that the brothers let fall a little of their corn meal and each in passing touched his fingers to brow, lip and breast in a gesture Samson had not seen before. He waited to see if Jemuel would do the same, but he hurried on, as if glad to leave the place behind him.

The rain cleared toward evening when they came to the shepherds' encampment, the dogs running out to bark at their approach. One of them lifted a leg against a post struck into the scrubby grass and bearing, like a windless flag, what looked like a dead bat. It was a moment before the boy saw that it was a human hand, severed at the wrist.

"Shalom! You've had thieves, then!" the brothers called by way of greeting, and a bald man from the tents, shouting at the dogs, broke off to spit expressively into the ground.

"Shalom," he called back.

"Lost many sheep this time?"

"Seven. And one man." The shepherd's teeth were suddenly white in the blackness of his beard: a sinewy man, tough as blackthorn, in a striped chalouk with a dagger stuck in his waistband. "Who is the lad?"

They told him, Samson of Zorah, and he looked the boy up and down.

"The Nazirite. Aye, I've heard of him; though I've never heard of a baby Nazirite before." The boy stiffened, and their eyes met. A moment, and the shepherd grinned again. "You've a temper, I can see that." He clapped a hand on Samson's shoulder, steering him toward the tents. "No offense, lad: that's a fine cloak you have there. You'll not take wine, being a Nazirite. But we'll warm you up with our *shechar.*"

This was barley wine, not drunk in Manoah's house: a light beer made from fermented bread and drunk from earthware pots of enormous size. No one told Samson that *shechar* was as much forbidden to Nazirites as wine of the grape, and for the first time in his life he got drunk.

Awaking before dawn in the unfamiliar dark of the tent, the boy remembered little of it: the bawdy singing, the women's voices behind the tent wall. He was still wrapped in his cloak, with someone–Jemuel?–still as a corpse beside him; but there were others breathing and snoring. It was the lice and fleas that had woken him. He went outside to scratch and relieve himself, into an alien, misty world, the mountain ridges immensely black against the reddening sky. Cold winds flapped the edges of the tents. The ground was wet with dew, and he crinkled his feet at the shock of it. Now he could make out two or three sheep watching him, their heads turned his way. The dew was silver on their fleeces.

Samson had to walk a long way down the mountainside before he found what he was looking for: a rock pool holding sufficient of the previous day's rain. He stripped off his tunic, touched forehead to ground and recited the morning prayer, half attentive to the sheep bells all around him. He washed himself in the icy water, disposing of a couple of lice in the process, and combed his hair with a small bronze comb he had found in the pocket of his girdle. Then he wound his hair about his head and secured it with his headband, searched about for a piece of twig from the shrubs and stood, scrubbing his teeth with the frayed end of it. None of these things occupied his mind, and when the cry came through the mist he was instantly racing toward the sound as if he had been listening for it.

Under a lone terebinth tree a heap of fleece lay twitching. Standing over it was a ram, its curved horns lowered to attack; and facing the ram a ferocious mass of fur which rose on its hind legs almost into the tree itself, an enormous bear, waving its paws slowly like a drunken man.

The cry had come from the tree, where the watch had shinned, leaving his staff on the ground almost under the bear's feet. The watch and the bear saw the boy at the same time. Samson had never seen a bear before; he felt his bowels loosen inside him. The man in the tree was shouting: "Run for your life, child! Run for help!"

As the ram stood, so did the boy, the word *child* slowly exploding in his chest. The man was out of reach: all his hate concentrated on the bear, the great grinning mask that seemed to mock him as if to say, *The child, the boy Nazirite.* Samson lifted a heavy stone with a short prayer uttered through closed teeth: "Yahweh Adonai, avenge me now!" And he ran forward and smashed the stone against the brute's head with all the force of his two hands.

The bear howled in surprise and pain, and swung a paw

as a man might brush off a troublesome fly, backhanded, sending the boy crashing against the tree, where he fell winded. He was dimly aware of the watch slithering down the trunk beside him, shouting all the time; of the ram's blood splashed over his knees as it passed, the shepherd's staff threshing wildly, and the bear's fetid breath; then the answering shouts from behind and above, and the rocks falling like rain, the bear shambling off, as if offended.

They came down with their slings in hand, and there was Omar, the shepherd chief—a dark bull of a man with the left side of his mouth elongated by an old scar, which gave him a malicious look—scowling at him and shaking his shaggy head in wonder. The ram was lost, but the watch saved; the bear might have had him out of the tree if it had had a mind to climb up after him. If the watch had not climbed down and retrieved his staff, the bear would have killed Samson for certain. And Omar said he ought to have run for help straightway, as he was told.

"You are a fool," he said.

But he said *shotté,* which is not the fool who is witless or simple, but foolhardy: because it is written that all young men are *shottéhim* until they learn caution. You do not say *shotté* to a child.

□

The encampment was on a high plateau broken up by smaller, rounded hills, scattered with buckthorn and coarse winter grasses everywhere between the rocks. There were few trees, and little shade. Here the shepherds had already led the flocks in, so that in daylight they seemed as many as maggots in a windfall. Apart from keeping a watch at night, the shepherds took their pleasure in the way of men long denied it, drinking and fighting, storytelling and womanizing among themselves.

The bald-headed shepherd gave Samson a sling, a hollow pouch of hide with long cords attached to opposite sides.

"If you mean to fight *bears,* it's well to keep your distance."

It had a more common use. A stone slung just beside an erring sheep could turn it any way the shepherd wanted; a series dropped close in front of the leading ram could bring the whole flock around. But it took a deal of skill. Jemuel showed Samson how to wind one cord about his palm to anchor it, taking the other in the fingers of the same hand, to hold the stone looped in the pouch.

Samson's first shot went high and wide, and the leathern sling with it. But at the end of the three days, when the flocks were ready for the droving, he was able to hit his target once in three or four shots. A light snow fell as they started down: the black tents vanished into the hillside, the groups of shepherds losing distinctiveness, still shouting their farewells. They would meet again in the spring, in four or five months' time. The Danites drove more than six hundred beasts, and Samson walked behind the last of them with Jemuel, feeling very different from the youth who had come up this way with the brothers, a hanger-on in his stiff *Maddim* cloak. The two walked hand in hand, in the way of men in friendship, Jemuel a head taller, dark with the beginnings of straggly beard; Samson seemed to be growing sideways, very broad at the shoulders and thick of thigh like his father, but with none of Manoah's heaviness: he padded like the lion that was his birth sign, tireless and relaxed, missing nothing.

He missed Tamam, however. They camped one night, and the next afternoon came down through the Shephelah, the sheep flowing like a white river to the villages. The men were out ploughing with oxen in the valley, but left off to come and help pen them. Climbing to his house, Samson kissed his mother's cheek as he embraced her, and went at once to wash, knowing her eyes followed him. Afterwards he found a clean tunic, his best with the brown and white stripe, which Tamam must have put ready for him. But she was not in the house. He parted the veil to the harem, and it was empty. He wanted to tell her of the fight with the bear, and the drinking, and show her his sling. But she was nowhere to be found, and he went up the hill to Uzziel.

It was Uzziel who told him that *shechar* was forbidden to Nazirites.

The old man was almost blind now, seeming hardly able to tell the day from the night; but his wrinkled eyes followed every movement Samson made. Uzziel's eyes rolled backward in his head, and his lips moved urgently as if he was talking to someone, but it was moments before he spoke.

"Yahweh," he said. "The Lord protect you, my son, for I don't know who else will. What did our father Moses say concerning the man separated with the vow of a Nazirite?"

"He shall separate himself from wine . . . and shall drink no vinegar of wine . . . neither liquor of grapes, nor eat moist grapes or raisins–"

Uzziel stopped him. "Separate himself from wine *and strong drink,*" he said, his voice rising in spite of himself. It was not the way to talk to Samson; but at least it kindled a spark. Uzziel said, "You will never make priest, if you cannot hold the law in your head from one day to the next."

"I don't want to be a priest."

"It is not what you want, but the will of Yahweh that matters," Uzziel reminded him tartly. Was it Yahweh's will? It was certainly Manoah's: sending the boy to him, not knowing what else to do with him. *Better he should follow your ways than mine.*

"If Yahweh wanted me to be a priest," Samson said doggedly, "he would have had me born a Levite."

"How many young man are there in Dan? In Israel? And Yahweh Adonai chose him Samson, from his mother's womb. The first time you leave the villages like a man, what do you do? You get drunk."

"Yahweh chose Noah," Samson said. "Out of all mankind, not just Israel, to save him with his kin. And Noah got drunk."

The old man stiffened. *"Noah?"*

"You told me yourself. After the flood, when he planted a vineyard and drank the wine. He was so drunk, his sons found him naked in his tent. . . ."

Uzziel sucked his gums, masking a grin, and rubbed his chin.

"Noah was not a Nazirite," he said. And he said, "It may be you will make a priest after all."

But when Samson was gone from the tent, the hermit sat looking blindly at the place where he had stood, sure in his mind that he would not be.

But if not a priest, what then?

□

She would be down at the wine presses treading the grapes–why had he not thought of it before? His head was so full of the bringing in of the flocks, he had altogether forgotten they were still at it: the whole village would be there.

The singing led him down; it had been in the background all the time if he had stopped to listen. So much for Uzziel's railing against drunkenness: there were hardly any sober. Where was Manoah to allow such a thing? And he remembered he was at Shiloh. A girl–it was the sister Abigail–tugged shyly at his arm, and he shook himself free, plunging on. He was recognized, and a shout went up. They had been dancing, and broke off to look toward Baasha the hunchback, him with the lyre, grinning and calling for the song again.

"It's Samson! He's here!"

And Baasha, while the boy stood puzzled, struck a chord and threw his head back, with a hiccup.

> Behold, he comes like a lion from his den!
> From the garden of Jordan, the pride of the river!
> He stands among the sheepfolds
> As a strong tower in the vineyards.
> The bear's blood is upon his hands
> And the blood of the beast an offering to Yahweh.
>
> The strong men have slain their jackals.
> But Samson the king of the bears.

He stopped with Samson's forearm across his throat and no air to breathe, let alone sing. The lyre smashed in a jangling discord. The silence spread outward like rings on a pool, returning to swell the throng about them.

"What is it? I can't see."

"It's Samson. He's killing Baasha."

"He thinks he's a bear."

"Shame on you!–and him with a crooked back!"

"Stop him! *Stop* him!"

This last a woman's voice, shrill and sobering; and two of the men at last pushed through and laid hands on the boy, half in jest, but with some roughness. Samson swung the limp Baasha by the neck like a club and felled one man to the ground, letting the hunchback go flying over him. The other man he hefted over into the wine vat with his mouth still in an astonished *O*. The rest crowded backward like the waters of the sea of reeds when Yahweh divided them, and he walked between like Moses, turning aside only to take the still form of Baasha on his shoulders in the manner of a shepherd carrying a lamb, with none hindering him.

The light was going as he climbed the terraces, between the oak trees. A thin, soaking rain began to fall again, blurring the first lamps in the houses above, before the shutters were drawn, and he veered to the left uncertainly, the rain clearing his head. He was taking Baasha home; but where did the singer live? Sometimes here, sometimes there: in a ramshackle hut in the vineyard, in a makeshift tent among the home flocks; sometimes he seemed to go to ground like a fox.

"Baasha," Samson said.

There was no answer, and Samson bore him across the terraces and down to the well instead. There was no one there at this hour, and in the rain. He set his burden down and drew water. There was blood caked at the side of Baasha's mouth, and he unwrapped his headband and wiped it clean as best he could. There was no need of the well water, the headband was soaked through. The mouth moved slackly with the movement of his wiping, but that was all.

It was there that Tamam found them, in the darkness beside the well: the sodden bundle propped against the low wall, and the boy seated on its edge some way round, staring down at his open hands. Her lamp picked him out, but he did not look up.

"Where have you *been?*" she cried. "I've been looking for you everywhere. Your mother's had a meal ready these past four hours. Who is that?"

He did not answer, and she swung the lamp back, close to his face. It was drowned in misery, though whether from tears or the rain she could not tell. She said sharply, "Are you going to leave him there?"

"You know I cannot touch him, as a Nazirite."

"You brought him here. You must have."

"He was not dead then."

She took the lamp to Baasha. "He is not dead now. Come and help me!"

Samson came to life, leaping up to hold the lamp and shelter it with his hand while she tended to Baasha. Turning his small, misshapen body over and holding him while he retched. He was manifestly alive, and Samson's cry of relief turned her head.

He said apologetically, "Yahweh answered my prayer. I never thought he would."

"Pray him to stop the rain, then. He is like to die of the cold. Give me the lamp."

He handed it to her meekly, and she said, "Now pick him up gently . . . no! Not like that, idiot: in your arms."

The faint beat of Baasha's pulse against his breast was as welcome as the wakening of spring in the dead earth; it was true that Yahweh had answered his prayer, whatever Tamam thought. But he was too relieved to argue.

Tamam said, "We shall take him to Dorah, she will know what to do."

The midwife Dorah was the nearest Dan could boast to physician. Her house smelled of herbs, mingled with the rancid oil smoke of the one lamp. Dorah's wrinkled old walnut face greeted them with disapproval, scowling at the wet they brought in with them.

"Stupid girl," were her first words to Tamam. "I tell you to be careful, and you are soaked through. What are you doing out in this weather?"

"It's Baasha."

The old woman made them lay him straight on rush matting, and began peeling the psalmist's clothes from him like the pelt of an animal. Tamam wrung her shawl out in the doorway. Dorah said, "He is badly bruised. And one arm and a leg is broken. He will have to remain here. Samson!—go by the door, you are making a pool on my clean floor. Tamam: mix me some oil and wine; you know where it is. He has some deep cuts, too. Then take your wet things off."

She seemed as much concerned for Tamam as for Baasha, leaving him and taking the lamp to rummage in a chest. She produced a voluminous shift, holding it up. "It's old," she said, "but it is clean and dry. You can go, Samson; we do not need you now."

"Baasha will live," Samson said.

"Yes, yes. He will live."

"I would rather wait for Tamam."

"Wait outside then."

Because there was only the one room, Dorah told him to shelter next door, but he was not bothered with sheltering. He walked up and down in front of the dark houses, their lights blocked off with mats or shutters, but there were cheerful chinks, letting the rain fall as it would: he could not get any wetter or happier, hugging himself and grinning privately like an idiot. Baasha would live, and Tamam was back. He was impatient to be called inside again; but he was not called at all. Instead, Tamam came out, her borrowed shift billowing, with her wrung shawl like a canopy over her head. The rain had petered away. Only the trees dripped, and the corners of the roofs. Samson looked at her in question, and she said, "He will be all right. He spoke to me."

They climbed toward their house, and she said, "Who could have done it to him?"

He was glad Baasha had not told her; and then thought it might be better if he had. He missed the sound of her bangles, and looked round.

"It was *you,*" Tamam said, very low. "Wasn't it."

"Baasha said that?"

"No; he was only interested in his precious lyre. But I am not a fool. You had him at the well and said nothing: not how he was hurt, not how you found him, nothing. But your eyes give you away. They always do. How did it happen?"

He told her. She would find out soon enough from those who witnessed it, which was most of the village. He might have been telling the story of Cain and Abel, or Joseph and his brethren, or any other far-off tale that had nothing to do with himself. It was like a dream, when you do impossible things that have no reality except in the remembering of them. But it was real to Tamam; she wrapped her shift closer as if afraid of contamination.

"Because of a song," she marveled. "A simple song. You would kill a poor lad for singing a song, and playing on the strings. A song in your honor."

She had misunderstood altogether. He blundered after her. "Not in my honor!" He was half angry with himself now. "They were laughing at me, all of them; don't you see? They knew I never killed the bear–it was more like to kill *me.* I hit it with a stone; that was all."

"Well, I heard you killed it. So did Baasha–all of them," Tamam said. "You know what you are."

And she said, "You are mad."

It was not true. If he were mad she would pity him. He had never known Tamam like this. She was changed. Her feet were flying up the path ahead of him. He raced after her and had a handful of her shift from behind. She struggled like a webbed fly.

"I am a man now!" he said close to her enflamed face. "You shall not walk ahead of me and shame me! I will not let you."

She beat his face with her clenched hands until he trapped them. She spat at him: "Brave fighter! First a hunchback boy, now a woman."

He let her go and she brandished her wrists, the white of his fingers in the flesh. She was dancing with rage.

"Mad, mad, *mad!*" she screamed at him. "You don't know your own strength. You would have killed Leah if I hadn't been by."

He had forgotten the goat. She made no sense, but her words stirred another recollection, and he said bitterly, "I'd not have harmed Baasha if you had been there. Where were you? I looked all over for you."

She did not answer, and he dropped his shoulders. "Oh, Tami . . ."

"Oh Tami," she mimicked. "Am I your keeper? Your nursemaid still?–and you a man, you tell me!"

There was more, but Samson was no longer listening. He felt suddenly cold, and tired from the long day; with the emptiness of hunger in his belly. He said, "Go, then."

But now she would not. "You want to know where I was? I will tell you. Where else would a woman go when she is with child, except to the midwife?"

He was stunned. "Dorah?"

"Yes, Dorah, Dorah. Who else? You might have guessed if you were clever. But you are not; you are slow and stupid, and think of nothing but your silly sheep and your wrestling games."

Understanding drenched him with relief, washing away his tiredness in a moment. In the darkness he was flooded with light and tenderness. Everything was explained: her fury, her contempt, her strangeness–everything. He had been off with the drovers, getting drunk with the men and singing their songs; and she had been at home sick with his child. He would marry her, Canaanite slave as she was, he was nearly of age. His father could not refuse him her, not when he knew. A son: he was sure it would be a son.

"It is Manoah's," Tamam said, "naturally. Sharah gave me to him long ago. You would have known if you were not so blinded by your own selfishness. Sharah is barren again I suppose. And no more angels this time! Or perhaps she did not want another monster like you–yes, that was it. Who can blame her?"

The earth smelled fresh and clean, as it always did after the rain. He heard the swish of her skirts as she left him, and the jingle of her ankle chains, and that was all. Only the cicadas chirring in the fields below, down toward the valley somewhere.

He did not follow her. He stood up stiffly at last, and began to walk back the way he had come, past the house of Dorah the midwife, down toward the well and out of the village.

Somewhere behind him in the new moonlight the ash heaps stood against the sky, marking the end of Zorah. It was here that the iron figurine of the Astarte had come flying on a day in summer, and the godlike Philistine soldiers had come out of the trees he now passed through. And it was as if somewhere behind him, in the broken ground, a boy stood still as a tree and watched him go.

4

AMALEK THE CANAANITE went to the small gate for the fourth or fifth time to scan the road which drew the eye south an unbroken mile across the plain to a smudge of myrtle trees: and it looked empty all the way. It was clear after the morning rain, the dust settled, and cold. There was a shallow dip somewhere halfway to the trees and he waited a full minute to see if anything would emerge from it; but nothing did. He might have had a better view from the main gate, further along the wall, but it was a considerable business unfastening the bolts and chains, and he did not want to draw attention to his own nervousness.

He moved away from the wall at last, barring the small gate properly behind him, and crossed the compound, a small man, walking with corpulent self-importance in and out of his own granaries and storerooms. The corner barn had been half-cleared, as he had ordered, to make room for the goods his son-in-law was bringing back from Ashkelon; but the floor had not been swept.

"Ahiman!"

He went out into the sunlight but his overseer was not

there: only Jaala the herd boy, crossing the yard with an empty yoke slung over his shoulder.

"You sent him to the watchtower, Master."

"Never mind: you will do. Fetch a broom and sweep the floor inside here."

Jaala hesitated, openmouthed. He was a Cushite, and his teeth and eyes showed white as fuller's bleach in the black of his face. Amalek said with asperity, "What is it?"

"Master, you said I was to fetch water for the house. As soon as I had seen to the goats."

"Don't argue!" Amalek shouted. "Sweep the barn afterward, then. And hurry; they will be back before we are ready."

The herd boy scurried off like a black beetle, and Amalek made his way heavily up the steps to the roof of his house, the better to see the road again. On the rooftop he found his eldest daughter Esther on the same errand as himself, leaning over the opposite parapet, her thin sari billowing in a small breeze. The fine green cotton did little to hide the ample fullness of her figure, and he found himself speculating, not for the first time, how long it would be before she grew as fat as her mother. It was the only resemblance. Were it not for his cropped black beard, the face she turned toward him mirrored his own: somewhat softer of feature, but with the same defiant bluntness, snub-nosed and double-chinned. Yet curiously, she was not uncomely. Her dark brows went up in slow astonishment. "Why are you got up like that?"

Amalek glanced down at his multi-colored robe, his embroidered slippers that curled delicately up at the toes; touched a heavily ringed hand to his wide turban; and scowled. Esther herself was untidy, as always. The shift beneath her sari was, on closer inspection, none too clean, and her hair unsuccessfully braided behind her neck. He said, "You know we are expecting Sheshai back any time. You would do well to look to your own appearance."

And seeing even this small irony lost upon her, he translated: "By all the gods, woman!–can't you pretty yourself up for once?" He was shouting, but it had no effect.

All she said was, "For Sheshai?" and went back to looking over the parapet, the way they would come. Sheshai was her betrothed husband, Amalek's adopted son-in-law. Her father's servants had found him half dead by the roadside, beaten up by Amorites it was said, which was odd, seeing that he was half Amorite himself. When she came to know him better, she suspected woman trouble; somebody else's woman no doubt. Like everyone else she had fallen in love with him immediately and obviously. Sheshai drew people to him as naturally as moths to a lamp, offering nothing in return but the luminosity of his feckless charm. Her mother, her sisters and the servants from overseer to herd boys became his personal slaves. Even Amalek, at first appalled at the young stranger's idleness, and the prospect of another mouth to feed, unbent eventually. For it was discovered that Sheshai, when driven to it, had a peculiar aptitude for the business of trading. Within a month the surrounding villagers, bringing their grain and olives, their wool and hides to the compound, were asking for Sheshai rather than Amalek himself, though he was no more generous.

When Sheshai departed during the night without farewells or explanation, the only one dry-eyed in the place, apart from Amalek, was Esther herself. She was sure he had gone off with a woman from one of the coastal towns he was so fond of visiting, and was nearly as much relieved as dismayed, having fully expected it to happen. She expected there would be money missing from the treasury, too.

It turned out that she was wrong. Amalek weighed out every last shekel and pim, and it tallied. True, he kept the key himself, chained about his girth; but it would not be beyond a plausible rascal like Sheshai to find a means of abstracting it. The thought of how nearly he had been robbed made Amalek ill. Nevertheless the young man was honest, and a shrewd businessman though lazy; and such a man is not found every day in these hard times. He allowed himself to be persuaded to go and fetch Sheshai back, taking a troop of armed servants a full day's journey up the north road until they overtook the tall, lean figure striding through the dust.

There was no woman, either; or if there was Amalek never mentioned it. There was instead a rueful tale of gambling debts and the threat of the Philistines' prison house. The amount was enormous–a whole year's wages–and Amalek grew agitated. What if the Philistines came and demanded the money from *him?*

Sheshai's grin was disbelieving. "They wouldn't do that."

"They might. After all, they must know you work for me. Unless I told them where you had gone, they might. May be they would put me in prison instead of you."

Sheshai appeared much moved. He put an arm round the older man's shoulders. "You would do this for me?"

"For myself I don't mind," Amalek said unconvincingly. "But my wife; my daughters . . ." He saw the servants grinning, and shook himself free. "Come back with me," he said with a gesture of capitulation. "I will pay your debts."

"You are a kindly man," Sheshai said: "and much misjudged. What do you expect in return?"

"Nothing! You are like a son to me. If you like, you can pay me back out of your wages."

"That will take some time."

Amalek agreed. "Five years."

"Two."

"Four."

"Three."

"Three then," Amalek said, this being the number he had had in mind.

"If you make me your heir," Sheshai added.

"My *heir?* To everything?"

"You said I was like a son to you. Now I will be your son."

After a show of protest, for form's sake, Amalek agreed. Esther, the eldest daughter, was thrown in to clinch it. Sheshai was to work without wages for three years, at the end of which time he would be given Esther and title to Amalek's estate when he died: his son-in-law and next of kin.

He had served one year now; with two more to run. Amalek never ceased grumbling, and Sheshai was restless as a caged lynx, according to their natures, but both men were well satisfied with the bargain. So, although no one thought to ask her, was Esther. On the other hand she saw no need to pretend it was the flower of her beauty that had ensnared this particular wandering bee. The nectar lay not between her patient thighs, but in her father's treasury. So she answered his question with another, "For Sheshai?" and watched the road as before. It was warmer now. The cold season was drawing to an end. Already the almond trees were putting forth their delicate white blossom. Sheshai had set out for Ashkelon three days ago to trade with the Philistines who had wanted to put him in prison and were now his friends. His mission this time was important, and secret: she knew better than to ask why. Sheshai had taken an unusually strong escort–nearly all the able-bodied men, in fact, leaving the compound virtually unguarded. But it was high-walled and secure enough: it did not seem to Esther to explain Amalek's jumpiness. He was unsettled as a dog with an itchy tail. And she wondered if Sheshai was in some sort of trouble again.

"What if he brings home a guest?" Amalek said, falling back on improbabilities. "That grand Philistine lord he is so friendly with–what's his name. Athol. You want we should shut you away out of sight in the harem, like the barbarians?"

"I should think Sheshai would prefer him to look on Athaliah or Miriam, rather than his espoused wife."

"That shows you know nothing about men," Amalek snorted. "And Miriam is only a child."

"Well, Athaliah isn't."

Athaliah, the middle of the three sisters, had inherited their mother's much-admired fairness, and was slender and vain. Nobody ever had to tell Athaliah to pretty herself up.

Amalek was gathering the skirts of his robe to leave. "Think yourself lucky to be firstborn, that's all. Athaliah is better looking than you, and younger, and she doesn't argue. Men cannot stand women who argue."

At the top of the steps he added: "Sheshai would have taken Athaliah, you know, if he had had the choice."

"Yes."

Esther watched her father's dignified retreat down the steps and round the angle of the house, not looking to left or right, which indicated something more serious on his mind. She wondered if it was true, that she knew nothing about men. She knew her father. The Philistine would never make the journey all the way out here to their modest house, but Amalek dressed himself up in his best raiment in case he might. Already he was mentally presiding over the nuptials of his second daughter, seeing her as one day a princess in a palace in Gaza. He was nothing if not an optimist.

She heard Miriam calling her name fretfully, and flew down the steps, afraid the child had fallen or injured herself.

Miriam had trapped her small fingers in the counting-house scales, but freed them herself before Esther reached her. There was no damage, only a little redness, an excuse to claim attention. Esther put the fingers to her lips, and returned them with a reproachful pat. "You know you are not allowed to play in here." But she could remember herself as a child, the irresistible attraction of the weights: the smooth carved stone and bronze figures of lions, oxen, ducks, frogs. There was even a little scarab beetle, the smallest of them all. She retrieved a porphyry sheep from the floor, blew the dust off it and replaced it on the bench.

"Papa said I could," Miriam told her.

Esther half believed it. Miriam was Amalek's one weakness.

Miriam was moving a green frog along the bench top in little jumps. "If the bad men come I will hide in the loft. And I'll *pull* the ladder up so they can't catch me."

"Good idea," Esther said.

Then she said, "What bad men?"

Miriam made a lion jump on the frog. "*A—morites,*" she said. "There's lots and lots of them in the fields killing all our sheep. That's why Jaala had to fetch the water. Papa wouldn't let me go."

"You're making it up."

Miriam was indignant. "I'm not either. Ask Jaala, he will tell you."

"Then Jaala must have made it up," Esther said with more conviction than she felt. "He is wicked to frighten you with such tales."

Not that Miriam seemed particularly frightened; more

cross at being kept in. And Jaala would hardly have invented a story which cast himself in the role of water-carrier, women's work and much beneath the dignity of a male, even a herd boy.

"Do lions eat frogs?" Miriam wanted to know.

Esther wasn't sure. Where was the child's nursemaid? She said, "It's time for your rest."

"Are you coming to rest too?"

"Yes, presently."

Miriam skipped out into the sunshine, and Esther went in search of Jaala, who was nowhere to be found. The emptiness of the courtyard was suddenly ominous; as if everybody had run away. It was Ahiman the overseer, peering over the edge of the watchtower in answer to her call, who confirmed Miriam's story. It was true: two men had gone out from the house in the morning to fetch in a fat lamb, to be held in readiness against the arrival of a guest. They had come upon a band of Amorite brigands, already feasting on a carcass from their own flock: wild men in sheepskin, armed to the teeth. They had returned empty-handed with broken heads, lucky to escape with their lives.

"Your father did not want to alarm the womenfolk. There is nothing we can do until Master Sheshai returns with the men. We bolted the gates, and he set me to watch here. You can still see their fires over the hill."

Esther climbed the ladder to look. The wheatfields were still green beside the river, over toward the far white walls of Libnah, the old Canaanite royal city. Their own pastureland was lightly wooded, rising ground that masked the hills beyond. At first she could see nothing; but following Ahiman's trembling finger just made out a wisp of smoke, and perhaps something moving out there. It was still difficult to believe; it must have been a decade since the Amorites dared to raid so far west into civilized country.

"What became of the herd boy?" she said. "Somebody must have been watching the flock."

Ahiman nodded gloomily. "He ran off. They say he went to Libnah for help."

They both knew he would not get it. There were chariots in Libnah, but they were for the safeguarding of the city, and those villages close outside its walls that came under the king's domain.

Esther went indoors to find the household in an uproar. Miriam had repeated Jaala's story, and their mother Bilhah had promptly retired to her bed with an attack of hysteria. She was there now, her plump softness heaving on the creaking cords, like a fair buffalo in the mud, her face flushed in sharp contrast to the ashen paleness of Athaliah, bending over her. The room was full of women servants, vying in shrill competition with remembered tales of famous Amorite atrocities, especially on women. Esther's attempt at peacemaking went unheeded. It was Amalek himself, storming among them with furious gestures, who restored the peace.

"Sheshai is back," he said furiously. "Up! Come!"–he was driving them like cattle–"You, and you! About your business. He has brought us a guest." He told Esther: "I am surprised at you. See to your mother."

He shooed the last of the servants out with Miriam clinging to his hand, shouting for the men to open the gates.

They were open already, with Ahiman bowing his head as Amalek bustled through, smoothing the folds of his robe. Sheshai was still a fair way off, riding the second-best mule, having given the white one–the best in the stables–to the guest who rode alongside him. Amalek nodded his approval. It was the Philistine, then. He was disappointed the princeling had not come in a royal chariot; or at least brought a fine mule of his own. Nor, it seemed, an escort; though it was difficult to tell. They had outstripped the slow-moving train of ox carts which, in fact, appeared to have stopped altogether. The men there were clustering round like ants.

"A wheel clean off," Sheshai explained, sliding his long legs to the ground to greet his father-in-law with his usual ironic kiss on the hand; a warmer kiss followed for Miriam. "These roads! Couldn't shift it–with all that weight aboard: we shall need a beam for leverage. I brought our guest on."

He was older than Amalek had expected: a clean-shaven, high-boned face, unmistakably Philistine; but the hauteur diminished by a bagginess about the eyes, a certain looseness of jowl and blotchiness of texture. Amalek did not like anything about him. It took an effort to embrace the man, pressing his costly embroidery against that unpleasantly stained and nondescript traveling cloak–a sensible precaution when traveling abroad, but not what one expected from the Philistines–and was rewarded with a whiff of alcohol so powerful that he involuntarily stepped back.

"A thousand welcomes to our poor house, my Lord. My servants wait to attend to your needs. We are doubly honored and fortunate to have you with us this day."

"How's that?" The speech was slurred.

Amalek took his arm. "Now you are here, I place myself and my house under your protection. My Lord, we have Amorite bandits in the sheepfold stealing and burning this very instant."

"In that case," the Philistine said, coming suddenly alive, "the sooner we get inside and bar the gates the better." He bolted through the gates himself, leaving his host speechless. Amalek sent Miriam after him. Sheshai was shaking with laughter.

"And this is your soldier-prince?" Amalek said coldly: "the famous Athol, son to the Ser of Gaza?"

"No, it isn't. His name is Jason, and he's in the wine business; though you wouldn't think so, he doesn't hold his drink very well, does he." Sheshai said, "Bear with him, 'Malek. Tell the servants to bed him down with a jar of wine, and he'll be happy enough–we'll talk to him later. He has extensive vineyards at Timnath. He will be useful to us."

He paused, to let it sink in, and said: "Now, what is this about Amorite bandits?"

Amalek told him briefly, impatient to ask: "You were successful, then?"

"Have you ever known me to fail?" Sheshai made it a reproach; then allowed himself a satisfied grin. "We have everything–ploughshares, mattocks, hoes, sickles: all of the finest iron. We shall be able to name our own price. They make our old bronze tools as primitive as flint or stone."

Amalek glanced back toward the line of stationary ox wagons, permitting himself a moment of jealousy that was like the first sip of new wine. Like the other Canaanite traders, he had been trying for years to persuade the Philistines to allow the carefully guarded products of their iron foundries to be sold outside their own estates. "How did you do it?"

"Drinking, mostly. They made conditions, however. The tools we sell must be taken to one of their own forges for sharpening. I tried to hire their smiths to come here, but they refused."

It was to be expected. Amalek was mentally computing the enormous profit. "And what do they want of us? Not silver."

"No. Barley, figs, olive oil, wool–the usual. Oh, and wine. Especially wine. That's why I brought Jason back. His wine is the best in Canaan."

"But he is a Philistine himself! So why does he need us to trade with his own people?"

"Don't let him hear you say that. Jason comes from one of the old families: they settled here generations before their 'sea peoples' tried to invade Egypt. He thinks them upstarts, these newly arrived, self-styled kings, the *Seren* of the five cities. He is indebted to me, by the way–if he remembers when he sobers up. I saved him from a tricky situation. He insulted Athol, no less. He insisted on addressing the prince in their classic Philistine tongue; and of course Athol didn't understand a word, though his grandfather would have. He took the point all right. He had already called his father's bodyguard and was all for having Jason flayed alive and his skin nailed to the door. He would have done it, too."

Amalek winced. "So what did you do?"

"I persuaded Athol he meant it for a compliment. I told him it was a form of address the old people reserved for royalty; though I'd no more idea what Jason had said than he had. Then every time Jason opened his mouth I poured it full of wine until he was too far gone to speak to anybody–well, he spoke to me, naturally: that's how I learned of his vineyards, and tasted some of the wine samples he'd brought with him. But he has no notion how to trade. I wanted to bring Athol back, as you know. But he was none too pleased with me by then. So I brought Jason instead, to keep them apart. I told you, this man will be useful to us."

"Well he's no use to us now," Amalek said. "And while you stand gossiping like a woman, our sheep are being carried away into the hills. Take half the men."

Sheshai straightened his aching back and touched his forehead in a grave salute. "My Lord." Then he said, *"Half?"*

"I shall need the rest to bring the wagons in. We cannot leave the iron unguarded. Take half."

Sheshai took none. It was less costly to lose sheep than men; and if he could bargain with Philistines, why not Amorites? Nevertheless by the time he was into the open woodland, riding the second-best mule up past the mausoleum where they laid their dead, with a purse of shekels in his waistband to buy the raiders off, some of his confidence had evaporated, and it was no small relief to find on cresting the ridge that they had already gone. A solitary peasant squatted by the remains of their fire, evidently scavenging what they had left. Sheshai mentally saluted a fellow opportunist. To his surprise the creature made no move to run off at his approach, but went on chewing unconcernedly at what looked like a whole haunch: one animal eating another, for he was huddled in an old sheepskin himself, his matted hair indistinguishable from the blackened wool; an ugly-looking fellow, and bigger than he looked at first.

Sheshai drew rein beside him. "That sheep you are gorging yourself on, my friend, belongs to my father-in-law."

"He is welcome to it," was the growled reply: "when I have finished." The peasant had not so much as glanced up, and Sheshai flushed. His long fingers edged inside his cloak for the reassuring solidness of his dagger hilt. The man seemed unarmed, at least.

"You've a bold tongue for a thief. Do not imagine that I come alone. My men are following me at this moment."

"They are still trying to get the wheel back on your ox cart."

Sheshai rubbed his chin. How long had the fellow been up here, watching? He said more amiably, "Come, we might overlook the sheep, if you will tell me which way the Amorites went. And how many."

"Amorites?" The man tossed the mutton bone into the ashes of the fire and wiped the back of his hand across his mouth, revealing himself as little more than a youth, with only the beginnings of a beard. "I saw no one. Save a couple of lads who came on me from behind with staves, and I knocked their heads together. They weren't Amorites. They went back into your city"–he pointed down to Amalek's house with its outbuildings. "And I'm no thief: I will pay for your sheep."

"With your life, it may be."

The man merely shrugged, and Sheshai said curiously, "With what, then?"

"With these." The peasant suddenly stood up and spread his hands with a rush of truculence, like a man not so much begging for alms as demanding them. He was uncomfortably close, and Sheshai drew his mule back a pace.

"We have hands enough already."

"Not like these," the man said, and disappeared beneath the mule's belly. Startled, Sheshai went for his dagger; but the next moment was clinging with both hands to bridle, mane, neck, as man and beast rose in the air, the mule's four legs kicking wildly on nothing.

He raised the ox cart the same way, though with greater effort, until it seemed his splayed legs must drive down into the earth: but the cart creaked and groaned and finally lifted with an almighty clatter of iron inside, while the men stood in a semi-circle of dumb disbelief. Amalek had taken four of them to the house to fetch a lever, and met the procession at the gates as he came out.

"Here is your band of Amorites," Sheshai said. "Samson the Hebrew, who has come to join us."

□

The Canaanite menials among whom Samson came to live at the end of that winter at first kept their distance recognizing, as Sheshai had not, that his savagely unkempt appearance betokened among his people the deepest mourning. He ate and slept by himself, adopting a corner of the bachelor house the others avoided because of a leak in the wattling. Only Ahiman the overseer, obliged to speak with him to allot his tasks for the day, ventured to ask if perhaps someone close to him had died.

"Aye," was the answer. "Myself."

If the reply meant nothing to Ahiman, withdrawing to

report the newcomer somewhat demented in his grief, it satisfied Samson deeply. To Jaala, materializing from the shadows of the barn to ask timidly if it was true, if he had really and truly been *dead,* he answered with fierce conviction.

"And in Gehenna." Samson looked at the herd boy and said, "That is where the dead go, and are eaten of worms."

"But you are alive now."

"Yes."

"That is a . . ." Jaala scratched the black wool of his head, searching for a word. He came out with *mystery,* and Samson scowled.

"No it isn't. Injustice and betrayal are mysteries, that eat at a man's soul like worms. There's no mystery in death; not even your own."

Jaala understood no better than Ahiman. They went in to the barn together and Samson relented, clapping a hand on the lad's shoulder. "More of a riddle: listen! He is born in his grave; and in his mother's womb he is buried."

"The seed," Jaala said; because Samson was sifting the grain through his fingers as he spoke.

"And all things growing," Samson said. "Man–the adam–he is no different."

He found a pitchfork and began hefting great bales of the straw up into the open loft. Jaala was up the ladder, scampering about like a dark spider, spreading it out. He called down, "Does it hurt much?–the dying part?"

"Aye. So does the being born, I'll wager, if we could think back on it."

Jaala said he would not like to die, and Samson leant on his pitchfork and chuckled for the first time.

"You don't want to be herd boy forever? Maybe one day you will be overseer; and where will the little herd boy be then, eh?"

And he said, "Dead and buried, Jaala; dead and buried like Samson of Zorah. And good riddance."

Jaala's face puckered with the effort of following this. "You were buried in Zorah?"

"Much of me," Samson said, and pitched up an enormous fork of hay that buried Jaala in the loft; and grinned at the black face that emerged. "But there was still enough left to frighten the wolves away from the sheepfolds in the hills between Dan and Judah: aye, and the Bedouin too."

Mostly, from preference, Samson worked among the animals, mucking out the stables, grooming the mules, watching the familiar sheep, feeding the oxen. The beasts were more to his liking than his fellow men, and more sensible. They accepted their lot without envy or complaint. They copulated among themselves, but they did not love. The men flattered him out of respect for his prodigious strength and despised him for his rough ways, and the beasts did neither.

The animals were few, however. In the Shephelah a man would be thought poor, whose sheep could be numbered at a glance; the Canaanites there lived much as the Hebrews, with their flocks and their ploughing and vines. These traders were a different breed. All life and living was confined within the circle of Amalek's own walls which, though they might have taken in Zorah with room to spare, extensive enough to be taken for a city when he first looked on them–still seemed crowded most days with the coming and going, the weighing and measuring and counting, the bartering of the Philistine ironware.

Sheshai's journeys to the Philistine towns became more frequent; even Amalek complained less as he saw his coffers swell. From his rooftop he noticed Samson sitting under a tree beyond the walls and called out to him, but Samson either did not hear or ignored him, and moved off. Amalek sent for his overseer in a high rage.

"That fellow"–his finger shook at Samson's distant back–"Why is he not at work?"

Ahiman peered nervously; then his brow cleared. "It is the Hebrew, Master. This is his holy day. It is the seventh day by their reckoning, when they must rest."

"Is that a fact," Amalek said through his teeth. "And does he not eat our food on his holy day, or shelter under our roof, or wear the garments we have given him on his holy day?"

He punctuated his speech with little needle jabs of his forefinger at the overseer's chest, his voice gradually rising with his color, driving Ahiman backward around the roof. Ahiman's uncertain protest–"It is their custom, Lord"–was drowned by his roar:

“Do not speak to me of custom!–you are growing old, I will find me a younger man.”

“Nay, Master–”

“Go tell this barbarian,” Ahiman hissed at him, “that he is not among his people now. Go tell him he will work with the rest. Or tell him to *go!*”

Ahiman fled with the message. But work on the Sabbath, Samson would not. He would have gone, with the easy compliance with which he received all instructions, but because he had by now accustomed himself to taking on many of the arduous and disagreeable chores the other men most disliked, he had many and unexpected allies. A deputation went to Ahiman who, not risking a second confrontation with his master, conveyed an elaborately paraphrased version of their complaint through Sheshai. Sheshai himself was more direct.

He told Amalek: “I would not make an enemy of this fellow. Remember what he did to our sheep herds. Moreover by employing him you buy the strength of ten men for the price of one.”

“Buy? You *pay* him?”

“When he has worked off the price of the sheep he stole,” Sheshai said smoothly. “And the garments he now wears. But only the same as the herd boys.”

As usual, when his bullying was to no avail, Amalek discovered an injury to his own good nature. “Must I work myself all the hours in the day, to feed a man who sleeps one day in seven? Do we not have holy days and festivals enough to satisfy the laziest among our people?”

Then he said, “Tell me. Do not the barbarians have the same festivals as we have?”

Sheshai said, “No.” In fact, he had no idea.

“Then he can work on our holy days, instead of on his.”

It was as a result of this decree that Samson first saw inside Amalek’s mansion, absolutely barred to all but the household servants. Even Ahiman, when he wished to see his master, must wait under the stone porch until Amalek came out to him.

It was on the first day of the feast of the goddess of the evening star–Anath, who was also goddess of women–in the dusk. One of the cows was in calf and Samson had stayed with her in the stable until the light faded, and looked for a lamp, and found none. He came out into the courtyard and almost collided with one of the women, who sped past shrieking, closely followed by a man he recognized as one of the priests of Baal, who closed with her and dragged her squealing pleasurably into the shadows. There were other shadows, heaving and grunting, and abundant sounds of carousal from the workers' lines beyond the house, but no one about to assist him. The torches in their sockets on the walls were burned down neglected in their clouds of insects, and useless for his purpose. He came to the house, pushing open the unlatched door to an unlit chamber, cool as a tomb. Beyond it was another, where lamplight outlined a half-open door beside a round gong that hung like a shield. Here were flagged stone floors softened with fleecy rugs and woven carpets that deadened his footfall, and a luxury of furnishings that held him amazed: carved chairs and footstools, a low table with feet like a lion's paws, swan-necked pottery and polished brass that burned with reflected flames; and in a corner a shrine like a little house with windows, sheltering, when he came up to it, a little fat goddess who sat invitingly, open-legged. She reminded Samson of a cow in labor, and he took the lamp and turned to go, to find his exit barred by Athaliah.

Apart from Amalek that first day, he had seen none of the family save at a distance. But even without the jewels at her throat and in her pale hair, there would have been no mistaking Athaliah for a servant. Wraithlike in the doorway, her white sari misty in the flickering light, she might have been Anath herself. Even her voice seemed to come from a great distance, or another world, though the words were common enough.

"I suppose you are drunk," she said with disgust. "No matter: that will not save you."

Samson lowered the lamp a little. Since she had made no move to veil herself, he had full view of a cold and beautiful face, that might turn a man's head if it only had a little more blood in it. He said, "Neither drunk, nor in need of saving. I came for the lamp, to save a calf halfway born. Move aside."

No man had spoken so to Athaliah in her life, let alone a black animal of a peasant with matted hair and the stench of cattle on him. She recoiled with a physical aversion. "I will have you flogged–*to death.*"

Without vacating the doorway she reached behind her, and the next moment the deep boom of the gong reverberated through the house. They both waited, and no one came.

Athaliah bit her lip furiously. She was confident that sober or drunk he would not dare force his way past; but she could not stand here forever. Nor would it satisfy her present mood to have him flogged in the morning, when the men returned.

"Very well then. I will do it myself."

She darted suddenly across the room, and when he would have passed through the doorway at last, was back with an evil-looking leather whip, slashing inexpertly at his face before he had the wit to lift his arms to protect himself; raining blows upon his upraised arms, his chest and shoulders until her strength was spent in a rush of sobbing, and she collapsed on the floor. Samson had offered no resistance. When she had done he stepped over her and walked out of the house unhindered.

There was so much blood from the calving that it was not until the spindly creature was safely delivered and being cleaned by its mother's searching tongue, and he went to clean himself, that he found an astonishing amount of the blood his own.

There was no reference to the incident the following day. Samson told the men he had fallen in a thorn bush, and if they did not believe him, there were too many with bites and scratches for it to evoke more than a sly wink. He guessed correctly that Athaliah had no business to punish a male with her own hand–the women were a different matter, and were slapped often enough–and would not dare report the matter to her father. Once, after some days, returning from the sheepfold he glimpsed Athaliah looking down from the rooftop and their eyes met. One at least of the marks–on his cheek–he would bear for life, and he saw the satisfaction in her face before she turned quickly aside. It made him laugh suddenly, and he went into the granary without looking where he was going, and banged his head on the lintel post.

The rains thinned and died away at last; the wheat whitened the riverfields and the figs swelled green, and it grew hotter. In the Shephelah there would be tulips, wild gladioli, yellow crocuses and blood red anemones; the women out pruning the vines and the men ploughing with the harrow for the spring crops. Only the turtle doves, with their familiar and intimate keening in the roof of the watch-tower, reminded Samson of the Shephelah. There were times when he forgot Tamam; he had long since forgiven her. But Manoah he had neither forgiven nor forgotten for a moment.

Sheshai came to him in the timber yard on a scorching afternoon, when most of the men were at rest, with a leathern purse and emptied silver and copper into his hand. "Your wages. What is the matter: have you never seen money before?"

Samson turned the little bars and wedges in his palm. "Aye, I've seen it. But we've not much use for money where I am from."

Since he had been working in the open, he had stripped to the *saq* about his loins. Not knowing what to do with the money, he stuffed it into his headband.

Sheshai watched him with amusement, seeing the dark eyes already wandering in search of the next task. The barbarian was much changed since he had found him on the hill. Say one thing for Amalek: he fed his animals well, if only to get the best out of them. The coarse barley meal had put weight on Samson; the wild shooting of beard over his face and the rich black mane of hair gave him a leonine look; Amalek would do well to breed from him. Sheshai said aloud, "Are you not going to weigh it?"

Not even the most ignorant clod accepted money without telling its worth on the scales; but Samson only shrugged. "What would I do with it?"

"Why, purchase something for yourself," Sheshai explained with rare patience; though he could not imagine what, come to think of it. Ludicrous to imagine this shaggy bear in fine raiment, soft leather shoes; fingering a delicately chased dagger in his great paw, even. There would be little in

Amalek's storehouses to tempt Samson. Sheshai scratched his long chin. A cloak?–a chalouk–something dyed in bright colors, such as could be had at a price in the town bazaars. He gave up. "You think, and tell me. And I will fetch whatever it is when next I visit the coast."

Samson wandered off without answering, and Sheshai gave him no further thought until Esther, who never made the smallest intrusion into his male world, surprisingly accused him of favoring the Hebrew.

There had been a family dispute over the evening meal started, innocently enough, by Sheshai himself. He had suggested that Amalek take a villa in Ashkelon on the coast for the summer season, where the family might enjoy the sea cool, and something of the social life there. He said it, as he said everything, half in jest; but Bilhah and Athaliah had taken it up greedily. That they could now afford such a luxury was not in dispute. But Amalek was adamant. The coast was unhealthy; it was well known that the plagues and diseases of Egypt were rife all along the coast. And since he would trust neither his family nor his business out of his sight, it meant they could neither go with him nor without him. Sheshai left them arguing to make the night rounds, checking the gates, storehouses and the watch. It was the first time Amalek had allowed it to be done by any but himself. Esther followed without being missed.

They were seldom alone. The night was starry, with a full moon that peopled the courtyards with deep shadows. Sheshai turned and said, "Ah, I hoped you would come," making it believable, and slid his arm about her, drawing her out of the moonlight toward the wall. He was so much the taller, she could see his expression only by tilting her head, which she did not do.

"I needed the air," she said to excuse herself. "My head aches."

"Mine too." His hand lifted to soothe her brow. "You think I am wrong, don't you."

"You seek my opinion?"

"It is the only one we have not heard."

She smiled to herself at that. "It would be a good thing for Athaliah to spend some time on the coast. Bilhah thinks so too. Athaliah will be hard put to find a husband here."

"You did."

"I was going to say: of her choosing."

Even Sheshai was affronted. It was a dangerously novel idea, like a slave choosing a master, or an ox a yoke. True, if the woman were well born, and rich and clever enough, she might have a say in the matter. Did she think her sister one of such woman? Esther shook her head.

"That is just it. She is the second sister; she will lack my dowry. The man who takes Athaliah must want her for herself. She has little but her looks, and that is a luxury only the rich can afford. Her worth is small among our people here. She should have some freedom to choose her way of life."

"In a palace, no doubt! Isn't that what every woman would *choose?*–if we followed your wild and discontented notions!" He lifted her chin with cruel fingers. "Or is it for yourself you speak, little Esther?"

She said with difficulty, "Can you see me in a palace?"

That marvelous face was no more than a span from her own, looking down like an evil god on her tormented flesh. His fingers sucked every drop of affection from her, as casually as a man squeezing an orange. She made no response; neither to the hurt, nor to his nearness; and this seemed to provoke him the more. He bent down and pulled her mouth impatiently to his, bruising her lips. His voice at her ear was shaken: "You don't know how much I want you, Esther."

Indeed she knew. Pressed against her, his need was evident; if not for her, for some woman; and she dropped her eyes. "You shall have me soon enough."

"Not soon enough for me."

"Until then," she said evenly, moving on within the wall's shadow, "try to be patient. With my family also. My father will never agree to leave this place, even for a season. He is lord here, the people bow to him. In your cities he would be another merchant, kissing the feet of your precious Philistines like all the rest."

Sheshai had paused to test the bars of the small gate; and caught up with long frustrated strides. He said between his teeth, "You are as blind as he is. What do you know of the Philistines? You see a few soldiers marching in column like sheep; their chariots out playing at hunting–a drunken old aristocrat: Jason! You don't know how powerful they are. You think they are few, and so they are; but they command the loyalty of half the Canaanites of the plain–and the obedience of the other half! They have their walled cities, just the five cities, and you think they are like our cities, which are many, but they are not. Ours are scattered, each one a little kingdom to itself with its villages, and each one's hand against his neighbor when it comes to it; when the Philistines move they move as one man. And their influence is growing all the time. It is as well to be numbered among their friends."

It was one of the longest speeches he had ever made to Esther; such as husband might make to wife. She concealed her pleasure with an innocent question: "Is that why you have cultivated the prince Athol?"

Sheshai's grin acknowledged her shrewdness. "He is the most dangerous of all, because he thinks; and he knows what others are thinking. I tell you, Esther, Athol will be their Lord of Battles before he's finished, and like to win his wars without having to fight any. Because in our time, Esther–yours and mine–the Philistines will place their mark in every corner of the land. Nothing can stop them, when they march."

He said, "And march they will."

"You say that as if you would welcome it."

He did not deny it. "Look how much better off the Canaanites are, under their rule. They will put a stop to the border raids, and the murder and the stealing; open up the country for free trading. The only ones who won't welcome it are the Habiru, who keep their women veiled and think all pleasure is wicked."

"What of your own people; the Amorites?"

"Sod the Amorites," Sheshai said cheerfully. "The Philistines will bring their laws and their ironware and civilization to the wilderness, and riches. And I want us to be with them. I want my children to grow up like their children."

"Perhaps you should marry a Philistine girl."

Sheshai did laugh then. "There's no talking to you, Esther. Am I not espoused already?" He kissed her again, but gently this time. "You see, I have no choice in the matter, any more than you, or Athaliah. Any of us."

It was then that Esther said what she had followed him out of the house to say: "Except only the Hebrew. He may come and go as he pleases, it seems."

"Samson?" Sheshai's dark eyebrows rose comically. "Esther, your thoughts are like butterflies. A man might run all day and never catch hold of a one. What has Samson to do with us?"

"He frightens me. I wish he would go."

"Then I will get rid of him."

"When?"

She was serious. He said, "In the morning."

Esther raised her eyes slowly. "Will you? My father gave orders that he should be sent away, and he is still with us. He broke into the house and threatened my sister–yes! Athaliah told me–and was not punished. The servants lower their eyes properly and stand aside when we pass them: he does not. He is not a servant; what is he?"

But she knew, from the way Sheshai withdrew within himself, that she had gone too far. Amalek was right after all: a man cannot stand a woman who argues. But she could not prevent herself from putting a last question: "Why do you befriend this uncouth ox?"

Perhaps because the Hebrew had come as he himself had: friendless and from nowhere, with nothing in his hand. But it was the unexpected tinge of jealousy in Esther that alarmed Sheshai. He told her not to meddle with things outside the house. She accepted the rebuke meekly, almost it seemed with pleasure, and left him. Afterward, Sheshai wondered if it was because she imagined she had her own way.

In the morning, busy with preparations for a visit to Ashkelon, supervising the loading of the carts with oil and grain of barley for the Philistine garrison, and skins for the market, he was still undecided when Samson appeared in the crowded compound with a request. He unknotted a bundle of cloth, and displayed the wages Sheshai had paid him.

"You said you would bring me something back from the city."

Mentally, Sheshai damned the fellow. If he agreed, it

would seem to Esther a deliberate slight. If he refused, his word was broken. "What is it you want?"

"A lyre," Samson said. And seeing Sheshai's blank look, went on: "With strings, to play on and make music . . ."

"I know what a lyre is! Very well, a lyre. But what sort of lyre? There are hundreds."

It was evident, after a moment's hesitation, that Samson had no idea. He knew only that he would recognize it if he saw it: the one he wanted.

"You had better come with us and choose for yourself," Sheshai said impatiently. It struck him suddenly as an inspired idea. At least it would get the Hebrew out of the way for a time; perhaps he could be found a place in Ashkelon, even. Then he looked at Samson again, doubting it. "You cannot travel with us like that; we take only picked men."

"Pick one better then," Samson said, and turned on his heel. Sheshai gritted his teeth; then broke into a grin, shaking his head. He called him back.

"We leave in the hour. Go find the barber if you want to come. Tell Ahiman I say you are to join the escort; he will give you cloak and spear and fresh sandals–whatever you need." It was already getting uncomfortably hot; flies were swarming about the patient oxen. The men began to assemble in groups, squatting along the ditch in what shade they could find. Amalek came down as usual to hurry the proceedings, and warn them to keep closed up for safety, and keep a sharp watch. Sheshai, listening with half an ear, gave the order to move off; whips cracked, the drivers shouted, and the solid wooden wheels creaked and began to turn. The spearmen fell in alongside, four to a cart, two on each side. Sheshai looked back from his seat beside the driver of the leading wagon to count their numbers; counted twice before he realized that Samson was among them.

□

The barber was a Libnahite who had found a ready trade with Amalek's ladies, since they favored the old conservative styles, and with his workmen, who knew nothing of fashion.

He washed Samson's hair and oiled it, and combed it until it shone, marveling at the unusual growth and richness of it. He sharpened his razors on an oilstone while the Hebrew gazed in astonishment into the mirror handed him, a circle of polished metal attached to a worn wooden handle. It might have been Manoah's face staring out at him, and Samson handed the mirror back in disgust.

"Now," the barber said, coming beside him with the bronze razor gleaming in his fingers, weaving in anticipation. "Where shall we begin? You wish to keep the beard? Trimmed so . . . and so . . ."

Samson covered his own mouth with one broad hand.

"Shave me here," he said, and drew the hand downward over his throat.

It was soon done. His mouth emerged, curling with the sting of the razor's edge, his throat reddened and sore; the beard gone. He held his hand out for the mirror again. He was left with the long side whiskers that satisfied Hebrew law, curling inward as if seeking lost friends. He touched them, and hesitated. At least he no longer resembled his father.

"And the hair," the barber said, lifting it from behind with expert fingers. "It's been long neglected."

Over his shoulder, in the mirror, the barber looked like a fatter Uzziel; not that he was fat. What was it Uzziel had said? *How many young men in Israel? . . . And Yahweh Adonai chose him Samson.*

But it was Manoah who made him Nazirite. Manoah who made the vows for the unborn child.

"To . . . *here?*" the barber said. And his fingers almost caressingly touched the base of Samson's neck.

The effect was alarming. Samson whirled as if stung by a hornet, so violently that the razor flew from the barber's fingers. The man took one look at his face and cowered.

Samson snatched a cloth to wipe his face, and gathering the full length of his hair over his wrist, wound it round and round his head, securing it with his headband. He snatched up cloak and spear and ran out into the sunshine.

Now, seeing Sheshai's gaze pass over him, and return in openmouthed recognition, he passed his hand over the unfamiliar smoothness of his own mouth and returned the Amorite's wondering grin.

"Why," Sheshai exclaimed, waiting to fall into step and smite him between his heavy shoulders: "Who would have thought it? You look positively handsome! You are one of us."

5

BEYOND THE MYRTLE GROVE, out of sight of Amalek's walls, the road wound among low hills, every so often with a village clustered over the crest, with its gardens and yellow flowering olives. This was the Philistine highway north and south from Ekron to Gath. Gath lay ten miles to the southeast. But they turned westward on a lesser track toward the sea. You could smell it already.

Samson surveyed the undulating moorland from the back of Sheshai's cart, his legs dangling. From the Shephelah it looked a uniform, dusty green; but it wasn't, it was carpeted with scarlet poppies and blue anemones, mallow and iris and narcissus–the yellow rose of Sharon–and everywhere the white daisy, which hill people called the lily of the valley. *Philistine country,* Sheshai had called it, turning his head, but he was wrong: it was the land Yahweh had given Dan for their inheritance, from the Shephelah to the sea.

They passed through the blackened remains of what must once have been a village, a desolate acre of scattered mudbricks and charred timber where nothing grew. The men, who had been singing, fell silent. Even the oxen seemed not to like the place, and quickened their step with no prompting from the goad. Samson commented that the

Philistines did not seem to keep their country in very good order, and Sheshai turned his head.

"On the contrary. This was no border raid. There was a dispute over taxes; the summer before last, after the harvest. They say the tax collector was killed in a brawl–anyway, he disappeared. The Philistines sent a cohort and burned the village to the ground. There has been no trouble since."

Samson surveyed the meager ruins. "So where did the villagers go?"

"Nowhere."

The village was behind them, the men chanting their slow song again. Sheshai said, "Remember it, Hebrew. There is a law here, and those who do not abide by the law perish by it."

"I will bear it in mind," Samson said.

In the forenoon they rested at a well, shaking stones from their sandals, dust from their clothes. A troop of women from a nearby village, who had evidently been watching their approach, filed down bearing pitchers on their heads to draw water for men and beasts. Unlike Hebrew women, they were carelessly veiled–one or two not veiled at all, exposing their faces shamelessly–and the men, who had passed this way many times, spoke slyly to them, calling them by their names, and pinched their buttocks for anyone to see. Manoah would have stoned the lot of them.

Afterward they came down through a series of great and golden cornfields, the granaries of the Philistines, the city clearly visible, and beyond it the sea; not at all as Samson had imagined it. From the heights of the Shephelah it was a dead blue desert; but it was alive. He was still staring at it, seated beside Sheshai in the front of the leading cart, when they came to the main coast road, a broad street of laid stones which Sheshai told him was part of that same highway which came up from Egypt on their left hand and continued all the way up to Carmel and lands beyond on their right. Here the traffic was heavy in both directions, a colorful bustling of travelers, mostly afoot but some with asses decked with bells and ribbons and baskets.

They crossed over at last, and now their way led straight to the city, through coarse and marshy grasses interleaved with long tongues of sand. The flies grew more troublesome, the flat stone houses more frequent, in twos and threes, with their vegetable patches and cooking fires; then clustered together along the wayside until they were passing continuously between them, the children standing to watch, and their unveiled mothers casting glances. They were approaching the great painted walls of Ashkelon itself, towering to the sky where the bulging house windows looked down like watchtowers.

The gateway dwarfed them, a massive stone arch five times the height of a standing man; but the great, iron-studded gates which would fill it stood back, and a solitary guard stepped casually into their path to signal them to a halt. He was a tall Canaanite in the uniform of a Philistine foot-soldier, with the feathered helmet and metalled leather armor Samson well remembered. Sheshai handed him a papyrus from his purse, and the man glanced at the writing and nodded. Nevertheless, it was not until he had walked down the column, prodding here, lifting the coverings there, that they were allowed to proceed inside.

"Who is this?" He was looking hard at Samson as they passed. "We haven't seen him before."

"He is my kinsman," Sheshai answered. The clatter of their cartwheels on the paved street cleared a path through the busy marketplace. Samson turned his head to ask Sheshai why he had said kinsman. He had to say it twice, competing with the cries of the street vendors.

Sheshai met his glance, which was merely curious; wanting to know. He shrugged. "It was necessary to say something."

"Why kinsman?"

"What else?"

"You could have said, he is a Hebrew."

Sheshai looked at him in disbelief; but he really did not know. "They would likely have seized you for a spy. Your northern brethren, north of Dan—what tribe is that?"

"Ephraim."

"Yes, Ephraimites. They've been giving the Philistines a packet of trouble recently. Hebrews are not too welcome here. What is the matter now?"

Because Samson was making a face. "The smell . . ."

"This is the street of the scent sellers."

It was a pungent aroma that assaulted the nostrils, overpoweringly feminine, penetrating even the oxen smell and the drains. It reminded Samson suddenly of Tamam; though in fact she had never had the means to buy scent. There seemed to be shops, bazaars and stalls of every kind, crowded with shoppers fingering linen, turning carpets and rugs, sniffing the fish, lifting brassware to the light. But it was the women Samson noticed most. Not since he was a child, admitted freely to the harem, had he seen women striding and talking like this, with upraised eyes and voices: for all the world as if there were not a man to observe them. Their voices dominated the street sounds. No God-fearing Hebrew woman would bare her face in public as these did. Only prostitutes and menial slaves. But these could not all be slaves and prostitutes. Many had the look of the well-to-do, rich in striped linens and jeweled hands and feet; not a few were fair to look on. He caught their eyes, and turned his head away in amazement. They turned in under a low archway, which Sheshai said housed the guardroom and barracks. There were also a few soldiers about; not many, and most unarmed.

"Ashkelon is a trading center," Sheshai said. "And far from the frontiers. You should see the soldiers at Gath . . . !"

They began the unloading. Sheshai disappeared into one of the buildings and presently came out again in his white tunic, having discarded his cloak and combed his hair. He spoke to the head man in passing, and took Samson by the arm.

"Come, I will show you the town . . . kinsman!"

□

It was in Ashkelon that Samson got drunk for the second time in his life. There seemed an endless succession of wineshops, khans, bordellos and even temples in ever narrower and darker streets, and Sheshai's innumerable friends, a great many of them women. There was much singing of unfamiliar songs, and dancing of near-naked girls in the shadowy torchlight. Finally there was the cavalry barracks, trooping men, women, and boys between the gleaming rows of standing chariots and up to the officers' quarters, at the end of the square next to the Ser's palace; and the young, aristocratic captains performing a weaving dance of their own in line, each man's arms over the shoulders of his fellows. Samson performed clumsily; and was easily persuaded to desist in favor of a display of feats of strength for the amusement of the company, lifting a girl in each hand, the way he had once seen the shepherd Omar lift two sheep.

He had eaten there, too: a gargantuan meal of rich and unknown viands, heavily spiced, which was worse than the wine to a stomach accustomed to country food.

He awoke to the sound of the surf like the slow breathing of an olden-day giant through the open window; which framed a single star, but he could not give it a name; not knowing which way he faced. He heaved himself off the cot, thrust his head through the window and returned the disagreeable contents of his belly to the night. The salt air cooled his brow with a refreshing spray, and he sucked it gratefully into his lungs, feeling better immediately. Wine from one of several cups he found to hand, rinsed around his mouth and spat out, completed the cure. The window was right on the sea, above a wharf; there was a torch burning below and to his left. By its light he could make out breakwaters that speared into the white lines of the spume, the black water, and the masts of ships in the harbor like leafless trees.

The woman on the cot had not stirred. But when he turned back into the room she was awake, and watching him. The room was large: the single oil lamp, burning fitfully before the statue of a heavily breasted goddess, did not light the corners: but they appeared to be alone. The air was heavy with incense. Samson said, "Where is Sheshai?"

"Your kinsman? He went off with Tuah."

He remembered Tuah as small and glossy; this one was a young lioness. The candid admiration in her almond eyes drew his attention to the fact that he was as naked as she, and he jerked a cover from the cot end to gird himself.

"Late for that now," she said.

The lyre stood against the wall. It came from Assyria, and was shaped like an oarless boat: the finely grained hull sailing the floor rushes, the prow soaring delicately like a swan's neck, from which he counted eleven strings that sloped back like rigging across an aperture to a ram's head looking aft, marvelously fashioned in live colors. The cost had staggered him. It occurred to him that he did not have sufficient left to pay the woman.

She rolled on her stomach to see what he did. "Why do you frown so?"

"I have never seen a thing so beautifully made by man."

"Nor I by woman."

It was a moment before he understood that she referred to himself. Considering her profession, it was no small compliment, and he left the lyre. "We have a saying: The lips of a strange woman drop as a honeycomb."

"Come. Taste my honey."

"Our hunters bait their traps," he told her, trapping her upturned face between the pillars of his arms, "with honey." One of her nostrils was pierced with a jewel in the shape of a tiny scarlet flower.

"What do they catch?"

He told her mouth: "The little foxes. Even bears."

"I prefer a bear." She whispered it, placing the words on his lips, her searching tongue through the uncertain barrier of his teeth, busy within his surprised mouth like a bee seeking nectar; then flying off to nibble at the lobe of his ear. The tightening circle of her arms, unable to bring him down, raised her eager breasts to him instead, their buds pricking him like spearpoints. She tickled him, and he fell on her. It was a trick of Tamam's, and for an instant he was back in the cave at Etam again, the twin rivulets trickling into the magic pool and one star in the cavemouth; the musk scent of the woman in his nostrils and his mouth to her breast like a child.

"I am your mother," she breathed, accepting the role with a swift change to tenderness; "I am Inanna, the bride of El, father of gods and men. I am your sister and your spouse. Do what you will with me, for I am bound by the rules to refuse you nothing, nothing. . . ."

The words had a ritual chant, and he remembered something. *Inanna* was the name of the goddess statue in the room. The girl was not a harlot; she was a temple prostitute who would not need to be paid. A moment's relief gave way to deeper misgivings, and he lifted his head. "I am of the children of Yahweh."

"Names." She pulled him back reassuringly, cradling his head as if he were in truth her child. "Yahweh, El, Baal . . ."

Her strong hands slid expertly down his flanks, lovingly as a herdsman with a prize bull, and explored inside the hollows of his thighs, lighting a fire in his groin that dispelled his misgivings wonderfully. His palms were upward under her shoulder blades, the softness of her belly flattened with his own. "I did not know you were a Hebrew . . . though you're not the first . . . I knew you were no Philistine."

Because of the circumcision. She moaned, and when he would have eased his weight her legs locked behind him, and he understood that she meant him to hurt her. Her eyes closed tightly to squeeze out a tear from each; and opened a little way knowingly, with no tears in them. A night breeze entered the room like a wandering spirit as they began to move in unison, bringing the incense smell and the musk together more strongly, and disturbed the lamp's flame. He saw the goddess move beside the wall, and twisted his head to encounter the same evil eyes again, half-closed and knowing. It was Inanna he was clinging to, seething together like the tides beyond the window to bring the seed to fertility in the rhythm of the seasons, the earth mother who must be violated to accomplish the triumph of new life. A voice called out that he discovered was his own: but whether *Tamam* or *Inanna* he could not tell; and then the fire was gone out of his loins, and there was nothing but the sweat, and the woman, and the smell of musk.

Afterward, she knelt by the goddess with a libation of red wine like blood, signaling him to join her as she placed forehead to ground between her hands at the goddess's feet; but he did not move.

"Next time then, Hebrew," she said. "Inanna is pleased with you nonetheless."

□

They returned to Amalek's house the following day with one dead, killed in a backstreet brawl. Sheshai made light of it: a small reckoning to set against their precious cargo of ironware. He told Samson, “The Philistines liked you! They want you to come back and wrestle with their champion.”

He picked up the lyre Samson had purchased and strummed a discord, swaying with the movement of the ox cart. He said slyly, “The women liked you too.” He put the lyre down again. “What did you think of them?”

“The women?”

“The Philistines, donkey. Our masters.”

“They are human beings,” Samson said.

It was laughable to recall that he had once thought them gods: unearthly tall to the child with their plumage, and the sun blazing on their armor.

Sheshai was laughing. “You’ll be saying women are human beings next. True; but there is a difference! Your *human beings* are no more able to stand up to their iron chariots than corn to the sickle. If you saw them–as I have–wheeling rank on rank, their horses thundering like fiery demons, you would understand why your people and mine took to the hills.”

“The hills are our home,” Samson said between his teeth. “Our God is from the mountains of Seir.” He reached behind him and brought out an iron ox goad, new from the Philistine forge. “The Philistines’ flesh will bruise and bleed like that of other men. As to their famous iron, it will bend if Yahweh says it will.”

He took the rod in his two hands, bending the metal like a sapling twig, and tossed it over his shoulder. It fell into the cart with a clatter. As always, the physical exertion spent his anger, and he grinned at Sheshai’s dismay.

Little Miriam, meeting them at the gate, bore the lyre cradled like a new birth into the house ahead of them, and because it was Miriam, none hindered Samson from following. In the cool day chamber he half expected to find the pale Athaliah barring the way; but it was the dark sister, Esther, rising from a low stool to a stranger with some attempt at arranging her garments. Her black brows lifted, and came down in a frown of recognition.

“You are back, then,” she said over her shoulder. “What do you want here? You look different.”

“My lyre.”

Miriam had vanished through the far doorway, which led to the inner courtyard. Esther had been doing something to her hair, part looped over the flesh of her bare arm, part fallen down in thick, blue-black ropes over her plump shoulder blades as far as the dimple of her buttocks, visible through her shift. Looking at her back, Samson wondered what Sheshai could want with a temple girl like Tuah, when he had Esther. The tresses flew out like a flock of ravens when she turned.

"*Your* lyre: it is yours?"

He nodded, and she turned again and called Miriam, using the pet name, *Miri,* which he had not heard before. There was no answer.

Esther had taken up a brush and began to draw it down the length of her tresses with slow, deliberate movements, her eyes on his face. "Tell me, Hebrew, do you consider all women stupid? Sheshai does." She turned her head aside to brush the back, and asked, "How many women did he have in Ashkelon?"

He saw that her arm paused in the brushing. From the inner courtyard came the first, tentative notes of the lyre, filling the silence with a rippling of notes like raindrops. Samson said, "Are you not his woman?"

"That is not what I asked you."

"I was not with him all the time. As to the lyre–"

"But most of the time," she said, and was still, as if listening to the music: "you were with him. Were you?"

He nodded, but she was not looking. "Nearly all the time," he said.

Her dark eyes returned to his face. She seemed satisfied. She said, "Then there were not too many," and stood up. "Perhaps you are good for him, after all. Tell Sheshai you may stay with us. There was no need for such a costly gift for Athaliah."

She smiled then over her shoulder, softening the dismissal, and walked through into the courtyard before he could reply. The lyre was like the first birdsong in Eden. Plainly Athaliah–if it was Athaliah–was expert. There came to him a picture of her slender fingers gliding over the strings, her wraithlike form bent lovingly over the cradled swan neck.

In the main yard outside the house the widow's wail lamented the dead nothing like as tunefully.

□

Unlike the Hebrews, the Canaanite communities buried their dead together in one place; and they buried them at night, this being the season appropriate to Mot, son of El and god of death and sterility. The mausoleum that served Amalek's people was set into the hillside, not far from the place where Samson had taken the sheep, making use of a natural rock formation which in the moonlight had the rough aspect of a house with windows, through which food was left for the dead. The procession went by torchlight, led by the widow. Samson followed out of curiosity to watch the sacrifice: a solitary sheep donated by Amalek, somewhat undersized, for the man had been of no importance and the widow was without money. The priests of Baal, who normally worked among the peasants, appeared suddenly in the glory of crimson robes, picked out by the flames of the torches, swaying and chanting, their arms uplifted like bare branches in supplication to their many gods. A cloud passed over the moon and a groan went up from the crowd, following by a swelling roar of approval.

"That is well," Sheshai said beside him. "Mot is come and gone, and the dead will follow after. Now we can drink."

He took a wineskin from a passing reveller and handed it to Samson. "They will be offended if you do not drink."

It was as good an excuse as any. Samson threw back his head and, his eyes being turned upward, met the eye of the night–which of the Baalim was it, the moon god? *Yareach*–and shivered. His dark angels trailed through the night skies, unpleasantly close to the earth. They were moving all about him, seething and twisting to the muffled sound of drums, in and out of the torchlight like phantoms without features, chanting to the drum beat:

What enemy has risen against Baal?
What foe against the Rider of Clouds?

Samson moved on, and found himself imitating the swaying of the dancers. There was the widow tearing at her clothes, already half-naked, as were many, and some more than half. Like all Canaanite ceremonies, it was becoming an orgy, with the priests ever to the forefront, shouting for more wine with hands raking naked breasts and thighs, drawing the young women out of the circle of light. They seemed to go willingly enough, seemingly half-drunken or carried away with the throbbing chants and drums. He felt himself touched, a woman's touch, and he turned. She was wrapped in a dark cloak, impenetrably hooded; but the voice was teasingly familiar: "It is true, as Esther said. You are wonderfully changed."

"Athaliah?"

"The same."

But she did not seem at all the same. Close to, an unsuspected smile revealed itself, puckering the edges of her marble mouth. "I have been watching you, Hebrew: you looked . . . disgusted. Do you not have such festivals in your dour hills?"

"Aye." She would not know of the wine feasts, the rape of the virgins at Shiloh. "But not for the dead."

She actually laughed. Samson had to look closely to be sure that this wanton creature, drawing him by the sleeve up the hillside, playing the whore with the rest, was the same cold daughter of the house who had whipped his face. She remarked that he was unusually ignorant, even for a Hebrew. "Do you not know that the passing of Mot signals the rebirth of Baal? A woman among us must conceive this night: it is the law of the gods. No one may stand alone as you stood." They sat on the slopes, drinking wine from an intimately shared cup. From what he could see, looking down, it seemed probable that more than one would conceive; likely the widow herself. Athaliah, following his gaze, asked him what would become of the widow among the Habiru, and he told her that she would be given to the dead man's brother. "That is our God's law."

She wrinkled her nose. "Your mountain god is too hard for us. We have more freedom."

Her head rested back against his breast. He touched a

strand of yellow hair, escaped from the somber hood. "Freedom for the Lady Athaliah to go with one of her father's bondmen?"

"Who is to recognize Athaliah this night?"

And then, catching the irony too late, she turned to scold him. "You are nobody's bondman, Shemeson! I spoke to the little black Jaala, and he told me your father is a great prince among your people."

The picture of Manoah made him choke on his wine. "Jaala said that?"

"He worships you more than all the gods. Is it not true?"

It was growing lighter in the east. He said, "My father's father was chief of a great clan that moved north. My . . . father has what is left. That is all."

"But he is still a prince," Athaliah said triumphantly. Her words were noticeably slurred. "You see, Hebrew, you are one of us."

It was what Sheshai had said. "Of the Canaanites?"

"Of the family."

She had the lyre with her; in the darkness he had not noticed. Her fingers trailed absently over the strings. "You brought me a princely gift, Prince Samson, and you shall not go unrewarded. You are to move your things into the house. Did Sheshai not tell you?"

He said, "The child Miriam took the lyre out of my hand. It was never a gift for you."

Below them, the people all turned one way, eastward toward the rising sun, where the land was streaked with light like incoming waves on the shore. There began a heavy chant again, louder and louder:

The noble Baal lives!
The Prince, the Lord of Earth, is at hand!

Either Athaliah had not heard him; or hearing not understood; or understanding disbelieved him. Samson took the lyre and left. In her befuddled state it was more than an hour before Athaliah found him in the ox stalls, and it was like the meeting the first time, in Amalek's mansion. When she understood that neither threats nor bribes nor cajolery could move him, she wept. As before, she wept for herself. She truly loved the lyre. She caressed the swan neck as if it were a living thing. He was taken in by none of it. But she was shivering, for the morning chill had penetrated the stall, and he put his arm round her. She clung to him.

"But I cannot break my oath," he said.

"What . . . oath is that?"

And he told her, since no explanation but the truth occurred to him, of the oath he had sworn to Yahweh Adonai, cursing Tamam and the hunchback Baasha in turn because of what he himself had done—maimed the boy and shattered the lyre in a moment of madness; repentant enough to swear to make good the loss.

Athaliah was moved to fresh tears. She lifted her face to say, "You love her still, this—slave girl? If I were you I would *hate* her."

"That too," he agreed. "Time was when I hated her, and myself, and Yahweh into the bargain."

She was shocked. "Your god? Are you not afraid he will punish you horribly?"

Samson rolled over beside her in the straw and surveyed her with amusement. The kohl that darkened her eyes had run down with the tears, giving her a comic look; but she was undeniably pretty. "Why should he do that? My hatred cannot harm him. Besides, he knows it doesn't mean anything."

"We do not . . ." Athaliah seemed afraid to utter the word, ". . . hate our gods!"

"That's because you don't know them. You don't love them, either. You are only afraid of them."

"Are you not afraid of Yahweh?"

"Yes," Samson said, his mouth on hers. "That is why I cannot break my oath." She had none of the skills of the temple prostitute but her mouth was softer, like an unbroken foal. He wanted her suddenly.

"Not here," Athaliah said. "In the house. Bring your things, whatever you have."

He let her rise, watching her shake the straw from her garments. Evidently he was still to live in the house, despite the business of the lyre. Had it been Sheshai's idea? Or Esther's? He doubted it was Athaliah's. He made a bundle of his few possessions and followed her across the still-empty yard.

"My room is here," she whispered. "When the house is quiet tonight you may come to me. But wait until the house sleeps."

She came close and held him a moment, touching the scar on his cheek with gentle fingers. "You could send my old lyre to your singer of songs. It is a good one, you have heard me play it; you must have." Athaliah's voice was as small as Miriam's, wheedling. "He would never know, would he? That way you need not break your vow."

His own room was tiny, a limewashed cell next to Sheshai's. He went in to Athaliah the same night for the first time while the house slept. She welcomed him like a greedy child. The next day he dispatched the old lyre to Zorah by the hand of a wandering peddler on his way eastward up to Jerusalem, his fat little brown ass laden with cloths and trinkets. Such a peddler as had bartered Tamam her purple shawl; perhaps the same one; but he was gone before Samson thought to ask him.

□

Though he had the Hebrew's contempt for tradesmen, who produced nothing of themselves and grew fat on the work of other men's hands, Samson found the new luxuries of Amalek's house by no means disagreeable. He grew used to the softness of carpets underfoot, to resting his backside on a cushioned stool rather than on his own haunches, the rich glitter of brassware and the extravagance of many lamps that turned night into day; even to the obscenity of their sacrilegious images and carved figures with their likeness to humans and animals, though he had none in his own chamber. The hazardous profusion of household objects and furniture, which at first made him seem clumsy, he learned to negotiate as skillfully as any of them, though not without initial breakages, to the delight of the child Miriam, finding someone more scolded than herself. They became allies. The business of bathing in the enclosed pool, with its heated water, even the intricacies of soda soap and scented oils, became as natural as a stroll down to the well. He grew accustomed to the yielding strings of a wood-frame bed–his own or Athaliah's–though preferring to carry his cloak onto the roof to sleep the night out under the stars after the evening prayer, until the rains set in. The Lady Bilhah who did little else was a devoted cook, skillfully flavoring her endless cakes with cumin, mint and cinnamon, the doughnuts with wild honey: the way Samson told her they were prepared in the Shephelah.

"You are getting soft," Sheshai told him.

It was a half truth: his great frame was visibly filling out, and might run to flesh on Bilhah's feeding; though Sheshai who ate like a wolf stayed lean as one. Amalek, for all his tubbiness, was a fussy eater, and returned his platters half-finished, though without spoken criticism. A bully outside the house, he was curiously subdued within it, contenting himself with a longsuffering self-pity and the chiding of his elder daughters. He accepted the new Samson with a tolerance amounting almost to affection (an attitude noticeably in contrast with his first reception of Sheshai), watching over his progress like a farmer with a fatted calf. Like Esther, he saw in the Hebrew a useful curb on Sheshai's excesses; in his formidable presence a sense of security no amount of armed guards gave him; and in his docile want of ambition, no threat to his treasury. Also, the menials afforded him the respect Ahiman never got. The men evidently liked him; or at least were careful to keep on the right side of him. Jaala was given charge of the animals, and Samson took over much of the overseer's work, when he was not abroad with Sheshai.

There was a plague on the coast that summer, and they traded inland to Gath, leaving the white walls of Libnah behind them and heading south into the Vale of Elah. Before noon a Philistine column overtook them: an oncoming train of dust which resolved itself into paired white horses drawing a single chariot at a slow, high-stepping trot; then the foot-soldiers four abreast, their spears nodding above the feathered helmets like barley in a poppyfield. Their regulation pace soon overhauled Sheshai's leisurely caravan, but the chariot pulled impatiently ahead, whip-cracking up the line of ox wagons with one wheel off the road. Over his shoulder Samson saw the Philistine commander lean precariously over the rail, shouting at Sheshai's drivers to the accompaniment of furious gestures: evidently no ordinary captain, and the wagoners made haste to obey as best they could, pulling in to the side. With his flashing, golden helmet and yellow cloak streaming like sunrays, he might have been the god himself. But it was his driver who caught Samson's eye. The man was dark skinned, and looked like a Hittite. Beside the swaying, shouting Philistine he stood still as a rock, never turning his head, miraculously controlling the rein ribbons in the fingers of one hand, the whip in the other snaking precisely over the horses' straining flanks at the twist of his wrist.

"Get those sodding things off the road!"

Sheshai complied, but not immediately. The chariot made a racing turn in the open road, vanishing momentarily in its own dustcloud, and returned. The Philistine sprang down angrily, and halted in surprise.

"Sheshai the Amorite!"

"Prince Athol!"

Samson lifted his head at the name. The two men were embracing like brothers in the road. There was little of the supposed princess about the Philistine now; but when he removed his helmet and shook his bright hair free, the face was the same. They stood back to let the marching column pass, the lines irregularly jostling close to, and talked of the plague–the cursed Egyptian boil, Athol called it; and said there were many dead. "You are wise to come up country, my friend. But you will find poor trading in Gath"–he clapped Sheshai on the shoulder–"and poor womanizing too!"

"And you?" Sheshai countered, with his vicious and innocent grin.

Athol turned abruptly aside to shout at a passing soldier. "My lord father sent me on this mission. These men are auxiliaries, local levies, they march like women. But we have to provide someone to keep the border with Judah."

"There is trouble?"

"Yes, but not here. In the north there is. Judah is a Philistine province now, under the eye of Gaza, and peaceful enough. No; I bring this rabble to relieve a regular company of trained fighting men, which I lead north to teach the Ephraim Hebrews a lesson. Who is your handsome friend, Sheshai?"

"My cousin, lord."

"Habiru," Samson said. "And not from Judah."

Sheshai flashed him a warning look, and moved easily between them. "But not from Ephraim! He has a fey sense of humor, my Lord."

"From Dan," Samson said. "On the borders of Ephraim."

In Zorah, on the slopes below the ash heaps, there had been three grown Philistine soldiers, one for each arm and a third with his foot on the boy's neck. Now there was none—the marchers having passed on—but the Hittite, climbing down from the chariot with his whip. Athol waved him back, but too late. Incensed at the brazen impudence of what he took to be a common wagoner to his lord prince, the Hittite at a distance of ten paces casually laid bare Samson's shoulder bone.

Samson had not moved. The blood ran down his arm. The Hittite was ordering him to his knees with a plain gesture, recoiling the whip. Sheshai reached hastily for Athol's arm. "Stop him. I cannot answer for my men."

The prince glanced at them in surprise; then at the receding dust of his auxiliaries. "Let your man pay his respect."

Sheshai looked at Samson, who shook his head. Athol grew impatient at this mime.

"Order him."

"You do not understand," Sheshai said apologetically. "Look at him! Nobody orders Samson."

The notion of a hireling—for the young giant was manifestly no kin to Sheshai—whom *nobody ordered* so amazed the Philistine that he did look at him, speechless while his own driver, taking his silence for assent, sent the whip a second time snaking venemously about the Hebrew's great chest and arm. Samson's hand closed on the retreating tail of it, twisting for a purchase on the bloody leather. It came taut. The Hittite, off-balance, scrambled to free his own wrist from the binding thong and could not. Samson drew him in like a man fishing. The next moment he had the driver by the waist in a bear hug clear of the ground. Athol's dagger pricked his throat.

"Enough!"

Samson looked past him at Sheshai's frozen face, seeing the Canaanite closing in, those at the far end of the wagon train running. He let the Hittite drop like an empty wineskin and walked away to find something to staunch his wounds. Athol sheathed his dagger and turned the driver over with his foot in mounting disbelief. "He is dead."

Sheshai knelt to reassure him. "He can't be."

But he was; and the Philistine told them to leave him be and get the wagons back on the road. He took the reins of the chariot himself, putting on his helmet in silence. Samson was up on the cart again, and Athol turned once to look at him more closely.

After a moment he said, "You have lost your goat smell; but not your evil humor." And to Sheshai: "Bring him to me in Gath." He whipped up the horses and was gone after his men before either could reply.

When he had stopped shaking, Sheshai began shouting orders in an uncharacteristic temper, haranguing drivers and spearmen as they passed and waving his arms like Amalek.

"I have made many mistakes in my life," he said, as he took the rope rein and prodded savagely with the goad, "and done many foolish things." The wagon creaked, and began to move. Samson looked at him. Sheshai said, "But I never regretted any of them until now. Even the gods make mistakes."

"I never heard of our God making a mistake," Samson said.

"Then he must want us all dead, if he sent you to us on purpose. I prefer to think it was a mistake. Your god should stick to the hills where he belongs, and leave the coast to our Baals: we've managed all right up to now."

"Yahweh is everywhere we are."

Sheshai had already reached that conclusion. He said gloomily, "That is why I regret ever bringing you into Amalek's household. I should have left you and your god out on the hillside, stealing sheep. *What are you doing now?*"

Samson had dropped down off the cart. Sheshai

dragged the oxen to a halt. Samson said, "You wished me gone. I am going."

"And have my head on the highest tower in Gath. You heard Athol order me to bring you to him. You are a good friend and brother, Samson-Hebrew!"

"And what will he do to me, if I come?"

"I don't know: have you impaled on a sharp pole, I hope." Sheshai suddenly grinned, and clasped the Hebrew's wrist to assist his painful return to the wagon seat. "Athol seemed to know you . . . maybe he will only have you flogged." He glanced keenly at him. "You didn't tell me you had met Athol before."

Gath was visible now, high on a broad plateau at the head of the valley of terebinths, commanding the pass that led up through Judah to Jerusalem. You saw the white limestone cliffs a long way off, rising directly from the broken plain like the walls of a house; then the towers and the line of the walls along the crest. They could just make out the dust of Athol's column, showing a way up the scarp.

"It was in another life," Samson said.

Sheshai waited, but seeing the Hebrew lapsed into one of his surly, uncommunicative moods (a side of him Athol knew something of, evidently), let it pass. He would find out eventually.

The wounds inflicted by the Hittite's whip had gone deeper than Samson knew. The seepage of blood under the rough bindings, aggravated by the sun and the flies and the bone-jarring movement of the cart, brought on a fever which dissolved the countryside to a likeness of Sheol, the shadowy land beyond the grave: himself and his companions moving through it like ghostly *nephaim,* with all sound gone. But the pain remained, and the thought came to him that it was not true, as some affirmed, that not even the anger of Yahweh could reach you in Sheol. Because I am a Nazirite, he thought, and here was Uzziel in his tent saying *What did your father Moses say concerning the man separated with the vow of a Nazirite?* But his father was Manoah, not Moses: Manoah standing with his threatening arms against the sun shouting *A Nazirite! A Nazirite! Have you forgotten?*—those great muscular arms descending in cuffs and slaps, not on the boy

Samson but on her, the slave girl Tamam, who was not brave and whose howling filled the house; Tamam squirming and writhing in the rapacious arms of her master, whose monstrous lust nailed her to the ground, indifferently annihilating the flame of her spirit, whose death throes sounded in the twitching of her ankle chains.

Sheshai, drowsy with the tinkling of the ox bells, was almost too late to catch him as he slid from the seat sideways.

□

The fever which raged through the Hebrew's great frame for eleven days would undoubtedly have killed a normal man. In the event, it saved Samson's life. In persuading him to continue with the wagon train into Gath, Sheshai knowingly gambled Samson's life against his own; but as a gambling man weighed the odds in the Hebrew's favor, half-cynically invoking the Hebrew mountain god to justify the Nazirite's colossal self-confidence; more than half counting on Athol's capricious favor to spare a second time the life he had spared once already—perhaps more than once, if they had met before; and seeing nothing to protect himself if he came to the Philistine empty-handed. What Sheshai did not know was that the Hittite had been more than charioteer to Athol. He had been Athol's lover, and Athol meant to avenge his death the same day. However, there being no satisfaction to be had from insensate flesh, he had the Hebrew merely flung into the prison house to await recovery or death of the fever and afterward, having more pressing things to occupy his mind, forgot him.

When Samson's mind became unclouded, he had no idea where he was. He had lived so long among Canaanites, the dialect of his jailers confused him until he recognized it as his native Hebrew. They were in fact Judahites, and being more or less of his own faith, and reasonably bribed by Sheshai, not ill-disposed toward him. He lay on clean straw in a chamber to himself, and was unfettered; the bread and fish, when he came to it, was coarse but wholesome; the water brackish but drinkable. Nevertheless, what little money he carried had been stolen with his leathern girdle, and his sandals. Predictably the jailers professed ignorance of the matter, and when he asked them bluntly how they came to be guarding one of their own kind, the question remained unanswered until a new prisoner was ushered in to join him, the third day of his mending.

"These men are mercenaries," the newcomer said; "serving none but Mammon." He spoke directly to Samson as if the jailers were not there.

It was noticeable that he walked in unmolested, like a guest in a friend's house. The Judahite guards stood aside, and beyond shifting their feet showed no particular resentment at his contemptuous speech, though they rattled the bolts home in the door behind them uncompromisingly as they left. His flowing hair and glittering eyes gave him a slightly mad look, which might explain the guards' tolerance, from that half-fear, half-respect accorded to those afflicted of God, and Samson regarded him warily. Yet he was a young man, no older than Samson and half his size. His hairy, rope-girdled cloak gave him bulk, but under it his thin legs stuck out like a pigeon's, splayed into downtrodden sandals.

His name was Samuel ben Elkanah and he was not mad; though he was a prophet. Samu-el is the *name of God,* and he seemed put out that Samson had never heard of it.

"They told me I would find a Hebrew here."

"You have found him," Samson said, rising on one elbow to return the stare. "And a Nazirite like yourself. But no prophet." He had never met a prophet before. Samuel was still standing there, looking at him with his disconcerting eyes. Samson said, "Is it true you speak to Yahweh?"

"He speaks to *me.*"

"What does he say?"

"That in Gath of Judah I will find me a young man who will kill more Philistines with his right arm than all the bows and spears of the children of Israel put together."

"They will hear you outside."

"They have heard me before: that is why I am in prison. *Are you the man?"*

"I don't know," Samson said. "Why do you want to kill so many Philistines?"

When Samuel was angry you forgot that he was a small man. He was, as Samson learned in the two days and nights they passed together in the prison house, a man hugely devoid of doubt, fear and tolerance, and plainly took such ignorance from a fellow Nazirite as an affront to Yahweh himself. He set the cool chamber afire with vehemence: not by volume, for he scarcely raised his voice; but by the intensity of his convictions. He tortured his girdle in his long, nervous fingers, lashing invisible hordes of the uncircumcised as he strode the confines of the cell, cramming it with visions; he rushed the bemused Samson from his bed of straw to the rocky heights of Mount Ephraim, there to look down on the burgeoning camps of the Philistines spreading like thornweed north and inland from their coasts, encroaching on the Land in every direction, their banners coming up like thistles.

"They must be cut back: cut back they shall be. *They shall be utterly destroyed out of the Land Yahweh gave his people, as tares before the scythe.*

"Ephraim alone cannot hold them. Every one of the tribes must be summoned, north and south and east across Jordan, as we summoned them against the sodomites of Benjamin; as Deborah summoned them in days past against the Canaanites, whom Yahweh delivered into the hands of the children of Israel, and spat upon their nine hundred chariots.

"This is the message I Samuel deliver to all Israel, even as Yahweh spoke it to me in Shiloh."

It was the word *Shiloh* that entered Samson's aching head with the force of a slingshot. If the prophet came from the central shrine, it must be with the sanction of the chief priest, Eli himself. No man's authority in all Israel stood higher than Eli's, and Samson realized that what he had just heard was not so much a prophecy as an open declaration of war. He shut his eyes in disbelief.

Afterward, he told Samuel that he was from Dan but not that he was Manoah's son; only that he had left his tribe to work among the Canaanites, seeing the disdain in the prophet's eye for a *hireling,* another sheep strayed from the true flock. Samuel had been with the Danites less than a month before, and had got on well with Manoah (who clearly had made no mention of his lost son). Of Zorah, Samuel said only that Uzziel still lived, Baasha's fame with the lyre was widespread–indicating that he had received the replacement safely and was presumably recovered from his injuries–and Manoah's wife had recovered from a long sickness. This much Samson gleaned from listening; and that the southern Danites were seemingly committed to Samuel's cause. Samuel said directly at last, "You must return to Zorah before it is too late; before the Philistines swallow up Dan as they swallowed Judah." And then, "You will go?"

"If they open the prison gates," Samson answered drily; "I will think on it."

The daylight fled from the window, and in the doubly imprisoning darkness–for they were given no lamp–Samuel's relentless voice held him like the fetters he had been spared. Shifting on the prickly straw, Samson felt his head ringing with wars and battles, most of them intolerably familiar. He was thinking of Bilhah's honeyed doughnuts, an irrelevance brought to mind by the rumbling of his stomach. It was the first time he had felt hungry and a sure sign of his improving health.

□

Despite the difference in stature and temperament there were odd, unlooked-for, similarities between Samuel and Samson. Samuel's story was remarkably like Samson's own: his mother too had suffered the affliction of being barren; she had prayed Yahweh, at the yearly festival at Shiloh, at the temple. So intense was her unspoken prayer that Eli himself, seeing her lips mouthing, thought her drunk. But the child came, and like Samson was consecrated a Nazirite from birth. Unlike Samson, he received a second call in the dark of night from Yahweh himself, and became a priest of the temple. Eli, growing old now, was openly grooming him to take the place of his own two sons, notorious for their manipulation of temple funds and loose living. The dangers inherent in such a scheme did not seem to have occurred to Samuel: any more than the presumed resentment of his elder brethren; for his father had taken a second wife already to bear him children while the first was yet barren, never thinking that she would conceive.

"A handmaid," Samson suggested, chewing a straw.

"No; a proper wife to my father–both." Samuel shook his head reprovingly with a rare, close-lipped smile. "You are thinking of Abram: when his wife was barren and he took the Egyptian maid, who was afterward turned out into the desert with her son Ishmael. Those were rough times. We were never like that."

"I was thinking of Manoah," Samson said.

"Ah, Manoah." Samuel conceded his mistake. "You are right: it is the same story–is it not?–in our own time. But Manoah was justified in sending the girl away."

"What girl?" Samson put the straw away.

"How do I know what girl?–wait: I remember. They called her *the last straw.* Once she bore Manoah a child, they say she openly despised his wife, Sharah; Sharah fell sick in consequence, even unto death. Manoah had no choice. The girl was not even of the children of Israel. So he sent her away with the child." Samuel had not seen her. He had heard the story from one of the elders of Zorah; and Sharah's sickness he had seen.

So Manoah had sent Tamam away.

Samson lay awake that night for the second time. In the morning the jailers came early to fetch him to Athol. He left the prophet asleep.

The Philistines' quarters displayed none of the marble and gilding he had seen at Ashkelon. Athol's chamber, approached by a narrow stairway cut into the bare rock, was little better than the cell Samson had just quit. A folding stool and a trestle table and bed were the only concessions to his exalted rank. The table was covered with what looked like maps. Athol stood beside it, his naturally pale complexion almost white with fatigue. He wore the same gold band over his blond hair that Samson had first seen at Zorah; the same cloak of yellow watered silk, which Samson now knew to be the Philistine royal color. His feet in contrast were housed in the stout sandals worn by the marching troops. The guards, making deep obeisance and discovering their prisoner upright, leapt to seize Samson's arms. Athol dismissed them.

"The Hebrew nobody orders," he observed drily. "Prison has not improved your manners."

Samson shrugged. “If I am to die, I will die on my feet.”

Athol looked genuinely surprised, as if the Canaanite tongue eluded him for a moment. “We are not barbarians, you know. I should have thought Sheshai had taught you better. He has returned to his master, by the way, with his wagons. Before he left he paid a fine of twenty shekels for the loss of my charioteer. The matter is closed.”

Athol moved to the stool and gathering the skirts of his robe seated himself gracefully. He had to raise his eyes to the height of Samson, who in the same moment took his own tunic at the neck and ripped it open over his shoulder, exposing the livid scar beneath.

“How many shekels is this worth?”

The Philistine’s shout of laughter fetched the guards again. Athol waved them away, still smiling. “No–wait! Fetch me a purse of . . . ten shekels.” He said to Samson, “You are an amazing man. We could use men like you.”

“To fill your prison house?”

“To fill the ranks of our army,” Athol said, and stood up. “But I had to be sure you were no danger to us.” He placed a slim hand almost gently on Samson’s arm. “The Hittite you killed was my personal bodyguard, the nearest of all my men to me. You could take his place. Do you accept the honor?”

Samson said slowly, “I will think on it. What makes you think I am no danger to you?”

“You paid no heed to the rantings of the rabble-rouser.”

Samuel! There had been eavesdroppers, then. How was it that Samuel, so wise in the ways of Yahweh, could be so unsuspecting? Why else, come to think of it, should they have shut him in with a fellow Hebrew? Samson glanced over his shoulder, turning back to ask what would become of the little prophet, and read the answer in Athol’s face, the good humor dying like a lamp turned down. Uzziel had said once, when Samson had denied the possibility of the priesthood for one such as himself: Do not imagine only the high-minded can serve Yahweh. If you cannot be his eagle, be his ass.

“If I agree to serve you as you say,” Samson said, “will you let the prophet go?”

To his surprise, Athol agreed. “He is like a fly that

buzzes about your head. It is no matter to me whether he is squashed here or flies away to irritate someone else." And he said, "It is settled, then."

Samson said, "But there is a condition more. I have a thing to do first."

To this, too, the Philistine agreed, though with a show of weariness. He sent for Samson's few belongings from the prison house, and told the jailers to find new sandals for him.

With the promise of returning within the month, Samson gathered his things and the ten shekels and left Gath, taking the country road north to Zorah.

6

HE RETURNED TO ZORAH as he had left it, by night in the aftermath of rain. He passed by the well where Tamam had discovered him with Baasha, and found himself listening for the swish of her skirts leading him up the path beside the midwife Dorah's house, where he had waited for her. There was no one about. He left the path and crossed the familiar terraces by a circuitous route which brought him out through the olive grove above the village. He thought for a moment the tent was gone, for the heavy goatskin was the color of night, and no light showed within. Then he stumbled against a tent peg, and the hermit's voice called out. When he understood that it was Samson, he lit the lamp. He held his frail, almost transparent hand over the flame for a moment. "Come close to me: for I am blind now."

Leaving his new sandals at the tent door, Samson kissed the old man's palm, and took the lamp from him. "I know. I met the prophet Samuel in Gath; he told me."

He stood awkwardly while Uzziel embraced him, fearful for the lamp. All the way up from the valley he had been rehearsing the formula beginning *Shalom alekh hem,* proper among Hebrews, determined not to disgrace himself with the loose idiom of the coast. Uzziel's directness put it out of his mind, and he stood scowling like a boy who has forgotten his lessons.

"You have grown tall," Uzziel said. "And strong! My two hands can hardly circle your arm. You have shaved your beard . . . but not your head. That is good. It means you have saved something of yourself at least for your maker." He used Samson's strong arm to steady himself as he felt his way back to his blankets, and eased himself down to sit. "You have heard the word of the prophet, and are come back to fight the Philistines."

"I am come back to find Tamam," Samson said.

Uzziel made no comment, and began to speak of Samuel's recent visit to the villages, in the way of an old man following the narrow path of his own thoughts. Perhaps he had forgotten who Tamam was. He raised his head, with its fringe of white hair and wide, blank eyes to ask: "What did you think of Samuel?"

"He is a fanatic." Samson did not want to talk of Samuel.

Uzziel nodded. "Perhaps. This day perhaps we have need of fanatics in Israel. Things have changed since you left. Listen . . . What do you hear?"

At first nothing. Then Samson said, "It is only the tent flap, grandfather. There is a night breeze on the hill."

"It is the breath of Yahweh, my son; which walked in the garden of Eden. Without it, we are dead men. It is said that Yahweh himself draws breath from the Land: is it not long and narrow, a fitting windpipe for a god?" Uzziel was mumbling to himself again. "Between the desert and the Great Sea, a narrow land, and long. And two hands round the throat of it: on the one side the Bedouin tribes, and on the other the sea peoples . . . ready to crush the life out of Yahweh's people. And they slumber; they do not waken. Yahweh neither slumbers nor sleeps, but his ways are mysterious to us. Out of the noonday he sends his servant Samuel to judge his people and call them to war. And Samson out of the dark to seek a common slave girl."

And he said, interpreting small sounds, "Why are you putting on your shoes again?"

"I'll not stay to be mocked," Samson told him, feeling

the blood rising and deadly afraid that Uzziel's feebleness would no more protect him than Baasha's hump. He turned his back to hide his thoughts, as he had done as a child; forgetting Uzziel's blindness; but it was no use.

"Baasha never mocked you," Uzziel told him. "If you had not rushed off like Nahor's bull, you would have known. After your fight with the bear, the shepherds found the carcass with your stone still buried in its skull. The young men still sing the song of Samson's bear in Zorah. There are many who would have fetched you home, but your father is a proud man, and would not suffer it. You are a legend among your people, my son."

It was raining in gusts like handfuls of pebbles flung against the tent walls.

Samson sat down quickly beside Uzziel and took his arm. "Who *are* my people, grandfather?"

He could tell from the way the hermit drew in his shoulders that he was moved at last. Uzziel said, "Your father and your mother are here with us. But you have not"–he realized it aloud–"visited them."

How could he know?

Samson said, "They have been strangers to each other since the business in Benjamin; to me too. You have been my father, Uzziel. Tamam is my mother and my sister and my spouse. What have I to do with their wars and quarrels? I came only to see you and to find her."

Uzziel covered the broad, muscular hand with his own. About to speak, he sensed Samson's whole body go rigid, and lifting his head heard the tinkling of bangles outside the tent.

A woman came in out of the rain with a dish of lentils sheltered under her cloak and goats' milk in a beaker, which she nearly dropped on seeing Samson there: a slight, slant-eyed girl with an olive skin, sallow with fright.

"Tabitha," Uzziel addressed her, though she had not spoken. "Run, child, and fetch another portion for our guest, who has come all the way from Gath of Judah to visit an old man." The girl fled.

"She seemed terrified of me," Samson commented.

"I expect she thought I had summoned you out of the

ground: an *ifrit,* a demon! She is of Canaan; not one of us . . ."

"Aye; like Tamam."

"Like Tamam."

"She is nothing at all like Tamam!" Samson roared, on his feet and pacing the tent, with Uzziel's expressionless eyes following the sound of his footfall, lifting again when the girl Tabitha returned, driving Samson into sullen silence while they shared the meal. The old man ate little himself, pressing the food on Samson formally, as with an honored guest, and speaking in his husky voice of the crops and rain, the flocks, and a lion that had taken a woman at the well at Eshtaol. Samson listened with impatience, answering Uzziel's questions of his life among the Canaanites briefly.

"You will go back to Gath, then?" Uzziel asked finally.

"When I have found Tamam," Samson said. "Where did she go?–when my father put her out."

But Uzziel did not know. "To a family farther down the valley; somewhere beyond Timnath, I heard. What will you do when you find her?"

"Take her for wife."

Uzziel was shaking his head. "You cannot. She bore your own father's child."

"My mistress, then," Samson said. "I'll have her one way or another."

No doubt Uzziel, with his unfailing knowledge of Moses' law, had objections to this too, but he did not wait to hear them; he excused himself and went out, farther up the hill to relieve himself and make his late evening prayer. The rain had stopped, but there was a dampness in the air that made the stars look like stars in a river. When he returned the old man lay still, his eyes closed. Samson snuffed out the lamp and rolled himself in his cloak across the tent door, where none could enter without disturbing him. In the darkness Uzziel said, "You truly love this Canaanite slave?"

"Love!" Samson opened his eyes to nothing; which was how it must look to Uzziel all the time. It was a horrible thought. He said, "I thought I did once; before I knew what love was."

"Do you know now?"

"I've not thought about it. I've thought about *her*. She's haunted me like a bad dream ever since I left the village. There is something of her in every woman I see. She won't leave me alone. I only know I have to have her."

"That is not a good answer, my son. You know that."

"Aye, grandfather; but it's not a good question either. You told me the story of Adam and Eve when I was a child: but you never told me he loved her. Loved her, hated her—what difference did it make? There was no one else."

Uzziel made no reply, and after a moment it was evident, from the rhythm of his breathing, that he slept.

In the morning at first light, Samson found a fresh round of bread to hand, warm from the oven, and water in a skin: the victuals for traveling. The slant-eyed girl had come and gone. Uzziel was making his ablutions noisily at the back of the tent, and paused when he heard Samson stir. He greeted him, and asked again if he would not see his father before he departed; and receiving no answer at all, said, "Do not think too hardly of Manoah, my son. When you are older, and less hot-headed, you will understand that he took the maid only to keep her from you. Manoah is a man of the law. It was unthinkable to him that a Nazirite, set aside from birth, could be tempted to take a woman from among the heathen. You were headstrong, even then. So he removed the temptation."

"You mean, he *knew.*"

"When we are young, we always think the elders are hidebound and ignorant. He knew."

Samson had his cloak on, and his sandals. "We have much to talk of still. I will be back."

"I may be dead before then."

"Live forever, Uzziel."

The hermit detained him with a last word: "This Tamam. There is much wickedness in her."

"I know."

"God go with you, my son."

□

Somewhere beyond Timnath.

It was not much to go on. Timnath was just over the low

hills, no more than an hour's journey for a young man in a hurry, down at the elbow of the valley, in no man's land. The Canaanites had farmed it and trellised their vines longer than anyone could remember, latterly under the eyes of Philistine Ekron and Ashdod both, a day's march westward and within easy reach of their patrols. Manoah had forbidden the town to his clan; but many went there all the same.

It came to Samson, striding down the broken road, his bread and water slung in a cloth over one shoulder, walking briskly to keep warm and whistling through his teeth; it came to him that he didn't even know her name, to inquire. For no girl calls herself *the last straw* if she may use a proper name, and he had no idea what her name had been before it was Tamam.

"A girl," he asked a man ploughing with a harrow at the edge of the valley: "a young woman from Hebrew Zorah with a boy of . . ." what? "Three or four years old, it must be. Alone and without husband." But the man shook his head and went back to his ploughing.

A group of Timnite women were scrubbing their household linen in the valley stream, frothing the clear water with their soda stones and chattering like starlings. They fell silent as the brown young giant paused beside them, veiling their faces with many a bold glance; but Tamam was not among them; nor any word of her. Their interested gaze followed him as he took the short cut, springing lightly atop the stone wall to plunge into the vine terraces.

The vineyards were heady with fragrance, though the blossom was nearly over, and the vine dressers already about with their pruning knives. Was it on a spring day like this that Tamam had come this way with her anklets tinkling, and Manoah's brat on her hip?

"If it's a woman you're after, friend," one coarse fellow accosted him at the edge of the town with a sly wink, "I can find you one for a price." Encouraged by Samson's amiable attention, he added unwisely: "A nice clean girl; not one of your village sluts."

Samson pitched him down the town well, where his cries rapidly gathered a crowd.

The smell of the dried fish and seasoned meat in the marketplace reminded him that he had not broken his fast, and he turned aside into an inn to eat his bread and purchase wine. It was nothing like the taverns of Ashkelon: a simple walled square, a smelly caravanserai where animals were penned, with a roofed verandah on three sides, with wooden benches for travelers, a few rooms for the wealthy; but he chose a bench. It was there that the town watch found him asleep in the early afternoon: three stalwarts with broad staves, shaking him roughly with questions about a man in the well. When he got to his feet and shook himself, and they saw the size of him, they rephrased their questions with a great deal of civility. Samson paid for wine for the four of them with one of Athol's silver shekels. The tipping of a man into a well, from constituting a serious crime became casual horseplay, and eventually an enormous joke. The fellow was a scoundrel, and doubtless deserved a soaking. One of the watch recalled a young woman who answered Tamam's description near enough, and certainly hefting a child, who had gone to work for one Joshua, the lord of the western vineyards, though it was a year or two back, and he had not seen her again.

In his impatience Samson lost direction in the labyrinth of small houses and courtyards, but everyone knew the lord Joshua's house, over beyond the western edge of the town on the Ekron road. Timnath was not properly walled, but the house was, like Amalek's but of less size and in the old style, deeply enclosed by vineyards, whose many watchtowers overtopped the green roof of the trellises; and cluttered with many outhouses. Joshua, whoever he was, was not a poor man. Samson came down to the hollow where the house stood by way of the servants' quarters, and there came upon a brown child playing with a doll in the shade of a twisted fig tree, who knew Tamam's name.

The fig's shade is a favorite haunt of evil spirits, and he was shocked to find her there by herself; scooping her up under one arm to deposit her gently ten paces away under a friendly olive. She went back for the doll, but returned to him with no fear. Her violet eyes surveyed the stranger gravely, and she suddenly thrust up her arms.

"More!"

Samson laughed, and letting drop his cloth bundle, took her up in his arms like a lamb. "And what shall I call you?"

"Lilah."

"And what do you call *her?*" for she still clutched the doll.

"Rhoda. She is asleep."

"Then we must not waken her, your little rose." Samson set the child down. "And is this the house of the lord Joshua?"

The child nodded, busy with the doll. "She has wet herself." She said sharply, "You are a naughty girl. Tamam will be cross with you."

Samson said, *"Tamam!"* and the child dropped the doll and then, seeing nothing but pleasure in his face, took it up and cradled it again, watching him curiously. He squatted beside her and asked carefully if there was a Tamam here, and she nodded again.

"Take me to her," he said. "Will you?"

"She is sleeping too."

"Take me to her."

The child's hand rested in his own. She drew him toward the outhouses but then at a tangent, through shade under the high-trellised vines and past an outbuilding which might house the fieldworkers, into the open again, talking all the time in a whisper to the doll, whom she laid gently on a small mound for a cradle, soothing it like a real infant. Samson waited, but she made no move farther. He said presently, seated beside her until he judged she had done, "Come now, Rhoda has rested long enough. Where is Tamam?"

The child looked at him, puzzled; then down at her feet. His eyes followed hers. It was then that he realized what it was he was sitting on: exactly the mandatory fifty cubits from the nearest habitation—the outbuilding they had passed.

The mound was a common grave.

□

To Sheshai, riding ahead of his ox train on the white mule, his long legs dangling, the crooning of doves in the cornfields was the most peaceful sound on earth. He had expected sulkiness from Athaliah, knowing there was more than casual affinity between her and the Hebrew; but Bilhah was shrill as a widow at a wake, and Esther's tongue so uncurbed that he viewed his approaching marriage to her with increasing alarm. That she had once charged him with being too friendly with Samson, and nagged him to be rid of him, and that Athaliah had slashed him with her whip, Sheshai refrained from reminding them. The whole household was awry. Only Amalek had seen the virtue of abandoning Samson in Gath, rather than have his spearmen eating their heads off in idleness, the loads of copper lying unsold, merely for the sake of discovering whether the Hebrew lived or died. But even Amalek had indulged in needless criticism of the new overseer in Sheshai's hearing. None of the men had wanted to leave Gath. Their silent reproach had followed him as accusingly as a fart.

It was in any case a relief to ride alone. The journey was easy because the wagons were light; and they were light because they were empty. It gave him a moment's vindictive pleasure to recall Amalek, pulling his black beard in a fit of horror at seeing his wagons rolling out of the courtyard with nothing in them. Copper was in demand everywhere, for cooking vessels, door sockets, mirrors, window gratings–a thousand things; he had wanted to send the loads straightway to the coast. Sheshai had argued successfully that they would get a better price by showing only a few samples, stressing the cost of bringing it up from the Araban desert mines south of the Salt Sea–no need to mention that he had traded it close at hand in Gath, and it lay in Amalek's compound. Even Amalek could see the force of that. Sheshai had said also that the Philistines were short of wine, seeing that none drank the plains water because of the plague, which was true; and that Jason's vintage was ready to be sold, which was true as well; and that it would not keep–which was not true: Jason kept it in whole oxskins in the cool of his cellars where it would keep forever. Meanwhile a stroll up the Shephelah on a spring day would ease his men's humor. At any rate, it took Sheshai away from the women. He had brought the white mule partly to impress the Philistines and partly, if truth were told, because he missed the companionship of Samson's massive intractableness on the wagon.

Privately, he had no doubt the Hebrew was dead; and when he approached the junction, where the road swung left to Ekron and ahead to Timnath, and he saw Samson standing there like man risen from the grave, he turned pale. Samson had the look on his face he had the day he slew the Hittite, and Sheshai felt his bowels loosen. Since no man can escape his fate, he slid down from the mule at once and ran forward to embrace the Hebrew's unyielding form.

"Brother Samson!–live forever! It is good to see you. . . . I was coming back to Gath, only first visiting the Philistines here, the Seren–to plead for your release. . . ." And realizing this did not explain why his train was headed north instead of west to the coast, he added quickly, "I heard the Seren were gathered at Ekron for the campaign against your people in Ephraim. . . . Praise the gods that you are recovered!"

And then, seeing that Samson though silent made no move against him, he recovered something of his composure and the lopsided grin. "You don't know the trouble I've had with Athaliah and Bilhah! Even Esther. It seems a man must first die to discover how much he is treasured!"

"My father has murdered Tamam," Samson said.

The wagoners had caught up with them before Sheshai could unravel this saying. They crowded about Samson with cries of amazement and welcome, those who had scarcely spoken to him before now slapping him on the back and grasping his garments as if to make sure he was no ghost. Several, to Sheshai's wry astonishment, actually wept. That Samson's father was some sort of petty mountain chief, Sheshai knew. He had no idea who *Tamam* was. Afterwards, when the ox train had been sent on into the vineyards to load up with wineskins at the house, he listened to Samson's account of his quest, and the ending of it: here in the estate of the Philistine lord Jason, whom the local people knew by the Canaanitish name of Joshua. Why the death of a slave who had once been his nursemaid should so derange the Hebrew was beyond Sheshai's comprehension. But he set his arm about Samson's shoulders as he led the mule toward the house, and said encouragingly, "These people bury their dead all over the place! How can you be sure the grave is here?–on the word of some servant child."

"I *knew.* It was like sitting on my own grave."

Nevertheless Samson had inquired in an agony of uncertainty and the daughter of the house led him in to the lord Jason, whom he recognized as Sheshai's companion in Amalek's compound the day he himself first entered it. Jason neither knew nor welcomed him; but Sheshai's name and the daughter's persuasion gained him admittance. Many had perished in the Egyptian plague that last summer, and Tamam among them, though they had to send for a servant from the laundry where she had worked to be sure it was the one. She had kept the name, evidently. Samson had heard of Sheshai's arrival, and walked outside to meet him.

From this terse account Sheshai concluded that it was Jason's younger daughter Ishba who had taken the stranger in, this being her nature: a simple child, as fair and open as an anemone. But on entering the house to greet the family, with Samson morosely following, he perceived that it was Niobe the elder, and was taken aback. Niobe was not unlike a taller Athaliah in her flaxen, Philistine way, but infinitely more experienced. From the way her eyes went knowingly to the Hebrew, the pale lashes lowered just too late, you would not easily guess that they had met for the first time earlier in the day. She had done the same to Sheshai at their first meeting; turning away at once as if to conceal an intimacy between them. Now her gilded fingernails rested affectionately on his arm. "How lovely to see you, Sheshai! We have missed you sadly, have we not, Papa?" Samson appeared to have noticed nothing. As soon as he could Sheshai drew him out of the house by a side door, on the pretext of seeing to the loading–"We must be in Ekron before nightfall"–and to Samson, "Come with us. We'll have a good time; I have friends there."

"I cannot. Leave me alone, Sheshai. I gave my word to return to Gath."

"To Athol? That's worse trouble. Some of these Philistines would as soon have a young boy as a girl to bed any day; and I saw the way he looked at you. Besides, Athol is on his way north by now: he was going to Sharon with his regular soldiers, remember?"

Why do I fret myself? Sheshai wondered, looking at the Hebrew who was not listening; hunched there *cowering,* he thought cheering himself with contempt, like a whipped dog.

Except that he was more like a wounded lion, and as dangerous. It would never do to leave Samson here in his present mood, just when the wine agreement had been settled.

"Come," he said with a cheerfulness he did not feel. "There is only one cure for a dead woman, and that is a live one."

"For you perhaps."

"For me there is always Esther," Sheshai said, moving restlessly, waving the first wagons to form line. "I shall be too busy breeding grandchildren for Amalek's bazaar. Still, there's no profit to be had from spreading one's seed in the byways forever. Perhaps you too should find a wife."

Samson rose slowly and shook himself, stretching out his arms until the joints cracked like knuckles. Sheshai took the opportunity to thrust a cup of the wine he had been tasting into his hand, and seeing his head turned toward the open place where the grave mound was, asked him why he talked of murder, when the maid had died of sickness which no one could prevent. Samson answered that Manoah had taken her, put her with child, and turned her out of the house. "Else she had not died."

He had forgotten to inquire after the son; none in the house had mentioned a child. He half turned to go back and ask; and sat down again. What did it matter now? Of that unnatural and loveless union Tamam was dead and Manoah was alive.

"You have given me an idea, Sheshai. Perhaps I will marry. The tall one . . . what is her name?"

It was a moment before Sheshai could believe that he meant Niobe. He removed Samson's cup to refill it, though the wine was barely touched, peering into the black eyes in search of a twinkle, watching the grim mouth for a telltale twitch, and finding none of these things to reassure him. Surely Samson could not be simple as to imagine that Jason, who openly despised the new Philistine Seren lords of the five cities as upstarts, would look with favor on one of the *Habiru* as a prospective son-in-law? Or that Niobe's practiced glances conveyed more than an invitation to a romp on the cornfields?–and that for no more than her own vanity's sake. Niobe was like himself, selfish: he understood her very well. The men were looking toward him, waiting for the signal to move off. Sheshai said, searching for words, "Have you spoken to her?"

"Aye. Before you came. Not of marriage."

There was some humor there, at least. Sheshai said, "What did she tell you?"

"She has a lonely life in Timnath. Her father is strict; he will not suffer her to visit the coast. She is not a virgin."

"Oh, true," Sheshai said. "You know she is divorced? A captain of the Philistine cavalry–like her brothers. You know she has brothers?–but there was a scandal. More than one. And he put her away. Look, old brother, she is not for you. If you want a woman I can–"

"A wife."

"You could not afford her. The *mohar*–the dowry to the bride's father."

Samson shrugged. "She is divorced, you say. It cannot be so much."

"More than I could afford!"

"I am my father's son," Samson said flatly. "I can take my portion. It will be more than enough."

He was probably right, if his father had as many flocks as some of the clan chiefs. Sheshai began to grow alarmed. He said persuasively, "Even so. What do you want with Niobe? Ishba perhaps, if you must, but not Niobe. What can she bring you? Not peace or loyalty, or your sort of loving."

"I don't want loving," Samson said.

And he said, "I want revenge."

□

For all his deformity, nowise lessened by the awkward, open-kneed way he squatted against a rock there below the ash heaps, the hunchback Baasha cut an imposing figure. He crouched so as to make a taut lap in his kaftan for Athaliah's lyre: but it was the long coat as much as the skillful play of his fingers that held the attention of the dozen or so young men on the rough grass about him; the clutch of village girls a way off, their giggling muted: the new kaftan, richly woven in rainbow stripes of red and green, yellow and blue and white. Baasha, peddling his songs the length of the valley and beyond, had prospered.

In Baasha's hands the lyre went like a living thing, a plaintive fall of notes through which the psalmist's voise rose with a surer, stronger tone, telling of Baal, god of all growing things and patron of men.

Old Eleazar, on his way home from a meeting of the elders at Manoah's house, paused on the terrace, leaning on his staff, to listen.

The wildflowers had just recently appeared all over the hillsides, their colors sharp in the late afternoon light: sure sign that the winter was past, the rains over and gone. All the hope and vigor of spring was in the young men's voices–for they had joined song with the psalmist–and all the promise of the new year with a good harvest and prosperity, when a man might sit under his own fig tree and be at peace with the world. It was hard for Eleazar to recall that only moments before the talk had been of nothing but strife. Manoah had met them with a roll of names and itemized stores and foodstuffs, lists of weapons, orders of march, plans for the appointment of captains. He had reckoned that, allowing for the harvest work, they could muster sixty-three fighting men, whom he would lead himself up to Shiloh to join with Samuel's army. It must have been obvious to him from the start that the others were not with him, though except for Mordecai they listened patiently enough.

It was Mordecai who came up behind Eleazar now, walking like a man well pleased with himself. There was no avoiding him. Eleazar pulled his white beard to one side and spat on the ground, not particularly, but generally, which was as far as he dared go to demonstrate his dislike of the man. Mordecai, with his sharp, earthbound intelligence and ignorant dismissal of tradition, represented all that Eleazar most mistrusted of the younger generation.

Mordecai's thin beard split with a grin. "We did well at the council, old man."

"We?" Eleazar did not turn his head. Then he did turn. "I said nothing!"

"Exactly. No man can lead where none follows. If Manoah wants to go north to fight Ephraim's battles, let him.

None of my young lads will march with him, that's for sure." By implication he meant none of their generation either. There was no need to say it. "Look . . . there, at the valley fields: and there, beyond! Did you ever see a better harvest coming up? *That* is Yahweh's work for his people; not some foreign war."

The psalmist's voice came to them again clearly on the hill, and Eleazar said gloomily, "Half of them call it Baal's work, these days. They scarcely know one from the other. They even worship in the high places and the groves; I've seen them sneaking off. If Manoah knew he would go mad."

"Manoah knows well enough," Mordecai assured him. "He shuts his eyes to it as we all do. They are simple people; they do what they see others doing. There's no harm in them."

Eleazar believed none of it. But you could never argue with Mordecai, he was too quick. He had a way of finishing your sayings so they came out opposite to what you meant. Because the Canaanites were circumcised at least, he made them kin, which they never were. Not that Eleazar had anything against them; all the same, he did not like to hear their songs sung in Zorah, which was something new.

Mordecai said suddenly, "They have stopped." It was getting too dark to see what they were up to. "You don't see the Beth-shemites rushing off to battle with the iron Philistines. It's like stirring a hornet's nest with a naked hand. So long as they leave us alone in Dan . . . *Now* what are they singing?"

. . . a lion from his den!
From the garden of Jordan, the pride of the river!

A boy came quickly up the hill, brushing past in too much excitement to notice the two elders there until Mordecai's angry shout halted him momentarily.

"It is Samson!" he called back, and was on up the terraces in great leaping strides. "I go to tell his father. Samson is returned with a wife!"

They watched until Samson followed up the path, his arm about Baasha's shoulders and the young people dancing and shouting after him. Eleazar did not at once recognize

Manoah's son, he had grown so tall and broad, a head higher than any of them. The old man chuckled, thrusting his beard forward and stroking it with glee. "See how they welcome him, Mordecai! If our Nazirite goes north with his father, do you still say they'll not march with us?"

Manoah's welcome was very different.

He stood at the door of his house neither coming forward nor giving ground, and the young men fell back and dispersed.

"What is this I hear of a wife?"

Sharah at his elbow, forcing past to greet her son, looked into the black eyes of a stranger, and faltered.

"Aye, it's true enough," Samson told them. "I have seen a woman in Timnath who pleases me well. I want you to get her for me to wife."

Sharah said, "Timnath–" and glanced nervously at her husband. "Not–"

Father and son were of a height now, but suddenly in the gathering shadows Manoah seemed the smaller. He broke the small silence by turning to Sharah with a familiar impatience to say, "*What is it, woman?* Is not our son of an age to take a wife?" And to Samson gruffly, "Timnath, you say. Do we know the family?"

"No. She is not of our people."

Manoah's countenance changed. "You are never thinking of bringing a Canaanite woman here to Zorah."

"Neither a Canaanite," Samson said. "She is of the daughters of the Philistines."

And he walked in front of his father and his mother, which he had never done, and entered the house alone. He lit the lamp, and discovered that his arm was bleeding from someone's clawing nails of welcome, which brought a smile to his lips. He found a discarded scrap of cloth to wipe it clean. It made him think of the calving that day, when Athaliah's little toy whip had opened up his flesh and he had not known it. The cloth was darker than the blood, though faded, and when he carried it to the lamp he saw that it must have been torn from Tamam's old purple-red shawl for a rag. Even a little of the fringe remained.

Then the tears came at last in great silent waves of agony, coursing absurdly down his cheeks to form globules on his chin; though whether for Tamam or himself he could not tell. He buried his face in the wretched cloth that somehow for all its misuse still smelled of her, afraid that Manoah would walk in and he would kill him. But neither his father nor mother came.

The young men made a feast for him that night, and when he returned to the house Manoah was gone up onto the rooftop to sleep alone. But Sharah waited up for Samson in the house. The lamp had burnt out, or she had extinguished it. Even in the dark he could tell that she was afraid of him. Once, she would have taken his head to her breast, and called him her lamb. Her voice said, "Why did you leave with no word?"–accusing him with her hurt. He had shaken his hair down, loosing it to the cool night air, and drew it back with his fingers. She said, "You have kept the vows we made for you, your father and I."

"Aye," he said, and hiccupped. "Most of them."

Sharah said, as he knew she must, "But this girl. This Timnite . . ."

"Niobe. Her name is Niobe."

"Oh, son. Is there never a woman among the daughters of your cousins, or among all our people, that you go to take a wife of the uncircumcised Philistines? It would shame your father to bring a heathen girl to the village."

Samson stirred himself to tell her there was no need. "They have different customs. She can stay in her father's house, and I will go visit her there. It's no distance."

"What kind of a marriage is that?"

"It will do," Samson said. Remembered household smells troubled him with a sense of unreality: the warmth of bread and the mustiness of bedding, mingled with the strong scent of the goats out the back. He did not want to talk to Sharah. He put out his hand and found the wall, and said, "I came for my father's blessing. And he will not give it, I'll take my portion and go without."

From her labored breathing he knew she wept. Well, that made two of them in an evening, and no comfort for either here. He turned to leave and her voice followed him. "Stay, son. You know Manoah cannot refuse you. We are no longer young. What is an old man without sons?"

"I'll give him sons. Grandsons of the Philistines. It will serve him right for rejecting the Canaanite."

Now it was the indrawn shock of her breath; but he had no wish to shock Sharah. She was saying, *"You have taken wine,"* in disbelief; because of the vows, as only his mother could say it, since it must be obvious even in the dark.

"A libation. They are off . . . offended if you do not take a drop of wine at a wake."

"What wake is that?" She said it carefully, humoring him, seeing that it was a feast of welcome he had come from, and he told her plainly, "Tamam's. Who else?" and still she did not understand. "The girl, Tamam: she is dead?" And he told her, "Aye, long since, and buried, and eaten of worms by now."

And then he remembered something. How Sharah had jumped when he said he had chosen a woman out of Timnath; where she must have known Tamam had gone; not knowing the girl was dead. *Not Tamam!* she had been going to say. Had she?

Sharah was moving, coming out of the blackness to where he stood in the doorway, and touched him. In the moonlight her face was tranquil and cold, like someone dead after much suffering.

"It is Yahweh's vengeance upon her, my son: do not trouble yourself. She was a slave, purchased by your father out of pity, for she had been cruelly mistreated. He always said I was too lenient with her, with her wild and disobedient ways; but she was more like a daughter to me; this you well know. It was at my asking that Manoah took her to himself for a second wife. Because Yahweh had given us but the one son. Wife of the chief of the clan! What stray kitten ever had such honors heaped upon her? And she repaid us by flaunting through the villages like a king's daughter and despising her betters. Me she was jealous of, and hated and despised most of all. Then she tried to poison my cup, and Manoah put her out. It was an act of mercy; if he had taken her to the council she would have been burned. This is your Canaanite you say Manoah *rejected.*"

"I meant her son. Hers and my father's."

"There was no son."

The image of Tamam's son was so firmly in his mind, he could only stare at her. "I heard there was a son." (Was it Uzziel who said it?–or Samuel in Gath?)

"Do you think Manoah would cast out his own son?" Sharah said. "After you had left, we knew not where; whether you were alive or dead! Do you believe that?"

But he did not know what to believe any more, and left her to make his evening prayer, which even Sharah could not hinder. He stumbled up the hill again, and it was as if Yahweh had departed from the place altogether, and none to hear the words he spoke. It was not possible that Sharah his mother could lie to him. But all he could hear was Tamam's voice saying *You might have guessed if you were clever.*

□

In the morning Manoah dressed with care, taking up the garments Sharah had laid out for him one by one: his best shirt of fine cotton to the knees, his green and yellow striped coat, followed by his ceremonial cloak, handwoven in brown and green stripes of softest wool, drawn in with a broad girdle of embossed leather; soft, jackal-leather shoes, and on his head a woven headcloth with its silver thread: every inch a clan chief. Sharah, joining him with a critical eye, was no less impressive in her way, in a black *khurkah,* embroidered at the neck with scarlet thread, with a matching veil that fell to her ankles, and all her jewelry. Samson fetched the ass down, already laden with gifts of olive oil and fleeces.

"You will follow us," Manoah said. "After the noon hour."

And he looked at his son, and said, "You will not change your mind?"

"Get her for me."

7

THE LION lay at the foot of the vineyard wall where the sunlight, filtering through a canopy of leaves, suffused the earth with a brownish-yellow shade, exactly the color of his coat. Under one paw was pinned the bloody remains of a fledgling partridge he had surprised on the terraces, which with a frog and some half dozen small rodents was all he had eaten for three days. A single feather fluttered from his jaws.

There had been a scarcity of game in the Jordan valley, and his pride had foraged far into the wilderness, making their lair in the rock caves and taking strays from the Bedouin flocks, and one shepherd boy who attacked them and gave them their first taste of human flesh; and afterward, when the flocks were gathered in and close guarded, venturing more boldly up to the hill villages about Jerusalem, until a hunting party came out of the city itself and the lion was separated from his older companions. Thirst, before hunger had brought him into the Vale of Sorek. The woman he had taken at Eshtaol was the only one he had found alone, and without companions.

His head was still as stone, half-turned to where the women scrubbed their bright linen in the stream below.

Their sound came up to him in a gust of laughter, and one ear twitched. It was the women, chattering down the road from Timnath, that had driven him to cover. Flies crawled over his muzzle undisturbed.

One woman had left the group and was walking directly toward him, her faded blue shift still tucked up between her legs that trailed wet footprints in her wake. She vanished below the first terrace and he followed the small sounds, the displacement of a stone, the brushing of her thighs as she walked. When she reappeared the lion's head was pressed to the ground, his ears flattened. She circled a thornbush, careful for her bare feet, and freeing her skirts gathered them above her waist and squatted to relieve herself, her back to the lion. A vine dresser, calling to another somewhere beyond the wall, saved her life. The lion was already moving, scrabbling his hindquarters under him with a sensuous excitement for the killing charge; and froze. The woman gave a startled look over her shoulder, not seeing the lion, and with one movement rose to her feet and ran back down the hillside.

Nobody came out of the vineyard, and presently the women left the way they had come, all together, their washing on their heads. The lion watched them go with a show of unconcern, cleaning the underside of his paw, between the pads; pausing only momentarily when one dropped a garment and ran back, before catching up the rest.

He watched Manoah and Sharah approach from the other end of the valley, the man mounted on the laden ass, the woman perched sideways behind him. But they passed at too great a distance, and the lion mistrusted the stout staff the man carried, tipped with metal, like the hunters. Moreover there were now dogs barking, and signs of activity across the valley, where there was the smoke of a fire. When they were almost out of sight, the woman got off the animal and walked behind, approaching the township.

The lion dozed, and rolled on his side to ease the wind in his belly. When he woke, alert to some disturbance close at hand, the sun was approaching its height and Samson, coming up the short cut by the thorn bush like a mountain goat, was nearly upon him.

The lion's roar, close to the ground, seemed to come from all directions at once.

Samson stopped as if he had walked into a tree. He jumped back, looking everywhere, half-crouching on the open terrace with nothing in his hand and no refuge but the wall behind the shade of the overhanging vines: and out of the shade between the wall and himself came the lion in no hurry at all, with a leisurely shambling gait like a man with shoes too big for him, sure of his kill. Onyx eyes looked into black, and locked.

O Yahweh-Adonai, remember your servant the Nazirite!

The lion was coming on at a trot now, ready for the man to turn and run; who neither turned nor ran, but loosed and let fall his girdle where he stood without taking his eyes off the lion and stepped out of his heavy cloak, gathering the bulk of it wrapped over his left arm in time to take the full weight of the lion's charge on that side. The tremendous impact would have rolled a full-grown bull over and down onto the next level but the man, though his braced leg ploughed a backward furrow through dust and stones a full walking pace, and his back arched like a bow, held him, body to body, the lion taller than the man, hindclaws clear of the ground scrabbling to disembowel him, ripping the cloak in streamers. Samson's right forearm was across the lion's throat, forcing the snarling mask back from his averted face, the fetid breath from his nostrils; his left hand downthrust for a fistful of fur somewhere in the contorted flanks. He had it in mind to pitch the beast into the thornbush, hoping it would entangle itself; but its fangs and claws were everywhere, like an armful of vipers, less manageable than Sheshai's mule with Sheshai on it: he dare not risk a change of grip. Then he felt the claws come through the cloak, and heaved upward. One forepaw, desperately seeking purchase, clawed into Samson's newly healed shoulder, where Athol's Hittite had stripped the flesh, and he let out a roar to rival the lion's. He had not felt anger until now. It clouded his vision and went through his veins like new wine. He swung the lion like Baasha the psalmist, and let go.

The lion turned catlike in midair and landed facing him to rebound instantly in a spring at full stretch. Samson dropped to the ground under the rush of fur and caught one hindleg clear of the claws as it went by; swung round, carried with it, and had hold of its mate; and with one mighty wrench on his feet jerked his two arms asunder, separating the beast's limbs as a man tears cooked meat at a feast. The lion's broken roar was his last, and his entrails splashed at Samson's feet.

When he had his breath, he flung the carcass into the ditch beside the vineyard wall and walked down to the stream to cleanse himself. There was no one to witness it. The ruined cloak, which was borrowed and must be explained as lost or stolen, he threw atop the lion. Then he refastened his headband and climbed the wall as he had first intended, to make his way into Timnath for the second time.

□

Surprisingly, Jason put no difficulties in the way of the match.

Samson found him close in conversation with his father like two friends, standing at the window from which the shutters had been thrown back, arguing the merits of high-trellising the grapes between fruit trees, as against the usual hill method of cutting the vines back close to the ground, where the dust took off the bloom, but the labor was less. It was the one bridge between opposites. The Philistine, for all his wine-sodden arrogance, was expert in husbandry; it was no accident that Jason's grapes were the finest in the district; and to the Hebrew the Land was everything.

Sharah was there conspicuous in her black among the white or gaily colored tunic-dresses of the women, one eye on Manoah and plainly ill at ease to be in the same room as the men. She would have preferred to be seated outside on the honest ground, Samson knew. Her altered gaze took in his appearance with dismay. He grinned at her and looked for Niobe, and after a moment she came forward, swathed in rare purple lawn, to greet him with modestly downcast eyes, offering him wine in a low voice inaudible to any but himself.

"You are to be my husband, then?"

Her directness still startled him. When she raised her eyes he saw that the modesty was not for his benefit. She said in the same low tones, "I am sent to fetch more wine. You will come with me?"

Samson glanced at her father, who seemed to pay no more attention than if they were brother and sister. "It is permitted?"

"It is expected," she said, and led him out by the same side door where Sheshai had taken him before. "A man of our people does not take a wife without first seeing if she pleases him."

Walking in the herb garden–for they never fetched the wine–he learned that Niobe's mother, long dead, had been Jason's second wife, and he had three sons by the first: Niobe's half-brothers, one married in Gaza, the other two both captains in the Philistine army, with the border patrol north in Ephraim. They came seldom to their father's house –there was more than a hint of ill-feeling–"But they will come to the wedding feast," she promised him. "I will see they do."

"If you please me."

She took it in jest, her laughter low and confident. "When we are married I will please you any way you want. What have you done to your clothes?"

"I was attacked on the way here."

Her eyes widened in concern. "You are not hurt?"

"No. Does your father not mind your marrying a Hebrew, when he has two sons going out to fight Hebrews?"

She shrugged eloquently, running her fingers possessively down his bare arm, thinking it would be a brave man or a foolish one to attack Samson. "No, why should he? Papa has no time for the New Philistines, as he calls them, the mindless warrior caste. Besides, you are from Dan, are you not? The Danites are our neighbors. If there is war, as the men say, Papa will be glad enough to have you here when the soldiers come by: soldiers are soldiers, friend or foe, nobody is safe in war. And Sheshai spoke wonderful things of your father. He said he was a great chief, of ancient lineage, more ancient than the Seren."

Samson did not tell her that Sheshai had never met

Manoah. He took her hand and turned it over. "Jason would have me as son-in-law to spite his true sons, perhaps."

"Perhaps. And perhaps he thinks you will keep me in order." And she lifted her eyes and said innocently, "Will you beat me, if I am bad?"

"We beat our women every day," he told her, chewing a blade of grass. "Did they not tell you? Our women and our olive trees."

She sighed, and pressed her cheek to his shoulder. When she smiled a dimple appeared at each side of her mouth. She was as unlike Tamam as it was possible for a woman to be.

He told his father and mother: "She pleases me very well."

□

Sharah, bemused with the free ways of the Philistine house, so far forgot herself as to walk alongside Samson on the return to Zorah instead of following at the normal female distance. But the loss of the cloak troubled her, and before they left the valley Samson turned back on her insistence to make a last search for it.

The thought crossed his mind that there might be something to salvage, even now; for he had not paid much attention to it after the lion. He mistook the place, traversing the terraces again, and was drawn to it by the to-ing and fro-ing of bees, which had made a nest in the rib cage. It was almost all that remained, still enclosed in a covering of skin, dried out to leather. Jackals or hyenas had dragged the cloak some distance, chewing it in holes for the dried blood taste, and stripped the rest of the bones bare and scattered them. The skull lay under the thorn bush, still fearsome-looking, and he hefted it back with his foot to reunite it with the ribs, sending up a cloud of bees. There were honeycombs in the nest, and he scraped one out with a long stick, collecting three painful stings on his hand, but the taste was delicious. He ate part on the return journey, and the rest handed to his parents without telling them how he came by it. Adonai, who had given him strength to put the lion asunder, would surely forgive him, Nazirite though he was, for touching the body of the dead beast this once; but Manoah never would.

He told his mother the cloak was nowhere to be seen, which was true. He had covered it with a good layer of earth.

□

The choice of best man–Friend of the Bridegroom–fell naturally on Sheshai. It was a function that called for all his resources of diplomacy, tact and natural deviousness.

In the first place, not knowing how Athaliah would take Samson's marriage to another, he thought it prudent not to tell her; and this meant withholding the news from all of them, including Amalek himself; and in turn inventing elaborate excuses to explain his own absence for the seven days of the feast, especially to Esther. This he had done by inventing an Amorite custom, that supposedly entitled a man to a period of carousing with his bachelor friends before his nuptials. He was due to marry Esther after the coming wheat harvest. And it occurred to him that he had slaved three years to gain Esther and her portion, whereas Samson took the much more desirable Niobe seemingly at will with nothing but the most casual bartering over the mohar. Jason's compliance had staggered him. Not that Samson would inherit all Jason's extensive vineyards; but with two brothers soldiering and one married–and all out of their father's favor–he would end up with the lion's share.

The same thought had occurred to Niobe's brothers, Phicol and Hanno, who were out to make trouble from the start. They arrived without warning, before Sheshai could intercept them, in full plumage as Captains of Charioteers, impressive enough to intimidate any ignorant *Habiru* bridegroom from the wilderness. When they saw Samson, some of their swagger departed, until they had the happy idea of summoning their fellow Captains to join them. No less than twenty-eight arrived during the course of the day–all those not on active duty. The place began to look like a military camp.

"Have you no wedding clothes?" Niobe demanded uneasily. "People will think my brothers are come to a battlefield, not a betrothal feast!"

"Come, sister; shame on you, to insult your guests before they are hardly in the house, and bringing gifts, too."

This from Hanno, sprawled on a low bench with one golden arm carefully cradling his helmet, stroking the brilliant feathers, his long legs outstretched with their bronze shards a hazard in the crowded room. He raised his eyes over the rim of his goblet to add: "What? Did they not bring gifts? Well, no matter: they will have them sent on. Not extravagant gifts, I dare say: not jewels and rich garments–it's the thought that counts. We be poor soldiers, we cannot afford all this wedding finery."

And he looked straight at Samson, winked at Sheshai, and buried his nose in his wine, amid a murmur of laughter.

Sheshai had done what he could for Samson, smuggling the Hebrew's best tunic from Amalek's, with an embroidered headband of his own he had been loath to part with. The tunic had been a gift from Bilhah, or more probably Athaliah, of fine Egyptian cotton the color of the sky at night, and if it emphasized the darkness of his brow, the headband cheered it. The rest Sheshai had borrowed locally, but it was not easy to match Samson's size. The gaily striped kaftan threatened to split any moment across his shoulders, and was too short by a span at least. Nevertheless, with his hair oiled and bound up, and youthful sidewhiskers curling across his smooth cheeks, he was handsome enough, and Niobe's pride in her new possession was obvious.

Sheshai moved easily between them, filling Hanno's cup with a joking aside, and raising his own to Niobe with open admiration, not altogether feigned. She wore her hair elegantly in two slim braids woven wtih anemones, like a temple goddess. "The truth is," he announced loudly, "I believe we are all a little jealous of your man, Lady Niobe."

"The truth is," Phicol said, "that we are on our way north; and if your man's friends interfere with our patrols again we may in truth go from feast to field before the wedding is done."

He was shorter than his brother, but broader and heavier, a champion with javelin and discus. He said again, "The truth is–" and stopped with Samson's hand on his shoulder.

"You are all my guests," Samson told them over his head. "Though I didn't invite you. We shall see you lack for nothing: especially wine"–there was laughter at this; in

Jason's vineyard—"But none of you leaves before the wedding is done. *No one.*"

Phicol's hand went to his dagger, which like all the Philistines he had strapped to his upper arm, but the appearance of his father in the doorway, and the lack of response from his brother Captains—some of whom had encountered Samson in Ashkelon—made him hesitate long enough for Sheshai to make light of it with a suggested diversion: a trial of strength in the traditional Philistine manner—Atlantean wrestling. Phicol stripped off chest armor and dagger and was defeated, though not immediately. It was like pressing against a house wall. The veins stood out at his temples and his face went dark with blood and rage. It was at this point, when Samson began to bend the Philistine's arm like a barley stem, that Sheshai, leaning over to shout encouragement—it could be to either—trod with all his weight on the tendon behind Samson's ankle.

Samson found him afterward talking to the child Lilah, who was seated on his knee outside the house eating a piece of honeycomb. She had evidently succumbed to Sheshai's charm as readily as the older womenfolk, and had broken off a piece of the sweet comb to feed him.

"Why did you stamp on me?" Samson demanded. "I nearly lost." He was still limping.

"I was hoping you would lose," Sheshai said with his mouth full, and swung the child to the ground. "Phicol is famous for his wrestling. Make him look a fool in front of the others, and you will set them against us like wolves. Phicol is leader of the pack."

"Wolves," Lilah said, and looked from one to the other. "Samson is not afraid of wolves. Samson is not afraid of *lions.*"

"It's not Samson I'm worried about," Sheshai said.

Not all the young Philistines were hostile to Samson. Several had been his drinking companions with Sheshai before, and a number, having suffered defeat at Phicol's hand in the wrestling themselves, were not sorry to see their self-appointed champion bested by the Hebrew, not only at wrestling, but later with the javelin throwing and raising of weighted planks. At the end of the first day, with few sober, and the women away to prepare the evening meal, their jesting was not ill-natured. Since he was their peer in strength, they decided on a demonstration of his slow-wittedness by the time-honored pastime of concocting riddles.

"He who steals it, can neither keep it nor return it."

"A woman's virginity," said Samson, who had heard it before.

> "Neither man nor beast,
> Having six legs:
> Two to stand on,
> Four for running.
> Who comes out of clouds
> Yet is wingless."

This was more difficult. A god? The Philistines had some queer gods, one with a fish head; but none Samson could remember with *six legs.* A spider? A spider may come out of the sky and is wingless.

A roar of derision and slapping of thighs told him he was wrong. A spider has eight legs, not six. In the tumult a well-wisher muttered *There are clouds not of the sky,* and he thought: Locusts? But they came out of the sky. *Dust.* Out of clouds of dust, running on four legs . . . but two standing . . .

He said, "If you had told me, half man half beast, I'd have known. One of your charioteers."

"Very clever," Hanno said after a moment. "Now let us hear a Hebrew riddle. See if your country wit is as fine as your raiment."

The mention of clothing gave him an idea.

"Aye, I'll give you a riddle," he told them; "on a condition. If you can tell me the answer within the seven days of the feast, I will give every one of you a shirt, and a coat of honor fit for a wedding. But if you cannot, then each of you must give me the same."

"Done!" Hanno cried.

"Done!" The rest of them echoed it, cheering.

"You are out of your mind," Sheshai said later in alarm, drawing him aside. "What if you lose? There are *thirty* of them. It will cost a fortune."

"I'll not lose."

"What is your riddle?"

Samson looked at him in surprise. They were outside the house now, and the cool evening air had a sobering effect. Nobody in Zorah had ever owned more than one shirt, the fine light overgarment kept for special occasions; only one or two had a kaftan, the mark of a rich man. He told Sheshai, "I will think of one. Tell them I will be back within the hour."

He walked the length of the vineyard and back without meeting anyone, remembering all the riddles he had ever heard since childhood, starting with those connected with weddings: the pillaged vineyard that described a cuckolded husband, the rooster and the fox, the fatted calf . . . one at least of the thirty would be sure to have heard them. The barking watchdog, the lame grasshopper . . . The hour was up when he returned to the house with an empty head, and he sat on a broken wall and shut his eyes. *Forgive Samson, Adonai: blame the wine I was sworn never to touch. I am well punished. Only save me this once more, or these Philistines will spit on us all.* He put his hand down to raise himself, with no answer from Yahweh or anyone, and his hand came away sticky with the remains of the honeycomb piece he had given the child there.

Inside the house he told them:

> "Out of the eater came forth meat,
> And out of the strong came forth sweetness."

The second part of the saying was a boast, they were sure, of his sexual prowess, but no one could unravel the first. Samson would tell no one, not Sheshai, not even Niobe, though she pouted prettily and insisted there should be no secrets between husband and wife.

"You are not my wife yet," Samson reminded her, though she sat on his lap in the midst of the company, more like a harlot than a wife, pressing on him, her head rested back on his breast, and he could feel the sap rising mightily. He kissed the top of her head and said, "Three more days; then I will come to your bed and you shall have more than a riddle from me."

She lifted her face. "Tell me. Whisper."

"I've told no one: not even my own father and mother. Why should I tell you?"

"You don't love me," she said, and left him.

The unsolved riddle cast a pall over the festivities. Even the more friendly of the young Philistine Captains drew apart from Samson, growing truculent and critical of the musicians and dancing girls brought in from the town, comparing them unfavorably with the professionals of the coast, and brawling among themselves. They treated the women and even Jason like servants to wait upon them. Jason himself, if he noticed, tolerated them with a certain stiffness, intervening only when they became too familiar with Ishba, to dispatch the child on some invented errand. Samson's presence maintained a semblance of order, but it was the lid on a boiling pot. He seemed oblivious of it, spending most of his time with the women, still a novelty, despite his time with the Canaanites, or drinking with the musicians and jugglers. Sheshai, seeking him out, passed Niobe half-running, her face wet with tears, and asked Samson what was the matter with her.

Samson passed the back of his hand across his eyes. "She is sulking. Because I'll not tell her the riddle. Tell me, does Esther plague you like this?"

"In her way; they all do. Let me speak with Niobe."

He returned after a short interval, his face long and serious. "Her brothers have been at her. They are convinced she only invited them so that you could rob them of all their savings. They say if they lose the wager they will burn the house down and Niobe with it."

"And she believed them," Samson said.

"She is frightened. I have never seen Niobe frightened before."

"But she is their sister."

"That is why they say she had betrayed them."

"Niobe told you this?"

"Yes."

"Why did she tell you," Samson said, looking hard at Sheshai, "and not me."

"Because," Sheshai said, growing annoyed, "she is not afraid that I will trample through the house like a herd of mad bulls and smash their heads in."

Samson, who had got to his feet with just such a thought in mind, sat down again.

The truth was, he was already half-regretting his first impulse. It had seemed a grand idea, to destroy Manoah through his seed. He wished he had taken Niobe farther into the vineyards and had done with it that first time; except that it would have done nothing to Manoah. Now it was too late. It was the fourth day, and he was no more husband than on the first, and would not be for another three. She was shepherded like a ewe lamb, with Ishba, or another of the females, constantly close, Jason watchful, even when he seemed not to be, and the thirty Philistines, calling themselves the *sons of the bridechamber*–ostensibly there to protect the company from marauders–in Timnath, in the town itself!–the uninvited guests endured for Niobe's sake, wrestling and bantering with them like friends; who repaid him by mocking his country burr and looking down their long Philistine noses. And watchful, ever watchful, like jackals around carrion.

He could smash their heads, as Sheshai said. He could pull down Jason's house about their ears. With the wrath of Yahweh tingling in his arms there was nothing he could not do. Uzziel had said once, that Yahweh gives to some men little, and to some much, but to none everything he wants. He could walk under the vines now past the outhouses to that lump of adamantine earth and open it with his fingers like a seed cake. But he could not bring Tamam back to life.

Someone came out of the house, pausing in the frame of the lighted doorway, and he had a sudden vision of how it might be, if it were Tamam, and not Niobe, who waited for him there.

□

The fourth and fifth day were no better. Niobe took to materializing in his way, or breaking away from her companions to question him. "Out of the strong: the strong–that's you, isn't it. There is nobody in the world stronger than you." And she squeezed his arm, waiting for him to say yes.

"No."

Or on another occasion: "Is it the calf from the mother?

The meat out of the eater. That must be it!" He shook his head, and she burst into tears. Nothing he could say would comfort her. Every tenderness she saw as contrived, every assurance false. She was the most miserable of woman, having lost one husband, to be tricked into wedding another who had only despite for her, and nothing of love.

He did not believe in her tears, any more than he believed the threat that her brothers would burn the house. But he could not endure them, either. A red-eyed bride was a bigger insult than any her brothers had the wit to invent. In the end he revealed the riddle to her, though indirectly, and only on the last day, at the great feast where the men and women sat together. Niobe was beside him in her brightest garments, incongruously veiled for the first time. At least it hid the shadows about her eyes; but for the moment only. He thought by then it was too late for harm, and when she put the all-too-familiar question to him for the last time–for he was due to declare the answer to them all before they rose to go to the bridal chamber at last–he said, "Though I have told no one, as I said; yet there is one who knows."

Her eyes were suddenly alert over the veil. "Who?"

"The child," he said; "who brought me here."

It had been among the gifts he had brought: a honeycomb for Lilah, the servant's child, wanting to include her and not able to think of anything more appropriate. She had asked him where it came from, and he had told her the story of the lion, to amuse her–and it had amused her–though it was not the same honeycomb. The child knew nothing of the riddle. Jason was rising unsteadily to make a speech. It was a commonplace speech, and the audience grew restless, their comments more ribald by the minute. An altercation broke out at one side of the room, where one of the charioteers had spilt wine over another. When Samson turned back, Niobe was gone. The interruptions became more frequent, and gradually it became apparent that the atmosphere in the chamber had changed. Jason made an end at last, and to his surprise was warmly applauded, every man slapping his thigh, and some standing to applaud.

Among them was Phicol, coming forward from the back.

"What," he asked them all, turning his back to Samson

and throwing open his arms, "is sweeter than honey? And what is stronger than—*a lion?*"

It was greeted with a bemused silence; without an explanation the answer made no more sense than the riddle itself. Behind Phicol, Samson saw Niobe in the doorway.

Phicol faced him, his teeth clenched in a grin. "Am I right?"

Someone shouted, "Come, Samson! What do you say?"

He said, "If you had not ploughed with my heifer, you had not found out my riddle."

And he walked through them and out of the house, passing Niobe without looking at her, his face black with anger.

□

Risking a backward glance from the chariot, Ptullis could still make out the skyline of Gath, but nothing else: the countryside and the following column vanished under their dustclouds, unpleasantly pinkish in the sun.

Athol said, "I was a fool to let him go."

"You mean the big Hebrew."

"Samson?" Athol's head came up. "No. I mean their little priest, the one they call Samuel. You told me never to trust small men, did you not, Ptullis."

"I said you should not overlook them. It is a weakness of tall peoples, like yours and mine."

Athol said, "I wasn't going to overlook Samuel. I was going to have him strangled in the prison house. I knew he would go back and stir up the Habiru tribes, and he has. They have already twice attacked our patrols at Aphek."

"Is that why we are marching north?"

"We were marching anyway. But now there is haste."

It was the first indication he had given of their destination or the reason for their abrupt departure from Gath. The bald dome of the Egyptian's head nodded with the slow rhythm of a scale pan, weighing it up. Athol knew what he was thinking: that the military citadel of Ekron was nearest to Aphek; then, coming south, Ashdod. Even Ashkelon right down the coast was closer than Gath—at least by road. Only Gaza, southernmost of the five Philistine city-states, was farther away. If Gath was on the move, they were all moving.

Ptullis said slowly, "I see a lion that roars at a mouse." He lifted his eyes. "Does the iron might of Philistia march against a handful of rebels? Or tell me, do the Seren seize the excuse of a border skirmish to extend their borders northward."

Athol was watching the road impatiently. "This is no handful and no skirmish either. We could have an uprising all along the frontier, if it's not stopped quickly. *Now.*"

"Did I not teach you once, that haste is the father of all errors?"

"You are a wise man, Ptullis; but you are ignorant of the ways of soldiers. If we do not settle the matter within a month we shall lose half our men. Most of our Canaanites are farmers: they will slip away in the darkness to their villages to bring the wheat harvest in. Ah, here they come now."

He rested the column briefly by the roadside, where the already sweating footsoldiers found what shade they could in the ditch, there being no other. By mid-afternoon they were at the fork where, instead of keeping north on the Ekron road, they swung left toward the coast. Ptullis, looking back over his shoulder, saw that the move was unexpected. The leading file faltered, and a captain ran up to wave them to follow on. The column stretched back a great distance along the road, and reminded Ptullis of nothing so much as a hairy, red-and-white caterpillar, winding along on a thousand legs.

Athol caught his eye and laughed. "You look puzzled, Ptullis."

"Why this way, Lord Athol?"

"What does the sage say?"

"That Ekron lies north. And Aphek well north of Ekron. And the soldier?"

"The soldier says Libnah lies north also, between us and Ekron. The white city pays no tribute to Ashkelon—*yet.* How do we know what the king may do, if he sees five companies of our fighting men approach his gates? Or if we pass in peace, how many spies will count our heads?"

There was another reason for the change of route; but one Athol kept to himself. At Ashkelon they would join up with his own men from Gaza. When he fought the Habiru he wanted to fight from his own chariot, with Phicol and his friends around and behind him.

The moorlands were a blaze of color, and the standing corn, when they came down through it, already changing hue, the ears swelling white in readiness for the harvest.

"We have still two or three days' march to the war," Athol said.

Ashkelon was hidden by a fold of the ground, but now you could see the blue margins of the sea, the villages between, and their own road winding on through the marshlands.

"*War,* is it?" Ptullis said.

And then he said, "It looks as if the war has come to us."

Athol followed his nearer gaze.

Immediately below them their road was crossed by the coastal highway, at first sight deserted, for nothing moved. It was the wheeling vultures that pointed to the place, fifty paces to the north of the crossroad, between high banks: first a chariot overturned, its empty shafts pointing to the sky. Then another standing. There were five chariots in all, but no horses; and scattered all over the road, up the banks and half in the ditches, a multitude of heaps that had once been living men.

Athol did not go down at once. Because of the wheeling vultures, which kept their height, he guessed that there must be living as well as dead somewhere in the area; and he was right. He sent two cohorts under a captain to make a wide sweep before leading the main body down to the highway; and they fetched back a frightened and stuttering huddle of some twenty survivors from between the hills. Most were women, and all richly dressed and adorned in festal garments; which explained why the dead men had been stripped to their undergarments. They had been returning from a coming-of-age feast—the young man was among them—with six chariots to escort them: this much Athol understood from the babble of voices that surrounded him. They were all Philistines from Ashkelon or its villages. Of the attackers there was no sign. When he tried to discover the direction they had taken, he was deafened by a clamor of contradictions through which only one word became understandable from its frequent repetitions—*ifrit.*

Despite the heat of the sun beating down on the white-stone road, Athol felt a chill spasm pass through his stomach. An ifrit is the most fearsome of the jinn—a demoniacal spirit that has the power to assume human shape. He saw several of his footsoldiers cross fingers to invoke the protection of the gods, and straightened his back grimly. His uplifted hand quelled the tumult for a moment.

"Describe this . . . *ifrit* to me."

"He looked like a man at first. . . ."

"But a great huge man . . ."

"A mad giant, with a great cloud of black hair . . ."

"Terrible to behold!"

"Who stood in the midst of the way, like this"—the speaker stood with his hands on his hips and puffed out his chest, with a fierce look.

"And demanded that all the men take off their shirts and their coats, and hand them over."

There had been fourteen women in the caravan, two old men, and the youth: the rest, numbering two and forty, no less, had been able-bodied men. The ifrit—and they were all sure of this—had been alone. Not knowing he was an ifrit, but seeing just the one man, even a huge giant of a man, in their way, they had done what anyone else would have done. The first of the chariots had simply ridden him down.

What happened next was described in the hushed tones of the temple; of men and women in the presence of things seen and not understood; each turning to a neighbor for verification, wide-eyed.

They had expected the "man" to jump aside, but he seemed to go down under the horses. Then one horse appeared to rise violently into the air and across the back of its companion, rolling over and over taking the chariot with it in a confusion of hooves and screams and dust. The second chariot, too close to stop, went by the "man"—miraculously still on his feet—and he reached out and *with one hand* ripped the traces free as if they were no more than a handful of grasses, so that the horses bolted and the chariot skidded to a halt, the shafts ploughing into the road and the men spilled out over the sides.

It was then that they knew he was an ifrit, and no human being.

However, those behind on foot, not seeing clearly for the dust, were foolish enough to run at him in a body, with spears and daggers. He met them with one of the chariot wheels, iron-rimmed, which he whirled like a thing of no weight at all, scything them down to left and right like wheat at the harvest. What men remained, and all the women, escaped into the hills without looking back.

Athol left them keening over their dead, and drew his first captain aside with instructions to clear the road of all traces of the massacre before more travelers came on the scene. "And warn these people: I want no word of this published in the city on pain of death. Report yourself to the guard commander at the gates, and have the dead removed to the burial ground outside the walls–I do not want them taken into Ashkelon. Understand?"

Athol found Ptullis seated under a terebinth, it being beneath the Egyptian's dignity to assist in the work of carting the bodies aside, and asked him what he made of it.

Ptullis looked up, and slowly rose to his feet. He said, "I should like to see an ifrit."

"I should not," Athol said fervently. "We have enough devils of our own without picking up more from the Canaanites."

"But a creature, even an ifrit, who walks off carrying the garments of . . . what? . . . *thirty* men in his two arms . . . which would fill an ass's cart . . ."

"Or a chariot. He took the sixth chariot," Athol pointed out. "But first he drove off the remaining horses, so there could be no pursuit. And I think I know where he went."

"You are sure it was the Hebrew?"

"Who else?" Athol drove a fist into his palm. "If only we had arrived sooner!"

Ptullis closed his eyes with a profound prayer of gratitude that they had not.

□

There were thirty changes of raiment in the chariot; no more and no less. They made a considerable pile, and Samson had trouble keeping them from sliding off the open back. The horses he left much to themselves, with the result that they soon slowed to a leisurely amble. Darkness overtook them long before they reached Ashdod. As soon as he saw the lights of the town on its low hill Samson climbed down and led the horses off the road inland, stumbling over rough ground until the moon came up and showed him the track he was looking for, a rutted way between the low hills, passing at no great distance from Amalek's house.

He wondered what Amalek would say if he could see him.

At Timnath, he left the thirty sets of garments with Jason's sleepy-eyed watch. The house was in darkness.

Between Timnath and Zorah he loosed the horses, pitching the chariot into a ravine there, and followed the silver line of the stream up the vale. Outside Uzziel's tent he called softly; after a moment the hermit answered, and he went in.

"You are hurt, my son. I can feel the bruises . . . and there is blood. Where have you been?"

And Samson said, "To a wedding."

8

MANOAH HAD ALREADY LEFT for the annual harvest festival at Shiloh, though it was early in the month for him to leave Zorah. If the prophet Samuel was back at Shiloh, as they said he was, the gathering of the clan chiefs was more likely to be a war council than a thanksgiving.

Manoah had left word for Samson to follow, *if his own harvest is gathered in time.*

The barley harvest was already in, the wheat not yet; but he did not mean either of them. Nor was it like Manoah to soften a command with provisos. Some of this enigma was explained, however, when Samson discovered that only twelve arms-bearing men from the two villages–seven from Zorah and five from Eshtaol–had accompanied him, together with half a dozen hangers-on. There had been no open clash this time, for Manoah issued no command at all, taking only those who volunteered: those of his own generation who had fought in Benjamin. If their sons were to take up arms in the cause of what was still widely held to be Ephraim's battle, it would not be in the footsteps of Manoah, or even of Samuel, but a hero of their own ilk. Was this the harvest Manoah had had in mind?

Samson asked Uzziel: "Shall I take these up to join my father in Ephraim?"

"Why ask me?"

"I asked Yahweh," Samson said sullenly. "He doesn't answer."

"That is because you listen only with your ears."

In a corner of the tent was a small wooden casket, which Samson fetched and opened at the hermit's direction. Inside was a worn leather pouch, not much bigger than a fist, closed at the neck with a drawstring. Uzziel untied the knot, making a business of it with his shaky fingers, and tipped the contents onto the carpet by his bedding: two polished cubes of colored stone that clicked together and rolled, and were still. Samson had seen them once before, when he was a child, but he had never seen their use. He even remembered their names: the Stone of Lights, a translucent amber-brown, beautifully grained with greenish veins like marble; and the Stone of Perfection, which was white. They were inscribed with writing he had not understood, and did not understand now, peering over Uzziel's shoulder. Uzziel gathered both in his open palm, and signed for Samson to kneel beside him.

"What is your question, my son?"

"Shall I lead our young men north to fight the Philistines?"

Uzziel's lips moved as he repeated it, with many incantations. Then he tossed the stones into the air. They fell back onto the carpet again, and settled. The old man's fingers found them, and traced the etched inscriptions on the upper side of each. Then he lifted his head.

"No."

That was apparently all there was to it. Uzziel sat back and returned the stones to their pouch, drawing the neck tight, and dropped it into the casket casually. He might have been Amalek putting away small change.

Samson stood uncertainly. "But what does it mean?"

"It means you should return to Timnath, to your wife."

The next day Samson took a kid from the household flock and set off down the valley with it bleating across his shoulders. A kid was the proper gift a man gave his wife when the marriage was consummated. It lay warm across the back of his neck, and reminded him suddenly of Tamam's goat, which she said he had nearly strangled. He even remembered the name she gave it–*Leah.* Leah was Jacob's first and unfavorite wife, who was ugly, but tender-eyed. It was a good name for a goat. Tamam was good at names. Her Leah must have been dead these many years.

Like Tamam herself.

Uzziel was right: he said a man does not take revenge on women; and Niobe's perfidy was more than expiated by the humiliation of her unconsummated marriage. Striding under the oleanders, already cheerfully speckled with sunlight, he felt sorry for her. His quarrel was with her brothers; and their score was settled more squarely than they knew. It occurred to him also, climbing the vineyard wall, that Sheshai might have been left in some peril among them, which even his glib tongue would be hard put to avert.

Jason met him at the house door. He had evidently been hurriedly summoned, for his cloak was hastily drawn together, and his hair was tousled. He blinked at Samson and the kid, the slackness of his mouth pitifully exposed by the sunlight. His voice was querulous.

"Where are you going?"

"I am going," Samson said, looking at the puny arm that barred his way, "in to my wife; into the marriage chamber."

"You cannot come in here!"

Samson put the kid down. It stood a moment, and ran off. He asked politely, "Did not the thirty receive their change of garment I promised them?"

"They did; but . . ."

Jason seemed to shrivel visibly, like a leaf touched by fire.

He said, "Niobe is . . . I truly thought you must utterly hate her!" He wrung his hands. "We never thought you would come back. I gave her to your companion. He is with her now. So you see, you cannot come in. . . ."

"Sheshai!"

Samson could not believe it. He had shouted out the name, more in astonishment than anger, and Jason reeled back against the doorpost, one arm upflung to defend himself, his teeth chattering uncontrollably in terror. Samson lifted him by a handful of cloak, banging his head on the lintel and asked him if he meant Sheshai the Amorite, to be sure there was no mistake, and he shouted, "Yes, yes, your friend Sheshai!"

When Samson walked away Jason was still babbling, offering him Ishba instead: pointing out that she was younger, even fairer, than her sister. His voice faded, still calling out:

"Take Ishba, I beg you!"

Samson looked for the goat, but it was nowhere to be seen. Well, they were welcome to it. It was a small enough addition to the sum of thirty changes of raiment, a wife and a friend. But Sheshai! Had he been blind not to see how the wind blew?–the way the *friend of the bridegroom* had looked at Niobe during the feast? And he wondered who would tell Amalek. And Esther.

A group of Philistines had come out of Jason's house, no doubt to see if he had gone. Even at this distance it was plain that they flaunted their new festal garb, the colors bright among the green of the vineyard.

"You have eaten my meat," Samson told them silently: "you have drunk my wine. Now I shall be blameless, though I take a revenge that shall be remembered in Timnath."

It was the cornfields that gave him the idea. Over toward the coast the wheat harvest was already in progress: you could see the laborers like ants round an anthill, and the line where the reaping had reached, the sheaves dotted about the fields.

He returned to Zorah and sought out Jemuel.

"You remember the camp in the high pasture, where you taught me how to use the sling?"

Jemuel was heavier now, strongly muscled, and his beard a flamboyant black bristle. He nodded. "My brothers have slings, we all have. If you want more we can make as many as you like." He was ready to fight the Philistines' iron chariots with slingshot.

Samuel told him he didn't want slings: he wanted hunters. "You and your brethren and all the young men you can find in the villages. The sheep will be in the high pastures by now: meet me there in the camp of Omar, the shepherd chief. But tell no one. Only tell Omar I have need of as many men as can be spared for a short season, men skilled in hunting and trapping."

"Hunting!" Jemuel said. "What are we to hunt?"

"Jackals. Scores and scores of jackals."

Nobody ever hunted jackals, and seeing Jemuel's face Samson began to laugh.

□

The prophet Samuel, watching the Philistine column advancing up the coastal road beside the river, cohort after cohort as far as the eye could see, knew they had left it too late. If the Israelite army had taken the field as he had urged, two months–even one month–ago, there would still be the chance of rain, that could swell the river and make the moors a death trap for chariots. Now at the end of Ziv, the third month, even the latter rains were past, the skies cloudless. The air on the knoll where he stood was cool with a breeze off the sea, which stirred the grass tufts at his feet; but the ground between was bone dry.

The Plain of Sharon at this place was half a day's march across, from the Shephelah on Samuel's immediate left to the sea dunes on his right; a rolling moorland interrupted by hillocks and oak groves too scattered to form a bastion anywhere. Long tongues of sand ran inland from the sea, where only the coarsest grasses grew, but these too would be firm underfoot. The sand blew loosely across the path of the oncoming chariots which he could now see leading the column.

Barring their way, stretched thinly across the edge of the plain below Samuel and out of sight of the road, using hollows and rocks and any cover the ground afforded, lay more than five hundred men of Ephraim. Behind him, in reserve in the village of Ebenezer, was twice that number. It was pitifully few. A leavening had come up from southern Dan, a handful from Benjamin; none from Judah. Random sheep grazed among the lying men: Samuel, with his tall staff, would be taken for their shepherd. A too-deserted landscape would arouse suspicion. Surprise was their only chance; which was why he had rejected the idea of a rail of sharpened stakes; besides, wood was too sparse.

The waiting was the worst part. The dust rolling back from the leading chariots rose in brown banks, obscuring those behind, making it impossible to count their numbers.

Then abruptly it ceased, and Samuel, jerking his eyes to the head of the column, saw why. The leading chariots were turning off the road in pairs across the river ford, leading the train toward the walled town of Aphek. He saw Hamul ben Ishuah, a hundred paces to his right, shake his head angrily. Hamul was in command, and worried for the men, who had been in position before first light. The pallor of Hamul's face showed as he turned for confirmation, and Samuel nodded his head, mutely sharing his frustration. The Ephraimites were already crucified with cramp, suffering first the heavy dews, then the sun and wind and flies, with no water but what each man had by him. If the Philistine column turned in to Aphek to rest or reform, it could be hours before they came on. Even days.

It was a risk Hamul could not take. With a hurried prayer commending his forces to Yahweh Adonai, he made his decision. He cupped his hands to his beard and shouted orders to be passed on to the first hundred men on the extreme left to close on Samuel. And to Samuel himself:

"Lead them back through Ebenezer–fast as you can!"

Several of the Philistines in the first chariots turned their heads: you could see the plumes of their helmets nodding. It was doubtful if they could make out the words. It might still have been the shepherd calling to his flock. But when rank after rank of men rose from the grasses and began to run struggling toward Samuel's knoll, the front chariots reined in, and those behind came up at a gallop to right and left, fanning out into a long line as precisely as if they had been on the training ground. Hamul and the remaining four hundred stayed where they were, hidden. Before the first of the running men reached Samuel, trailing their spears and shields, the plan was clear. The Philistine line of charge–after the supposedly fleeing Ephraimites–would carry their chariots through Hamul's lines; and Hamul would let them through. At a signal, his men would rise out of the ground to confront the unsuspecting footsoldiers even now streaming after the chariots–obscured by the dust again but you could hear them cheering themselves on. He, Samuel, would lead the "fugitives" through Ebenezer, where the pursuing chariots would be ambushed by the Israelite reserve and destroyed in the narrowness of the streets. What Samuel could see, and Hamul could not, was that only part of the Philistine column had followed the leaders off the main road by Aphek. The remainder, and what looked to be the greater contingent, was continuing along the original route, with the obvious intention of making a sweep from the north, which would bring them up behind Ebenezer and cut it off.

There was no way of warning Hamul. To have shouted to him now, with the oncoming line of chariots already within earshot, would make his destruction certain.

It was certain anyway. The tall spears of the Philistine footsoldiers were massing like a moving forest. Hamul must be outnumbered at least three to one. His purpose must be to shock the front rank, and hold them until help came from Ebenezer: which now would never come.

It was the first battle Samuel had ever witnessed, and although he would see many more in the course of a long and full life, the one he was most vividly to remember. It was the day he cried out aloud to Yahweh on the hill top, and was stunned by silence.

He had expected the terror of chariots at full gallop, a shouting, shrieking wall of iron and hoof and spear. Instead, they came on at the same even trot and in perfect formation, scattering the sheep, the only sound the rumbling of their wheels, like distant thunder. He could see the controlled high-stepping of the horses, the plumes of the men's headdresses nodding in the breeze, their javelins still pointing to the sky as if they were on parade, flashing in the sun. Forty-one chariots he counted, in line right across the Israelite front and beyond, for they were well spaced out: some thirty paces between chariots, breaking momentarily like waves on the shore to circle a tree or knoll and joining again. He could even see the drivers glance to right and left to check their position.

Samuel slid to his haunches, still gripping his staff. "Come on. Come *on!*"

Because of the slow pace of their advance, the footsoldiers were much too close behind. Their columns, four abreast, would be on Hamul before the chariots were clear.

A flash of sunlight caught his eye.

In the center of the line one of the chariots had pulled ahead, the driver whipping the white horses on; the figure beside him half turned with one arm upthrust, whose movement exposed a breastplate like burning gold. In his hand he held a javelin bearing a yellow pennon, which he waved to left and right; then brought down in line ahead. At the signal, the chariots flanking him fell back, closing in, and held their place at a canter. The wings appeared to be losing ground, and turning in toward the center. The growling thunder swelled to a roar through the increasing dust. Samuel could feel the ground tremble under him. When the leader crossed Hamul's line it was at a gallop, the rest following in close arrowhead formation.

Inevitably not all Hamul's men evaded the first onslaught. Samuel saw a flying hoof come down on the upturned face of an Ephraimite still registering surprise, scattering bones and brain, and the iron wheel go over the result to bury a scream; a second man's leg was severed below the knee. From somewhere an arrow flew into a horse's flank, but without stopping it. Hamul was on his feet shouting for his archers too soon and finding the rear of the arrowhead upon him; but there was worse to come. From the front, each chariot appeared to carry two men. Now Samuel could see there was a third, seated to face backward, who dropped off to take the Ephraimites with sword and spear before they were properly on their feet. A dozen of these went down under a shower of arrows from the flank, and then the archers were streaming away from the field as the Philistine footsoldiers came shouting out of the dust to cut them down. From that moment it was no longer possible to distinguish friend from foe, save where the feathered helmets showed above the mêlée here and there. The last sight he had of Hamul was his hand, still clutching a captured sword, sinking into a mass of writhing, howling bodies. It was then that he called out to Yahweh to save them.

He did not see Ebenezer again, but a pall of smoke across the hills marked the place where the village had been. He fell in with a group of survivors, and learned that the main body of the Israelite reserve had escaped ahead of them, and were on their way to Shiloh. Those of Israel who with Samuel escaped the battle–more than a thousand with their arms–split into small bands to avoid detection, heading by various routes for the safety of the Shephelah; foolishly, since they were at the mercy of the Philistines so long as they were in the plain, their only hope being to keep together. It was a mistake Hamul would not have made. But surprisingly, none pursued them.

□

There was no pursuit because at the moment when Athol, his face blackened by the smoke, was indicating to his captains on a map the direction each would take to cut them off, a single chariot galloped across the ford with the message that Ashdod had been attacked; and within the hour Athol had fallen his Canaanite footsoldiers back on Aphek and was leading the chariots helter-skelter down the road south again.

□

Ashdod, like Gath, was no trading city but a military stronghold, with the greater part of its civilian population clustered in villages outside its walls, like chicks about a hen. Raised on a low hill dominated by its temple to Dagon, it guarded the coastal highway where it forked to Ekron, and inland commanded the most fertile plain in Philistia. It had been built on the conflux of two rivers where they joined on their way an hour's march to the sea; whose river waters were tapped in a series of wells and cisterns that made it virtually immune to assault. It was incredible that it should have been attacked.

Dusk overtook the cavalcade of chariots on the road, the sky changing from mauve to dove gray and then, in the direction they were going, orange. They had come from seeing Ebenezer burn; but Ebenezer was a local bonfire compared with this. It was as if the sun god had turned back in his course.

"It is Ashdod, for sure," Ptullis said.

Athol was suddenly less sure. The air was already tainted with the first smoke; the horses tossing their heads uneasily. Like the men they were exhausted, forcing a heavy trot, their chests and flanks creamed with foam. Ptullis was half asleep standing, his face a yellow skull full of downward lines. The sight of blood never failed to sicken him, and he had seen enough already this day to fill a cistern. Athol's elbow nudged him viciously awake. The smoke was a drifting wall across their front that joined earth and sky, extending well inland; and now you could see the flames at its base, and the unearthly figures of men like ifrits running hither and thither. A fox or jackal crossed their path howling like a demon and was gone, trailing smoke and sparks. Athol nearly lost control of the horses.

"It's not Ashdod," he mouthed. "The cornfields. We are too late."

The lights of the town appeared through the smoke high on their right hand; but the smoke was drifting harmlessly past and out to sea. Ashdod and its road, thronged with people who fell back to make a passage for the horses, were as yet untouched. But inland, the whole sweep of the valley seemed ablaze, the line of flames approaching at a great pace like incoming breakers on the shore, and with the same roaring sound. It was an old military trick, to fire an enemy's corn in the dry season just before the harvest, when it would go up like tinder; a single torch could destroy an army's fodder supply if unchecked: but this must have been fired from all points at once.

There was no time for questions. A human chain had been formed from the river with leather buckets to save the olive groves; but the buckets were too few. Athol sent the horses away, and his men into the nearer villages to fetch flails from the threshing floors. There was no shortage of men, but few soldiers, most of the garrison being at Aphek, and those that remained more concerned with the safety of the town itself.

Nothing could be done to save the standing corn. Only on the south side of the valley, where the harvesting had begun and the wheat was piled in shocks, was there any break in the fireline. Athol's flails beat a path through, enabling the townsmen to reach a part of the field; but by then the flames had reached the olive groves on the far side, and he left them to hurry across. The road itself, well soaked down from the rivers, was the only effective firebreak that saved Ashdod. By morning nine tenths of the corn was lost, and half the olives blackened and charred. Even the adjoining vineyards had not escaped, their leaves shriveled with the half-grown fruit.

Prince Raphah, Ser of Ashdod, was an old man, silver-haired and lame, one of the last of the old Philistine imperialists. Believing the town attacked, he had simply followed the routine procedure, ordered the gates barred and waited for reinforcements, leaving the villages to fend for themselves. Athol stood on the terrace of his palace, looking down on the blackened valley. He had bathed and changed into a fresh white tunic but not slept, a slender, almost effeminate figure beside the heavily robed Raphah. From here, the palace must have witnessed the holocaust from the beginning. But it was from the villagers, not from Raphah's watch, that he learned how it had started: by someone driving jackals - hundreds, they said, but that was surely an exaggeration—into the corn in pairs, tied tail to tail with a firebrand between; so that by the time the brand burnt asunder they were well into the corn, and spreading devastation in all quarters at once. The jackal that had crossed Athol's path was one of these. It must have taken a good number of men to bring the animals to the valley's edge: impossible to tell how many. From random questioning Athol had learned that they were not soldiers—*ruffians, habiru, brigands,* were the words; but a number of witnesses were able to describe their leader as a great giant of a man who stood and roared above the flames, waving his arms as if calling fire down from heaven.

Now that it was all over, Raphah was impatient for action. "When are they coming?" And when Athol raised his head, showing his weariness, he added: "Your men, your men. We have not sufficient here for a punitive expedition; you know that."

"No one is coming," Athol told him. "I sent word to them in Aphek to stand fast."

"On whose authority?"

They had never liked each other. The five Seren held equal status in name only; no question but that Gaza, by reason of its superior size and importance, outranked Ashdod. Athol of Gaza took his place in the council of princes second only to Ashkelon. With Raphah, the gulf of years was unbridgeable. Once, the old man had seemed a remote and terrifying figure. Now, looking at the reddening color of that noble face–the more startling because of the white hair–Athol could feel only a mild irritation.

"On the authority of Gaza, Ashkelon, Gath, Ekron . . . and your own, my Lord."

"By the gods you take too much upon yourself, young Athol!" Raphah was storming now; the face of a sentry appeared at the head of the steps, and vanished. He controlled his voice. "The Council appointed you Lord of Battles–in the north; and the battle is done. You have no authority to interfere in Ashdod. *I* rule here. And I want these barbarians punished!"

"I do not interfere, my Lord."

"Then where are my cohorts?"

"In Aphek," Athol said again. "And the battle is not done. This was a trick to draw our men south; else we had made an end in Ebenezer yesterday. Instead, the main body of the Israelites escaped us. Now they will regroup and attack us again. We must be ready."

"But what of *this!"* Raphah seized his arm and pointed with a shaking hand down at the ruined valley. "Are you going to let them get away with this? You have sufficient men with you–"

Athol freed himself. He said, forcing himself to be patient, "A handful of Habiru, safe in their hills by now. It would take all our armies together to smoke them out."

"Never mind smoking them *out*–we know where they are from. Burn their villages, burn their crops and vines, as they have burnt ours. Put a village or two to the sword, make an example–let them have a taste of Philistine rule! By heavens, your father would have known what to do!"

Athol stood against the parapet at the end of the terrace with his head on his arms, listening without hearing, only raising his head to signal to a charioteer of his own cohort, who presently appeared on the steps, past the sentry. The man saluted and handed him his javelin. Athol gave it to Raphah butt first, the yellow pennon in his hand.

Raphah looked at it. "What is this?"

"The symbol of my office, my Lord. The flag of the Lord of Battles. Take it, and do as you will."

"How can I take it? You were appointed by the council; and I am an old man. You mock me."

The butt slid to the ground between them, and Athol stood leaning on the staff. "Then hear me," he said at last. "All Israel is divided. They have neither kings nor princes to lead them. In the south Judah is subdued and under our rule. We have had no trouble until now in Dan, or Benjamin. Only in the north have they taken up arms against us; having neither swords nor chariots. Go burn and destroy their farmlands here and you will have the whole countryside united against us along the frontiers."

He took his javelin and went down the steps. He had his men bivouacked in the villages, and rather than endure Raphah's company any longer, went on down to join them.

□

Athol had told Raphah the burning of the crops was a ruse to fetch his chariots away from the battle; and if it was true, he was certain it was not the whole truth. If the Danite had sided with Ephraim, why had his tribe not come up for the battle itself? He knew from his spies they had not; or no more than a handful. And he said to himself, pulling on his helmet, "There has to be another reason."

He discovered it almost at once. The first of his captains came in answer to his summons, and among them was Hanno, son of the wine merchant Jason, bursting with news. Athol led him aside. "Well?"

"Athol, I know who fired the crops."

"You do?"

"My brother and I have been questioning those who saw him–the leader of the gang. Beyond doubt it was the Hebrew, Samson of Zorah, the same that was to have married our sister in Timnath. A great oaf of a . . ."

He looked at Athol's face, not knowing what was wrong. He had come seeking his friend and drinking companion, and he was looking at the Prince of Gaza.

Athol's voice was menacing. "*Was* to be married, you said. Why was there no wedding?"

"My Lord, there was a feast. . . . You *knew* of this?"

"Go on."

"Since it was our father's wish, we did our best to be agreeable; but the fellow was impossible . . . what could you expect? An uncouth peasant from the mountain tops. There was a . . . misunderstanding, and he walked away from the feast. To save our sister from public disgrace, my father gave her to another–a man of good family, and one of us, though not a Philistine; more suitable in every way. We never thought the Hebrew would come back." Hanno laughed uneasily. "I never understood why our father accepted him in the first place. None of us did."

Athol did not tell him it was because he himself had ordered Jason to agree to the match. As soon as word reached him from Zorah of the attachment, he had sent a messenger with a scroll under his personal seal, to warn that *on pain of death* no opposition was to be made. With Samson wedded to a Philistine woman, Dan would be halfway committed to the coast; or at least neutralized.

It was not the first time Jason had shown his contempt for the Seren; it would certainly be the last.

He sent the puzzled Hanno away, and called for one of his own Captains from the Gaza cohorts, the same that had borne his edict to Jason before, and gave him his instructions under oath of secrecy.

□

Omar the shepherd chief, though he took no part in the patient snaring of the jackals, had insisted on accompanying Samson on the raid. By then the flocks were settled in the hill pasture, and because the winter rains had been exceptionally heavy, the grazing was plentiful enough for several days before they would need to be moved on. So the shepherd's work was light, and Omar took thirteen of his ruffians with him down to the valley of Ashdod, leaving the sheep for the most part for the women to tend. From Zorah and Eshtaol there were as many again, though Samson could have called on twice their number from the young men Jemuel brought forward. Each man carried a pair of jackals in sacks, slung across the shoulders on a stick for a rough and ready yoke.

The jackals were vicious, and penning them as they

were brought in from the trapping a problem, until Samson remembered the cave in the rock at Etam, where he had gone with Tamam. With a boulder wedged in the cave-mouth, it served well enough.

They returned after the raid, and the place still stank of the beasts. They had laid in a store of grain and lentils, and more than enough *shechar* to celebrate their safe return, with the result that there was brawling between the Danites and the shepherds, and a lad from Eshtaol fell over the natural bridge at the back of the cave into one of the holes. They lit a taper over the blackness and shouted, but there was nothing save the echoes of their own voices.

"Can you not control your men?" Samson asked Omar angrily.

The shepherd shrugged. "They don't like being cooped up in here: they are used to the open air. What are we waiting for?"

"To see if we are followed."

"How long must we stay in this hole?"

Samson told him, "Another day; perhaps two. Then your men can go singly, at intervals. That way they won't attract attention. Mine will do the same."

"My men will go when I tell them. They will be needed to move the flocks on."

"And mine for the olive harvest. There is yet time. While we are here, no man is to approach the cavemouth."

"No man?"

Omar turned his head. The sunlight slid over the scar that twisted his mouth, and vanished behind his huge shadow; then streamed into the cave as he sprang down heavily on the floor, scattering rubble. His forward rush carried him into violent collision with Samson's retreating back, and taking advantage of this unexpected good fortune, he whipped his bare forearm across the Hebrew's throat and had it triumphantly in a stranglehold, bearing down with all his weight to block a counter-move. Nothing happened. He giggled, driving his heels into the bats' dung.

"Now let us see if these stories of your great strength are true!"

Still Samson made no move, his hands hanging at his sides. Omar let go his hold and walked round curiously to peer into Samson's face. "Where is the lad who slew a bear at one blow?"

The black eyes unclouded, as if Samson saw him there for the first time; and turned aside. "I will wrestle with you, Omar. But not now."

"Is the Nazirite afraid?"

"Do not provoke me." Samson said, "Can you not see that I am angry, because of the boy? Look at my hands."

They were shaking. He held them palms up, the fingers curling like rams' horns, and the thickness of his forearms flattened as if he cradled some gigantic, invisible burden.

"I tell you, Omar, I cannot control them. They would take you apart like straw. Now do you understand?"

Omar, ready to bluster, fell back, wary of a trick. He had seen men in a fit before, but nothing like this. He shook his head slowly, unable to take his eyes off the hands, and saw them uncurl and drop.

"Neither do I understand," Samson told him. And he said, "It is something that has come upon me at times, ever since I was a child, with this terrible anger that turns the world black. It was like it with the bear, that time. Only now I know the feeling, when it is coming upon me. My father has it; but with me it is worse."

From his distance Omar's laugh, when it came, was uncertain. "And is it gone now?"

"I think so." Samson laughed in turn, and threw his head back. "Aye, it's gone."

Omar came beside him like a man barefoot on thorns, accompanying him gingerly down the length of the cave over the bridge to refresh themselves in the pool, under the twin rivulets. He shook the water from his beard to demand, "Why should one man's death so afflict you?" To Omar, a man's death was written in his destiny, as acceptable a function as eating and passing water: unless he was kin. "Was this man your brother?"

In the water Tamam's face came beside Samson's as clear as his own, uplifted with that familiar, half-loving, half scornful look. He groaned and lowered his head, his eyes shut, and her lips were cold as ice, and gone. When he opened his eyes there was nothing but the pieces of his own image coming together in the water as it settled, and was still, alone. He felt a sudden fierce envy for the Eshtaolite, who would never leave this place again, or be quit of his youth. Aloud he said, "He was a child of Israel, and of Yahweh. The anger was not my own."

The naming of the god in this dim and unnatural place, with no sight of the sky, made Omar shiver. Water that came out of a rock was magic enough.

"Then I am glad we did not fight," he said, and clapped Samson cheerfully on the shoulder. "Though I fear no man, yet I would not displease your god!"

The following day, when scouts reported no movement of Philistines from the plain, they began to leave, singly: the shepherds to their encampment, Samson's little band across the border into Dan. Omar was among the last to go, and clasped Samson's arm.

"Send for me again when there is need."

"Aye, I will. And take the payment I promised you from my father's sheep."

Omar shook his head, with the crooked grin. "Not this time. Sacrifice one to Yahweh for us, when you return to your village."

It was evening before Samson left the cave. If they had been to Zorah looking for him, Jemuel would have sent word by now. That he had been recognized at Ashdod was certain: he had made sure of it himself. He pulled down a carob pod as he passed, and tasted the familiar sweet pith again. The night sky was full of stars, with hardly any moon, but he would have known these paths blindfolded. Long before he reached Zorah he heard the sound of keening in the village, like the howling of wolves round the sheepfold; and from the first villager he met, learned that his father had been killed at the battle of Ebenezer.

□

They had fetched Manoah home in a borrowed cart, and buried him the same day between Zorah and Eshtaol in among the oleanders. When Samson returned there was already a carpet of blossom, a pink and white starred mound to mark the grave.

The minstrel Baasha found him there in the morning, his cloak pearled with the dew; and nearly died of fright.

"Samson . . . ?" He let out his breath and said, "I thought you were *him.* Manoah."

And he stood on one leg and said, "I had not noticed until now. How like him you've grown."

"I am *nothing* like him, Baasha," Samson said between his teeth. And then, calming himself: "Why did they bury him here? It's too close to the stream."

"They considered it. The waters have never come up this far; not even after the rains."

"They might yet. Then you would really see him again."

The hunchback almost straightened with horror. "How can you joke about such a thing?" He told Samson, nervously following the stream down with his eyes and seeing nothing moving there among the corn stubble, that they had paced it out: it was exactly midway between Zorah and Eshtaol, the two villages of which Manoah was headman. "According to the word of Yahweh."

Samson scowled, and flung a pebble into the stream. "You are making up one of your lying songs, Baasha. What had Yahweh to do with it?"

"The elders asked Uzziel, and Uzziel had the answer from Yahweh through the magic stones–the *urim* and *thummin,* which he has kept ever since he was a proper priest. He keeps them in–"

"I know," Samson said. It baffled him that Yahweh had favored Manoah, after what he did to Tamam. He noticed for the first time that Baasha was barefoot, despite the dew, having left his sandals at a respectful distance; and wryly stooped to unlatch his own. "We used to pee in the water here, Baasha, remember? So the Canaanites would have the benefit of it downstream. Now it is a holy place, and full of ghosts. . . ." Samson straightened. "One ghost, anyway. Do you think the dead come back, Baasha?"

The psalmist, not liking this talk, drew his kaftan closer, half looking over his shoulder despite himself. It is not the dark which is to be feared, but the dawn and dusk: when there is just enough light to see what is not there. The remote sun drew the river mist up with the dew, veiling everyday things with unreality. Baasha's voice croaked. "They say, only if there has been great suffering . . . I heard he died quickly, Samson. An arrow, and he took it in the throat. They say he did not suffer at all."

Samson wanted him to suffer. It was monstrous that Manoah had escaped the revenge of which his marriage to the Philistine Timnite was only a beginning–not even a beginning, as it turned out, though at least Manoah never knew that. Samson had passed the night brooding on the unfairness of it, feeling cheated already without the unwelcome discovery that the tyrant's grave was declared a shrine. It did not occur to him to doubt Uzziel's decree. If Manoah was Yahweh's man, what was Samson the Nazirite?

He turned his head at last, to say, "I am big, like him, Baasha. Because you are big, men think you must be stupid with it, like the ox and the camel. Manoah was not stupid"–he scooped a handful of the blossom and let it fall through his fingers like colored snowflakes on the mound–"but he was simple. To him everything was day or night, good or evil, every man was a friend or an enemy. The *rightness* of it warmed him like a coal in his belly, too hot for anyone else to approach. The prophet Samuel was the same, only with him it was a flame that came out of his ears; I didn't like him much. If knowing you are right is wisdom, then I must be stupid, because my friends and enemies keep changing faces. I like enemies better: you know where you are with enemies, and what they want."

"They want to kill you."

Samson's scowl changed briefly to a grin. "You are little, Baasha, like a fox; nobody could call you stupid. Is that why you keep looking down the vale? Because the Philistines are coming?"

Baasha's eyes avoided his own. "They know you are here."

"So soon? They are well informed. Come to that, so are you. How do you know they will come this way?"

"There is talk of a gathering at Timnath. I was there last night. They know you must return to Zorah sooner or later, they are hoping to catch you here."

"How many?"

"Who knows? A dozen; maybe two."

It was too many to approach Zorah undetected; too few to surround the village and block the many ways to the hills. But it was enough to do in Dan what Samson had done in Ashdod, and he put his sandals on again.

"There is one more thing," Baasha said. "They have burned down the house of Jason the Timnite, and he and his daughter are dead."

Samson did not turn his head or answer. After a moment he left Baasha there and went on down beside the stream to meet the Philistines, running.

□

At the emergency meeting of the Seren which Raphah had called, as he had threatened, to challenge Athol's conduct of the campaign against Ephraim, Raphah had had the five chairs of State set up on his terrace between the colonnades in the usual circle, in the center of which he stood haranguing them in rising tones. He had begun with dignity, with a carefully prepared speech, but the empty chair distracted him, as it was meant to, and his gestures grew wilder, his yellow silks flying out, his face dangerously red. The empty chair was Gaza's. Athol had left it, breaking protocol with an arrogance to match Raphah's own, pacing up and down the terrace in a controlled fury at the delay. So far as he was concerned the meeting was a waste of precious time; but not even he dared join his army until the rigmarole was done. It was an error on Raphah's part to summon the Seren to Ashdod—though it was his right—instead of the usual venue in Ashkelon, in order to give them firsthand sight of his charred fields. Glancing sideways, Athol saw little comfort for Raphah in their faces: Abimelech of Ekron, middle-aged, tough and experienced, the most suitable to take over command from Athol, was too unambitious, nodding his agreement without listening; Maoch of Gath, a great, full-bellied man, sullen with resentment at being fetched so far at short notice; the handsome young Saph of Ashkelon, too preoccupied with the fleshpots of his trading and taxes and women to be much concerned. Not one of them wanted

Athol replaced. Raphah saw it too, and shrewdly changed tactics with a direct appeal to their self-interest.

"A caravan attacked and robbed in broad daylight before Ashkelon! The wheat harvest burned down here in Ashdod! *Who will be next?* I tell you, none of us is safe in his own city while this Hebrew Samson is allowed the run of the plains. Ask Athol why this man goes unpunished. Ask him why the punitive columns are kept like sheep in a sheepfold while the world laughs at us!"

Their heads turned curiously.

Athol said, "We are hunting lions in Ephraim, and my Lord Raphah would have us turn aside for a bee sting."

He walked back to his chair and stood behind it, leaning forward with his hands on the carved wood. "Well, it was Ashdod that was stung. When we have done in the north will be time enough to come back and smoke out this little hive. I say, leave Samson be. Leave him *alone.* Because his tribe is not with him; Dan does not follow this man, only a handful of brigands he has gathered; we have always had brigands."

There was a murmur of protest at this.

"Not on our doorsteps!"

"Not so bold as this!"

"Raphah is right. Where will he strike next?"

Athol held up his hand. "He will not strike again," he said confidently. "There was a reason–some of you have heard. He was both cheated and insulted by our kinsman, Jason of Timnath, and this was his revenge. Allow him this, and he will trouble us no more, neither will he stir up the Danites against us, as otherwise he might. You can blame Jason for what happened. He took the Hebrew for his son-in-law, and then gave the bride his daughter to another. I planned the match myself, to hold Samson safe and Dan with him, while we settled the northern business; and Jason disobeyed me in this."

Maoch of Gath leaned forward, willing to accept the scapegoat. "Then should not this Jason be punished?"

"He is dead," Athol told them. "We waste our time here; the matter is settled and done with."

But it was not settled, for while he was still speaking a messenger arrived from Timnath with the story of a new affray in the valley, with nine Canaanite soldiers slaughtered and scattered up and down the terraces and two Philistine Captains among them, one of whom was Phicol, Captain of the Charioteers and friend to Athol of Gaza, whose murder could not be overlooked.

Athol bowed his head, privately cursing the dead man and all his kin. Clearly Phicol had (how? but *some*how) got wind of the plan to do away with his father and sister, and must have rushed to intervene; no doubt too late to save them; and had gone blindly after Samson. The details no longer mattered.

He straightened and said, "Very well. I will have this Samson brought to the Council in chains, even if it takes half our armies. I will order the men back from Aphek."

9

SAMSON SPENT THE ONE NIGHT in his father's house, and in the morning was gone, long before the first of the Philistine patrols reached Zorah. They questioned Sharah roughly and turned the house upside down, but all the male things were Manoah's. When they understood how the woman had lost her husband they left her alone. "We have no quarrel with Dan," they said; "neither with Benjamin. Your man had no cause to join those who took up the sword against us." They did not ask where Samson had gone.

As it happened, only Uzziel could have told them. There were those who had pressed Samson to stay, and take his rightful place as chief of the clan, hotheads bloodyminded enough to stand beside him and face whatever came up from the coast. But the villages were without walls, and indefensible: to remain would invite certain capture, and worse. There was only one answer, and Uzziel said, "You have decided, then," as if that settled it.

They were alone. Samson had left his mother weeping out her prayers for him to be gone, before she lost a son as well as a husband, though the soldiers were to have no tears from her later. Samson stared at Uzziel's blind face, baffled. "I have decided nothing!–I have a choice? Does the earth decide to be wet when the rains rain upon it?"

And he said, grumbling, "First it was Manoah. Then the Philistines with whom I had no quarrel, pushing me this way and that."

"Is it not from Yahweh?" the hermit asked quietly, fingering his lip. "Remember the vows that were made for you."

"Aye, as a Nazirite. The prophet Samuel is a Nazirite as well, but at least Adonai speaks to him. He does not tell me what I should do."

"Perhaps he does. Sometimes, when Yahweh will have a man take a certain path, he closes all other paths to him."

"The Lord set Samuel on this path, and nobody listened to him. Why should they listen to me?"

"Your exploits are already famous, my son. These people are like sheep. Samuel was the Lord's dog that snapped at their heels, bringing in strays. But it is the shepherd they follow, the one who leads them."

The talk of sheep and shepherds made Samson think of Omar, and before first light he had crossed the stream and the Vale of Sorek skirting Beth-shemesh, where he stole a watermelon and the dogs barked at him, and made his way south again into the highlands to seek him out before going on to try where Samuel himself had failed: to raise up the sleeping giant of Judah against the Philistines.

□

The flocks were on the move, and it was several days before Samson caught up with them scattered over a steep hillside above the joining of two streams, not far short of Bethlehem. Omar, surprised to see him again so soon after their parting, greeted him with a bear's hug, and roared his approval on learning the reason for his flight.

"Would you had waited and sent word to us!"

"This is not your quarrel, Omar."

"Your fight is my fight," Omar said heartily. "Besides, these Philistines are all over Judah like flies on carrion. It is time someone squashed a few. They carry fine daggers, too, and fine raiment and jewels, some of them."

Samson's face darkened. "I will take food where I find it, but I am no thief!"

"No, but I am," Omar told him cheerfully. "Besides, I am talking of the spoils of war. All we had at Ashdod was a couple of wenches who came out to look at the fire. Right disappointed they were, I can tell you . . . the men, that is!"

He chuckled hugely at his own joke, leading Samson by the arm to where his black tent was pitched and shouting for shechar long before they reached it. He said, "What is it this time?–a fat village? A *town?*"

"A town," Samson said, though it had not occurred to him before. It was as he had told Uzziel, always others' ideas thrust upon him. But it was a good idea.

Omar pulled aside the tent flap for him, his crooked grin uncertain. There were others there waiting, ready with jars of the barley wine that seemed to be always on hand. After the sunlight, the tent was cool and dim. It was a moment before Samson recognized individual faces among those that crowded to welcome him.

Omar said, "Has it got a name, this town?"

"Yes. Gath."

"Gath!" Omar's ale exploded over his beard and chest. He reeled back against the man behind him, drenching his back as well, doubled up to slap his thigh, and threw back his head to bellow his laughter twice as loud at Samson's joke as at his own. He had to explain it to the others: that the Hebrew, not content with burning down the Philistine grain, overturning their chariots and scattering their dead up and down the vale of Timnath–would now have them believe he was ready to lead their little band to attack the strongest fortress town in Judah! Which was defended not only by stone walls and towers but a whole regiment of Philistine soldiers; all armed to the teeth. By now they were all laughing except Samson, who went on drinking as if he had heard none of it. Omar stopped. He said, "There is something you've not told me."

"Aye. Your regiment of Philistines is not there. They are away up north under the princeling of Gaza to war with my people. Gath is defended at this moment by nothing but a rabble of auxiliaries; half-trained farmers and shopkeepers, and from what I saw of them with only half a stomach for a fight."

They stared at him. Eventually Omar shouted, "This man is mad!" He shrugged and dropped his voice incredulously. "And if it's the truth; you'd still need an army to take Gath."

"That's why I am here," Samson told him. "To raise an army."

Afterward, watching the sun go down trailing a bright mist of stars, and listening to the reassuring tinkle of sheep bells somewhere on the slopes above them, Omar said, "I don't know how you do it. But if the Judahites listen to you as readily as my ruffians, nothing is impossible."

Samson stirred to ask, "You will come with me, Omar?"

"No. Your warring and your soldiers' battles are not for the likes of us. Our way is to raid, in and out and clear off with the spoils. But I'll not be far if you need me. And if I were you, I'd not go down to Judah; not yet. When their drovers come up for the shearing; pass the word and let them bring Judah up to you in the hills."

There was much sense in this. The Philistines would be watching for Samson; and any gathering of the lowland clans would forewarn them. If the Judahites rallied to him in the hills, they could achieve complete surprise.

It was only later, when Samson had made his evening prayer and lay with the warm smell of the earth in his nostrils, that a doubt assailed him. He felt immensely alone. He had loosed his headband and his hair was spread in the grass, and he thrust his fingers through it with a kind of despair. It set him apart from other men as surely as the brand on the forehead of Cain; and perhaps all the misfortunes he had endured–Tamam's loss and Manoah's intransigence, Sheshai's betrayal, and the wasteful death of Niobe –were all as Uzziel had said, doors closed to him, lest he live his years out contented with Tamam's children and grandchildren, and his thousand sheep and cattle, Lord of the Remnant of Dan and no worse than his father, and no better.

There were watches posted day and night to warn of Philistine patrols for Samson's sake, but they sighted nothing more dangerous than wolves. When the men came up from Judah for their sheep, Samson took them aside and made a speech. It was a good speech, made up of everything he remembered Samuel saying in the prison house in Gath, with bits from Uzziel. He told them, "Israel is the Lord's sheepfold, and the Philistines the wolf at the door. I give you a message to Judah, which is this: I will wait for you in the hills the first morning after the new moon at Etam. These shepherds will show you where."

And then, remembering the Levite of Mount Ephraim and the woman at Gibeah, he took a wolf killed by the watch and tore it as he had torn the lion, handing them four parts of it to carry to the four corners of Judah. If they would not come up for Samson, for Yahweh they must.

Waiting in the cavern at Etam, he thought ironically how proud Manoah would have been of him. The cavern was a good place for thinking about the dead. In the long hours of darkness they crowded about him like old friends, sometimes mingled with the remembered living, so that he could not distinguish the one from the other. And he thought–Sheshai: did he perish with Niobe and Jason her father? It would be no more than he deserved. But he hoped the child lived; seeing her there with the sticky honeycomb, who unknowingly betrayed his secret riddle to them all. On the appointed day the Judahites did not come, and after three days he sealed the mouths of the grain and lentil sacks, and the shechar jars, and prepared to leave.

"Lord, if you had wanted this thing, you would have sent them by now."

He could not keep the anger out of his voice. *What paths have we left now, Uzziel, old fraud?* Outside, the sunlight clubbed him dizzy, and he shook himself. He hesitated, then started on the upward track. The cliffs to either side were formed by a fault in the rock itself, which was one rock, greater on the left hand where the cavemouth was than on the right; and at the top of the track he abandoned it, and climbed up the rock face itself to the peak, for one last look. At first he could see nothing but the interlocking hills. He was debating whether to go down himself or to make his way up to Shiloh to join Samuel, when a movement caught his eye: in a defile at some distance the first dust of a moving column; repeated, when he looked for it, again and again where the road was visible: and not a Philistine feather to be seen.

It looked as if all Judah was coming up.

He went inside the cave again to wait for them, piling his few belongings inside the entrance: his cloak, waterskin, an old spear of Manoah's, tipped with bronze. It was another hour before he heard the sound of marching feet, and a parched voice shouting his name. He went to the cave-mouth.

"Shalom!"

The track was crowded in both directions with armed men, jostling one another like penned sheep, evidently unsure of the place. A hundred heads turned: but there must have been fully a thousand following behind. A man pushed through and stood below the cave, looking up: a man great of girth and arm, his beard bristling to match his voice.

"We seek Samson the Danite."

"You have found him."

"Caleb ben Abihu," the man said without further preamble, "of Hebron." The faces behind him were as hostile as his own and Samson, about to spring down to embrace him, stayed where he was.

"You had my message?"

"We had it," Caleb agreed grimly. "And so did the Philistines. They caught one of your messengers with his stick of rotten flesh in his hand. He was three days dying, staked out in the sun; and before he died he explained it. They have an army encamped in Lehi scarce an hour's march behind us."

This was evil news; because if the Philistines had the messenger, they knew where he was. And if they were on the edge of the Shephelah in the strength the Judahite said, they must have pulled back from the north while Samson was still making his plans. There was no chance at all of a surprise revolt in Judah.

Another path closed, Adonai? Where does a man go when every path is closed?

Samson leaned back on the rock and closed his eyes against the sun, feeling the sap drain out of him. Caleb was still talking, his voice loud with the blustering indignation of mob oratory for them all to hear, calling him madman; which was what Omar had said, *this man is mad,* so perhaps it was true. But with his eyes shut, without the distraction of Caleb's threatening beard, Samson could detect a shrillness, the smell of fear.

"Do you not know the Philistines are rulers over us?" Caleb was shouting. "They wait only for the signal to eat up our land like locusts. What is this you have done to us?"

Samson opened his eyes. "As they did to me, so have I done to them," he said mildly. "If what you say is true, why are you come up?"

"To bind you; and deliver you to the Philistines. Are you alone?"

But Caleb did not look at Samson as he said it, and shuffled his feet like a man with a thorn in his shoe. It was noticeable that he made no attempt to climb up to the cave-mouth himself. It would have been impossible for more than one man at a time. Samson began to laugh. "Who will be first?"

No one moved. There was no shade in the gully, and the men sweated visibly under a cloud of flies.

Caleb's face was tortured with impotence. "Will you kill your own people?"

"Ah, now you are my own people. Well, stay where you are, my people, and no harm shall come to you."

"If we do not take you back with us, we are all like to perish, and half Judah with us."

"Is that right?" Samson said, and went back inside the cave. It was empty as if even the dead had deserted him. *Where are you, Adonai?* He sat with his head in his hands, and argued fiercely: "These people have abandoned you; they are not worth saving. But I don't want the blood of half Judah on my hands. On the other hand, I don't want my blood on theirs either. Shall I go with them?"

He knew he must.

It was a temptation simply to walk out through the midst of them, for the pleasure of seeing Caleb's discomfiture. There was not a man among them who would stand in his way, if it was face to face. To be roped, like a heifer to the slaughter! There had been no lack of spite in their faces, festering in the sun from a poisonous fear for their own skins. They might find new courage, once they saw him roped.

He went outside and said, "Swear to me that you'll not fall on me yourselves."

They clamored forward, eager to swear by Yahweh, Adonai, El–and no doubt the Baals and Dagon if he had asked it. "No! But we will bind you fast and deliver you into their hands."

"But surely, we will not kill you."

He was unconvinced until Caleb came up against the rock to say privately, "They have ordered us to bring you to them alive."

He left his things in the cave and went down as he was, wearing nothing but a simple tunic of Manoah's, tighter on him than it had been on Manoah, and a headband to keep his hair out of his eyes. They were taken aback to discover his size, the tallest of them coming no higher than his chin, and two men who had brought forward ropes in readiness held back, until someone took Samson's unresisting arms from behind and drew them back. Hands pressing on all sides forced his elbows back until they almost met behind him, and bound them tightly round and round, working the rope down with many knots to secure his helplessly dangling wrists in the same way for good measure, winding the second rope in tightening ligatures about his torso again and again until he thought they would bury him with rope. It constricted his chest, making breathing an effort. The ropes were new and hard, and evidently had been chosen for the purpose. An end of a third rope was looped about his neck, though not tightly, and in this way they led him like an animal down to the Philistines.

Omar's shepherds followed them all the way down.

Keeping his men out of sight was the least of Omar's concerns, for the Judahites' kept to the road and deployed no scouts, evidently under the impression that their numbers rendered them safe from interference. Fatigue and the sweltering heat made them doubly insensitive to caution. It was not even necessary to watch them, for they trailed carelessly over the loose stones and talked among themselves as they went like a wedding procession; their progress could be followed from the blind side of a hill, a wadi, the lip of a cave. The problem was that their prisoner was in the center of the column, and could not be reached without great danger to himself. Moreover, being trussed and tethered, he could afford no assistance to his rescuers.

An instinct warned Samson that they were there. He turned his head slowly as he went, watching for movement among the scalps and ridges, the thorny scrub and scattered trees. For the first time, he began to feel alarmed.

"Caleb!"

The Judahite jerked his head up. A cloud of midges haloed the Danite's head, seeing he could do nothing to dispel it, and Caleb waved a hand uncertainly to relieve him. "What is it?"

"You will not get to Lehi on this road."

"Is this some trick?" Calbe glanced to left and right. "It is the way we came up: it is the road."

"It is the road to your death," Samson told him. "We are walking into an ambush."

He watched courage drain from the man like wine from a punctured skin. Caleb's whitening glance took in the scorched and broken terrain as Samson's had, and was no more reassured by its emptiness. The haze gave life to every shadow that moved with the eye, and he turned back with a shaking curse. "Who would dare come at us? Do you know how many men I have? Have you numbered them?"

Samson shrugged his trussed shoulders indifferently. "If Adonai were with you, you would have fought the Philistines with me, instead of running their errands. If he is not, it doesn't matter how many men you have."

And he added cheerfully, "Look at them."

The Judahites resemblance to a military formation had by now disappeared almost entirely. Exhausted by the unaccustomed marching through the blistering hours when no sensible man leaves the shade, they shuffled in sweat-sodden apathy, some trailing their bows and clubs, others leaning upon spears, with no thought but of getting home. Caleb cuffed those nearest and shouted in rising tones and a few straightened; but it was hopeless; he should have rested them before the return journey. For the first time, the disadvantage of their formation came home to him. The narrowness of the road frequently forced the column into defiles through which they must pass singly, or in pairs, or be so crushed they could not use their weapons. Both front and rear were far out of sight and hearing. He had issued no orders in case of attack. If he halted the march now, they would be no more secure. He ground his teeth and jerked the rope, causing Samson to stumble. "If I die, so will you!"

The same thought had occurred to Samson. The road was already declining toward the plain, lightly wooded on their right hand, and shaking the sweat from his eyes he saw what he was looking for: goat tracks down through the trees.

Caleb was moaning aloud. "It is the punishment of Yahweh on us, for what we have done this day!"

He was done, and took instructions from his prisoner without argument or protest. On Samson's instructions he sent word ahead for the column to proceed until they reached the plain and disperse, every man to his home; asking as an afterthought only when the messenger had gone: "Will they not be ambushed, as you said?"

"Not if I am not with them."

When the road turned a corner of rock, tucked into the hillside, Samson turned aside with Caleb and two of his men and was among the trees half-running. By the time Omar's shepherds noticed the Danite's absence, they were nowhere in sight.

The Philistines were encamped in a natural amphitheater among the foothills almost too small to accommodate the wide pattern of tents, each group with the colored banner of its cohort limp on the still air. The tents were of a light, lean-to type, such as could be divided and borne between two men on foot, open at both ends and providing little but shade. It was evident that their stay was not intended to be a lengthy one. The site was a sun trap, devoid of natural water, and chosen solely for its proximity to the road. Sentries patrolled the crests, but apart from the cooking fires, there was little movement in the camp itself. And because it was the road they watched, Samson's arrival through a screen of trees on their flank went at first unnoticed. It was not altogether by chance that the first to see him was Hanno, son of the dead Jason of Timnath.

Hanno had continued to scour the countryside tirelessly

since daybreak, long after the men under him had flagged and grown careless.

He was returning from a restless patrol of the road itself, and outpaced the dozen or so men with him, his body armor clanking across the edge of the hill, to wrest the rope from Caleb's hand as if only the physical contact could make him believe his good luck. He stared at the prisoner, his chest heaving with an almost sexual excitement, oblivious of the heat and his own fatigue.

"No wedding finery this time, eh, Samson?"

Caleb let go the rope uneasily. "You know him by name?"

"If it were not for this man, my father and my brother and my sister were alive today." Hanno wound the halter round his wrist until it came brutally taut. "You have done well, Caleb; you will be rewarded. Leave him to us now."

The Judahite said, "I didn't know."

But he said it to Samson, who lifted his head and nodded. Caleb turned, and led his men into the trees again without looking back, his eyes on the ground. Hanno composed himself, straightening his helmet and forming his men up in two files for the short triumphant march down to the camp. It would be nothing compared with the triumphant entry into Ashkelon, with the garrison out to keep back the crowds. He clenched his teeth to suppress an insane desire to grin and laugh, breathing heavily through his nose. They had been seen now from the camp; figures began to appear out of the tents like coneys out of a warren, and the cheering began, swelling to a great roar. It was then that Samson turned his head to see if Caleb had gone and Hanno, feeling the rope pulled in his hand, turned and struck him across the bridge of the nose.

The blow made Samson's eyes water, and for a moment he didn't know where he was.

The plumed helmets swam in the vision of a barefoot lad on the hillside below Zorah, who reached out in wonder to touch the cloak of a princess, and was backhanded in the face. In that instant all the remembered fury of the boy rose in the man. Hanno in disbelief saw the ropes part like flax in a fire, scattered in a whirlwind that plucked him off his feet and reversed earth and sky in a wheel of disintegrating limbs and armor, by no means all his own. One Philistine, thrusting his spear toward Samson's ribs, died with the shaft deflected against his own chest armor to penetrate his throat and come out a span behind; another took the sweep of the Hebrew's forearm on the side of his helmet and dropped like a broken doll. But those behind, casting down their spears, came on with daggers and Samson, his arms slashed in a dozen places, fell back and tripped, and the pack was on him like hyenas on carrion.

They had, even now, some idea of taking him alive. The fight was clearly visible from the camp, where the shouting had died away and was now redoubled on a different note as the slopes filled with furiously running men. It was necessary only to restrain the prisoner until they reached them.

Half-suffocated by the weight of men and armor and tortured by the razor-sharp iron at every turn, Samson reached out blindly for stick or stone to defend himself; his hand went in among the bones of some animal, scattering them to close on something sharp and hard; he turned his head and it was the jawbone of a wild ass, newly picked clean with the marrow still in it. His first stroke, hampered as he was, did no more than carry away a Philistine ear; but its owner's anguished howl and the sudden spray of blood shocked them off guard an instant, and the return swing took two teeth from the jawbone and seven from the face it encountered. On one knee, he took a dagger thrust in the buttock that flamed through his loins and nearly brought him down again on the slippery ground. He swung his new weapon in a circle at full stretch, clearing a space among the backward-jumping legs and brought two more down; and there was room to stand. Of Hanno's patrol, only two were on their feet, moving backward over the dead. One flung a spear that grazed his upflung arm, and was cut down; the other, when Samson turned to him half-blinded with sweat and blood, became two, and four and seven; and the men from the camp were on him beyond counting.

The jawbone flew like a flail on the threshing floor, piling the dead on the living, whose shrieks mingled with the battle cries of those behind and narrowed his senses to an awareness of disconnected things: the molten sun, a flock of birds that passed overhead, the jarring numbness of his right arm, the red and blue plumage that tossed like reeds in the *khamsin,* the never-ending faces that must be *struck,* and struck again, and continued to multiply. He meant to go on striking until he was dead, which was only a question of time.

He stopped with the jawbone raised and the blood running back down his arm, unable for a moment to grasp that there were no more faces to strike.

The Philistines were streaming back down the hillside in disarray, running half doubled-up, their faces turned upward as they ran and stumbled among the many already lying scattered, for no reason Samson could make out: until there came the whirring of birds again, which were no birds but a rain of slingshot falling like giant hailstones from the surrounding slopes. The Philistines had come up like hunters sporting after a quarry, expecting one man, lightly equipped, and their shields, which would have protected them from the slings, left behind in their tents. Men fell seemingly at random.

None but the shepherds could use the sling like this, and Samson, scanning the small figures on the sunblind crests, looked for Omar with a rush of affection that embraced the earth.

"Forgive Samson, Adonai! I thought you had abandoned me."

Since he could not help Omar's men, he turned with a hazy notion of finding Hanno; but the dead and dying were so entangled not even the captain's insignia was recognizable. He was amazed at the number of them, blurred in the sunhaze and the fly swarms, the scattered feathers like a chicken pen ravaged by foxes: there seemed no end to the dead. Maybe after all it was a pity Omar had arrived to draw them off, before he had finished. He said aloud, "I'd have managed, for sure!" Baasha would sing of it, one day: how Samson–

> With the tip of an ass slew a thousand or more,
> Ass over tip with the ass's jaw!

The earth tilted under his feet, and his last consciousness was of a patch of stubborn wormwood, the pungent smell of the crushed leaves, and the white flowerheads dappled with his own blood.

□

It was a carrion eagle that saved his life.

There was a score or more sailing the thermals that lifted from the burning ground; as many again already landed and busy among the dead; and one of these flapped onto Samson's shoulder and tore at his exposed back. He moved, and it rose in alarm with a flurry of wings that stirred the dust. The hot grains stung like bees, and his first attempted cough opened wounds in every part of his body. But it was thirst, when he came to his senses, that most tormented him. He thought for a moment that he was dead and in Gehenna.

The silence told him, even before his gaze cleared, that the Philistines were gone. His limbs felt weightless, and when he tried to stand his legs floated away, like a man standing in a strong current of water. Omar's shepherds were gone too, and must have drawn the main body after them; for it was obvious, when he looked down into the broad hollow even through the haze of his dizziness, that they could not have contained such a force for long. And because the eagles were thickest beyond the tents, on the far slope at a point nearly opposite himself, he could guess that this was where they had broken out. And the thought came to him slowly that the Philistines had taken neither their tents nor their dead with them.

Which meant that they would be back.

He turned his head to measure the impossible distance to the safety of the trees, and his knees folded, and he sat down cursing Omar through cracked lips for having left him. His tongue was leathery as a carob pod, and so swollen he could hardly swallow. The splintered jawbone lay red beside him, and with his last strength he hurled it bitterly aside. It struck rocks and bounced off into the wormwood.

"Adonai . . ."

He sat with his head on his knees. *You have given this great deliverance into the hand of your servant; and now shall I die of thirst, and fall into the hand of the uncircumcised?* The thought of the mutilations they would perform on his body filled him with a horror deeper than death itself. The crushed needle grass merged with the brown earth and took the shape of Uzziel's face, shaking its toothless disapproval; and he asked it, moving his lips silently, Why does he not answer Samson? And Uzziel was saying *you do not listen.*

So he listened, and at first there was nothing; and then there was Tamam's laughter quite distinctly teasing him: a light rippling, bubbling sound of merriment that persisted until he lifted his head and saw what it was: the well-spring flushing up from the hollow under the rock, where the strike of the jawbone had disturbed it.

□

For Samuel, the defeat at Aphek marked the beginning of a period of deep mental crisis that had nothing to do with recriminations or grief. The loss of life, with its epidemic bereavement, he accepted as a just retribution on a people fallen into backsliding and Baal-worship. But he saw, as few did, that the rise of Philistia could mean only the impossible—the collapse of Israel itself: the unravelling of the whole weave of Yahweh's handiwork from Abram to Joshua.

He did not return to Shiloh, but made his way deep into the wilderness for a prolonged period of prayer and fasting. And it was there that he remembered the word of Yahweh: *In Gath of Judah you will find you a young man. . . .* A man who bore the mark of Yahweh on his forehead as surely as Cain. A man to whom he, Samuel, owed his life.

His search for Samson took him into the Vale of Sorek and down into Judah, where he learned of the massacre of the Philistines at Lehi, and that Samson had escaped to the mountains, none could say where. It was said that he was with the shepherds; but by then it was already the tenth month, with the first rains falling, and the flocks long since brought down to winter folds, the encampments dispersed. In Bethlehem-judah he found the shepherd chief Omar, in whose camp the women had nursed Samson from his wounds, but the Danite had left them before they came down to the town. And it was in Bethlehem that Samuel received the bitter news that told him his quest was in vain.

In Samuel's absence, Eli's two priest sons at Shiloh had rallied the Ephraimite army again, and had returned to the battle taking the ark of the covenant with them this time at the head of a great column. It seemed as if all the north had answered the call, confident that the presence of the ark would strike fear into the hearts of the enemy; and at first they had met with some success, catching the Philistines between Ekron and Ashdod, the enemy falling back in awe, finding themselves facing the very god whose magic had struck down the Egyptians with plagues and death, as was well known; until the prince of Gaza rode out in his chariot and rallied them with threats and curses. It was too soon for details: but it was known that there were upward of ten thousand lost in Israel, and that the ark was in the hands of the uncircumcised.

The war was lost.

10

WORD REACHED SAMSON between Bethlehem and Eshtaol that Shiloh had been sacked, and there were Philistines encamped in the Vale of Sorek, and he turned back to consider the matter. Night was coming on, and a thin rain with it. Ephraim's war was one thing: but Shiloh belonged to all Israel, the central shrine of the tribes. It was unthinkable that Yahweh should have sanctioned its destruction. The burden of the news outweighed his natural caution, and finding himself in the vicinity of Etam and in need of shelter from the rain he went instinctively to the cave, without thinking what he was doing, and was halted in the act of climbing through its narrow entrance by a spear at his throat.

A torch flared up, that had been held covered, and he recognized the face of one of Caleb's Judahites, the same that had come up to capture and bind him before. A second spear pricked the back of his neck, though he had seen no one following him. A move in either direction and he would be spitted like a roast.

A voice said, "It is the Nazirite."

The spear was withdrawn. In the same moment the Judahite turned with a changed face to shout, *"It is Samson! Samson is here!"* The cry echoed through the cavern, disturbing the bats to a leathery whirring, and lights sprang up on every side to turn night into day. There must have been fully a hundred in the cave. Only when Samson was in their midst, and they crowded aside to make a path for his feet like thanes before a king, did he discover that they were gathered to honor him. Most of the faces were Hebrew, some from his own village and Judah; several bearing wounds from Ephraim, others with the dialect of Benjamin and even the northern Manasseh. A length of sackcloth had been fastened somehow across the cavemouth to keep the light in. They appeared to be well provided with meat and weapons, both. It seemed he had an army after all: though not from Judah, and not much in numbers. And not when he wanted it.

"Why do you come to me *now?*"

They told him, "Because Yahweh is departed from us. And we know he is with you."

He wished he was as sure. Some of them, on closer inspection, looked like men their own villages would be glad to see the backs of. There was at least one of Omar's lot, certainly an Amorite, and Samson pointed to him.

"What say you? Yahweh is not your god."

"Your god is my god."

During the evening meal it was plain that having banded themselves together and stocked the cave as a common base, they looked to Samson for a plan. To give himself time to think, he got up and went to rinse his hands and mouth under one of the twin rivulets at the back of the cave, where Tamam had once pushed his head under the water. He had had a plan once. He could still hear Omar's laugh when he announced it: to capture Gath, no less! But that was with the multitudes of Judah, which Yahweh never sent except as enemies: not a few score villagers. Perhaps because he was a Nazirite. But he was not the only Nazirite. He went back to them.

"Who has made me a judge in Israel? Why not seek out the prophet Samuel?"

They shook their heads, those nearest averting their

eyes. It was a man from Ephraim who told him that Samuel had gone a hermit into the wilderness, none knew where.

"What of Eli, then?"

"Eli is dead."

He had been an old man, nearly a hundred years old. When the Ephraimite army marched out of Shiloh under his two sons, the men bearing the ark at the head of the great column, Eli would not leave the city gate, but had a little stool fetched and watched there every day for their return. A Benjaminite was the first to return, his garments ripped and torn in the extremity of mourning, the misery of earth sprinkled over his bowed head. But the old man's eyes were too weak to see it. When the man told him plainly that the battle was lost, the ark itself taken, and his sons killed, the shock was too much. It was said that Eli started to his feet and fell backward, and broke his neck.

It was the first Samson had heard of the loss of the ark. He stared at them in horror. No one spoke, but he saw in face after face that it was true. It was as if every torch in the cavern had gone out. Their calmness nauseated him; he felt the bile of anger rise in his stomach, and clenched his hands to still their trembling. He heard someone saying there had been a child, a son, born to the widow of one of the dead priests, Eli's daughter-in-law. When they brought her the news that day she turned her face to the wall and never recovered. But before she died she gave the child a name, Dishonor—*Ichabod.* It was an awful name. There had never been another Ichabod in Israel.

"There has never been another Samson, either," Samson said. "Where have they taken the ark?"

They told him: "Ashdod."

He set out before daybreak the following morning alone, pausing at Zorah only to collect Baasha, with no clear idea in his head except to bring the ark back. Force, at that distance, and with the limited number of men at his disposal, was out of the question. He took Baasha because the psalmist knew his way about the streets of the cities, and because he didn't trust him enough to leave him behind. That the ark was held in a Philistine citadel stronghold, and doubtless heavily guarded, Samson saw as Adonai's problem, not his.

Ever since the day he had listened for Adonai's voice, and heard the most beautiful sound in the world–the water bubbling from the well spring at Lehi–he had never again doubted the wisdom of Uzziel's words.

In the event, the ark wasn't guarded at all.

The second day, in the afternoon, they came down the side of the familiar valley, whose rich brown earth, newly turned, showed no trace of the burning; but approaching the city they passed the charred remains of outhouses, and stunted vines, and the walls facing the road were noticeably discolored. Though they had both drawn their cloaks over their heads, like most winter travelers, and were somewhat hooded, Baasha followed the broad back of his companion through the jostling traffic of townspeople with growing unease. If there was one place where they had good reason to remember Samson, it was Ashdod. The next moment he lost him; to encounter with a start at the next corner the familiar black eyes unexpectedly on a level with his own. Samson had somewhere acquired a rickety staff, on which he leaned doubled over like an old man, shuffling his feet to complete the illusion. Except that he was grinning like an imbecile, he was unnoticeable in the crowd.

"The ark is in the temple of Dagon," he said. "Follow me."

There was no need to inquire the way. It seemed that all Ashdod was climbing the street to where the whitestone temple presently appeared against the sky, and looking back they could see a steady stream of men, women and children coming in on all three highways. The temple was a little city within a city, walled about with a single gate, through which they passed into a packed courtyard flanked with terraces of houses and storerooms, following the sluggish movement of the crowd that was sucked in like the backwaters of a slow river under the colonnaded arch to the inner court, where priests shepherded the sightseers past the open doors of the sanctuary itself. No loitering was permitted, and Samson had no more than a glimpse of the golden caskets, and the towering figure of the Philistine god behind, before they were moved on. There were no armed guards, and no need of any. To leave Ashdod the ark would need to pass through the midst of its citizens, in full view of all.

Baasha was for going home. Instead, Samson dispatched him to find lodgings and returned to the temple court alone. He had noticed the women before, two or three at the upper windows of the one house; but there were fully a dozen. You could see them only from the opposite side of the courtyard, since they kept back from the windows, while discreetly watching the throng below. Samson chose one and made a sign above the crowd, which was received with a look of disbelief. He straightened, and the woman stared again, lifting her little veil, and when he nodded, indicated an open doorway below.

She met him at the head of the narrow stairway, a sturdy girl decked like a bride in rainbow-layered shifts tinkling with jewelry, the veil in her hand, and not so young as she had looked at the window. Her black skin had the strength and sheen of polished wood. She knelt to kiss the mosaic floor between his feet, with a movement none the less graceful for its formality.

But her brown eyes were wide with curiosity. "Why were you doubled up like that? I took you for an old man."

"I had a pain," Samson said. "Tell me your name."

"Tahara."

She stood aside, and he went ahead of her, walking quickly down the marbled corridor past closed doors to the last, at the end facing him, his hand already on the latch before she could call out. She had paused halfway, and he dropped his hand. "Where does this one lead to?"

"The priests' quarters!"

The door she opened instead gave into a narrow, whitewashed chamber, well carpeted and almost as colorful as her garments, from the rich ornamentation of red and blue leather camel saddles to the vivid band of frescoes depicting various gods and goddesses in what appeared to be lewd sport, whose motif was repeated on a deep, painted chest. A pair of camel whips, ornately plaited, hung on one wall. He half expected to see the camel itself lurking in a corner. But it was the bed, itself strewn with cushions of every imaginable hue, that dominated the room. The twin heads of two lions, carved and painted alarmingly to resemble the real thing and not much smaller, rose threateningly to form the foot, their bodies stretching back—as Samson discovered, exploring–much elongated to end in tails that curled into rings for headposts. From the window where she had stood, he could see the inner courtyard still thronged with sightseers pushing between the columns, but not the sanctuary door. He asked if the bed was from Egypt, and she nodded.

"As am I."

She sat him on one of the saddles, whose wooden frame made a comfortable enough four-legged stool, while she poured water from a pitcher into a bowl and washed his feet, and dried them in her lap with soft linen, talking all the while to put him at his ease.

She came from a large family, once prosperous, her father having been steward to a grain merchant. Then came the great drought, when the government seized all the corn for the public granaries; and although there was compensation paid, it came too late for many; her father had been dismissed and there being no work for chandlers, was obliged to hire himself out for whatever work he could find, like so many others, until the tide turned. The wages were poor, and there were too many mouths to feed. The elder children had gone in turn to seek employment. Tahara and one sister were sold to a man who owned a troop of dancers, and it was with these that they came up to Canaan.

Samson half listened, encouraging her with a question when she paused, his ear turned to catch the courtyard chatter through the window behind his head. He tousled her black lambswool head in rough sympathy, wondering what she would say if she knew he was a Hebrew, whose forefathers had been little more than slaves in her Egypt; but she lifted her head with the grin only a black girl has, counting herself lucky. She removed his old leather girdle and his tunic with practiced hands, telling him how she had risen to be one of the solo dancers, performing up and down the country at wakes and weddings, and once in the court of the Philistines at Ashkelon. The bed, when he came to it, was heavily scented, the more pungent because she made him lie face down, while she massaged his back with cool oils. She had danced in the temples as well, and because she was good with men, and pleased them, in Ashdod the priests paid her purchase price and took her in as a temple prostitute, to replace a girl whose years were fulfilled. Her owner was reluctant to part with her. She shrugged: "But he could not argue with the Philistine priests. Besides, he got a good price. Why do you Canaanites cut off your little veils so immodestly?"

Samson had rolled on his back, still obedient to the command of her hands, which now smoothed the oils into the muscled ridges of his belly, the pink tips of her fingers pausing.

He did not correct her. "It is the custom," he said. And he said, searching for something to delay her, "I spoke with an Egyptian once."

Her fingers were busy again. "Many pass through Ashdod."

"Aye; I have seen them, by their dress. They all look like priests. But this was in the Shephelah, where they are as rare as figs on a vine. He was with the son of the prince of Gaza; him they call Athol."

"The Lord Athol has no son." She evidently found this funny; but was not distracted. "You are a lovely man. I have never seen a man with such a body." And she added slyly, looking sideways at him: "Except it may be one or two among my own kind. I am glad you chose Tahara. Tahara is a witch; she can make magic. Here is a riddle–

"She found a kid asleep in a thicket,
"And *lo!*–awakens a ram."

He chuckled, and sat up swiftly to fend her off, not altogether successfully–*"Tahara will sacrifice–the ram–before it reaches the altar!"* Her hands were slippery with the oil, elusive as fishes underwater. When she laughed there was a little gap between her teeth. She left him, and stood by the bed, beginning to remove her ornaments and beads loop by loop. He said, watching her, "I never said Athol had a son. I said he was himself son to the Philistine prince."

"Neither has Athol a father. He has only Ptullis."

"Who is Ptullis?"

"The Egyptian; his wazir."

He remembered then that Uzziel had mentioned the name; he had forgotten it. Tahara was writhing out of shift after shift with a dancer's movements, changing colors like a chameleon. Her head appeared briefly to say, "I met him once." Her whole undressing was artful, as if to the rhythm of unheard music: it might have been to the clash of cymbals that she flung high the last shift of all, and stood poised with her arms upraised while it floated to her feet; and he saw that she was not black, but the color of the dark grape when the bloom is on it, the purple roses of her breasts proud with the uplifted arms, without ridges or folds, but every part of her smooth in undulations, like riverstone shaped by the patient caress of immemorial tides. She came to him between the lions' heads, kissing his feet, and his knees, to lift her head with the grin to ask, "What shall I call *you?*"

"Ichabod," Samson said.

This time he captured her hands, and drew her up with one movement until her face came above his own, without letting go, and kissed her mouth lightly. The sounds from outside were dying away; he was sure of it. Tahara struggled, but it was no part of his plan to let her have done with him quickly, and when she began to move her belly urgently against his own he simply transferred her two hands into his one and turned on his side, tilting her onto the cushions beside him, her imprisoned hands between them. "Tell me of this Athol, and Ptullis. You say you know them."

She looked puzzled, frowning, and he stroked the bud of her breast until it rose like a little ram's horn, and she said uncertainly, "Does a temple girl know a prince? I have spoken with the Egyptian because we have one tongue. They have been here, that is all. Why do you ask so many questions?"

He asked another: "They came *here?*" and she giggled.

"Here in the temple–not in the women's house!" The absurdity of the thought, that a Ser of Philistia should visit a brothel, even a sacred brothel, suddenly convulsed her with laughter so violent that he was afraid someone would come seeking the cause. He gathered her hastily in his arms, smothering the sound. She raked his back with her strong nails in protest; it had no effect. "Ptullis is too old to have such needs. As for my Lord Athol, did you not know he would prefer the house of boys?"

"I have heard."

The image of that golden face came to his mind, on the

hill below Zorah, and again at Gath; and it was as if it suddenly came into focus for the first time. He said idly, "And where is this house of boys?"

"Across the court opposite. Will you let me go?"

"If you swear you will be quiet."

She laughed again, wriggling, and bit his shoulder. "The girls will pay no attention. We are used to hearing more than laughter here."

"And the priests? They must pass this door to go to and from the sanctuary."

"They go another way; they have their own staircase. If you do not let me get on with it, you will be too late to make your sacrifice there."

He loosed his embrace, and she shifted gratefully for a moment to let the cooling air come between them, stroking the hairs of his cheek with the back of her hand and discovering the scar Athaliah had made there; and he asked her teasingly if there were others waiting. She shook her head and told him no, unfastening the headband which was his only clothing, and marveling at the mass of hair thus released, taking it in her fingers. There had been no one all day; they were too busy gawking at the Hebrew god in the temple. "But the temple gate is barred after dark. We have not much time." And she sat astride him.

Samson put his hands on her waist, and sliding them down to the firm flesh of her buttocks had a happy thought. "Do you still dance?"

"Yes."

"Will you dance for me?"

"Yes." She pressed her palm over his mouth and whispered, "Another time."

He removed it, and said, "Now."

He thought she was going to refuse. There was no sound from the courtyard at all now; the light was beginning to fade from the window. He said, "Someone told me once, that temple girls are bound to do whatever a man wants."

She considered him then, wondering suddenly if this young god, so magnificently made for a woman's pleasure, was one of those shy of women after all; and made her decision. She said, "Did she also tell you that nothing may be refused *us?*" and slid her legs to the floor. She moved briskly, with a new purpose, turning up a little lamp and drawing shutters across the window. "Any man who enters this house joins himself in sacred union with the goddess Ishtar; and Ishtar is not mocked." She lifted the lid of the painted chest and took from it a timbrel, whose tinkling lifted his head; and searching within, two collars of bright red leather, such as the Philistines kept for their hunting dogs, and a longer strap which might have been a leash. She carried them to him with the ceremony of an acolyte offering the trappings of his office to a high priest.

"Ishtar's dog, is it?" Samson said, and fell back with his arms behind his head. He had heard of such games. If it took her mind off the lateness of the hour, so much the better. He said, "For Ishtar, no," and countered the sudden darkness of her frown with a cheerful grin. "For Tahara I'll be camel as well, if you fetch me a saddle. If you'll dance for me."

"I will dance for you."

"Swear it."

"In the name of the love goddess herself."

He thought the collar was meant for his neck, though it seemed scarcely big enough; but it went instead about his wrists, behind his back; his palms prised apart by her nimble fingers to admit another strap between them, which must be the leash. She rolled him like a log onto his back, to open his knees and draw his feet up under him with one movement, so that his ankles came together almost in line. The second collar secured them so, and was joined in turn to the leash, pulled down under his backside and linked to a ring set in the leather. Then she left him, and moved into the room without a backward glance.

It was quickly and deftly done. Samson made a small, exploratory movement, as far as the harness would allow. An instinctive attempt to straighten his legs jerked the leash painfully into the sensitive flesh between his buttocks and cinched the wrist strap like a vise; it was evidently joined in some sort of running noose that resistance only tightened. The shameless splaying of his knees did not permit him to turn over, and he could not close his knees because of the way his feet were strapped. He felt himself indecently naked, like an upturned frog, conscious of misgivings. Far from prolonging their sport, Tahara's little game was like to bring it to an abrupt conclusion, anytime she chose. He was in the hands of an expert.

Facing him, she sank slowly down cross-legged on the floor, and continuing a movement that was like the pouring out of a dark and precious oil, inclined her head forward between her knees in deep obeisance, her arms outstretched over her head bearing the timbrel in the manner of a wave offering, very slowly, until its colored streamers came to rest outspread on the carpet like the rays of the sun. It was as if the next movement began with the timbrel itself: a trembling of its little metal tongues that rose to a continuous chatter, following the contours of her thighs, the fluttering streamers exploring her with a sensuous caress that set her whole body in motion, drawing her to her feet like a black cobra in pursuit of its upward flight with the thrust of her hips, swaying her belly, twisting to present first one breast and then the other, until the streamers brushed her parted lips to soar to the height of her upstretched arms. She threw back her head to a crash like cymbals, rigid in a perfect mime of terror. Then the timbrel fell upon her like a wild beast, striking now on one side, now the other, while she writhed and weaved to keep her cleft in a frantic rhythm of protest too fast for the eye to follow, darting here and there like a dragonfly, desperate for escape and finding none. Faster and faster she danced, leaping and turning in concert with the flying twin of her shadow, enmeshed in the whirling ring of music that closed inexorably until at last she slowed and was still, panting, the gleaming darkness of her shape arched backward in an agony of submission, and the timbrel quivering down her naked torso unresisted between her two hands. With a sudden movement she locked it between her knees, sliding to the floor to cradle it like a mother, with a low moan.

Samson had never witnessed anything so lascivious.

It was not until Tahara lifted her head that he became aware of the numbness of his arms, the metal studs that bit like teeth into the flesh of his buttocks. Neither of these, nor the crucifixion of his doubled legs, troubled him so much as the one traitorous reaction he could neither control nor conceal, which gave the spectacular lie to his indifference. He lifted his eyes to meet Tahara's watchful grin, the little gap between her teeth.

For the next half hour she did as she liked with him, handling him with the insulting expertise of a village goat girl, absently nodding approval when he groaned aloud. He struggled, and she sat on his chest. And then, when he stopped fighting for want of breath–for she was heavily made–and shut his eyes to the inevitable, she turned and bit him strongly in the lobe of his ear. The sudden pain, doubled and redoubled in the violent creaking of the leather bindings, cleared his mind marvelously of all else and exploded in an oath, stifled under her waiting palm. The collars and leash strap, made by craftsmen for the purpose with layers of the red leather strongly sewn together with their broad iron buckles, were stronger than the ropes with which the Judahites had bound him at Etam, and he began to feel himself truly helpless. Tahara knelt on his open thighs, pinning his head down with her fingers laced through his hair, her tongue ransacking his mouth, then falling on him to bury his face under her cushioning breasts. She was rank with sweat from the dancing and her labors, half suffocating him with the strong smell of foxes. He began to feel his senses leaving him, and heard his own voice at a distance cursing, half laughing, cursing again and even begging her, without in the least distracting her from her purpose. She did things which he had neither heard of nor imagined, afflicting every part of him until his sweat mingled with hers to seal them together as if nothing would ever separate them again. She lay between his thighs then, and drew the last of his strength from him like a horseleech; and left him still as death.

She returned and released him, returning the bindings to the chest like a neat housewife, and said, "Go quickly"; but it was some time before he could straighten himself. Ishtar was another name for Astarte, and he understood for the first time why the Canaanites had the same goddess for sex and war. But Tahara was Egyptian.

He said, rubbing his wrists, "Ishtar is not your goddess. How can you serve Ishtar?"

"I serve the temple."

There was a curious politeness between them, as if they had just met. As if she read his thoughts, she said complacently, "Are you not purged of wicked thoughts? Go and make your prayers in peace of mind."

He did not tell her that his mind was far from cleared of wicked thoughts, so far as her temple was concerned; but it was wonderfully cleared. It was stifling hot in the chamber and she opened the window, to stand dismayed at the darkness outside, the sudden stars. "The sanctuary will be shut!"

"The priests will admit me."

"There will be no one there!"

It was exactly what he had most hoped to hear. He found his clothes and dressed, winding the headband, and asked her where he could relieve himself of a pressing need; and she told him to go down the way he had come up, there was a latrine in the courtyard; and she told him where. "But don't make a noise! And hurry back."

He closed the door behind him, and having satisfied himself that the corridor was empty, went the other way. There was a sound of women's voices behind the doors, but none to hinder him. The door to the priests' quarters opened to the latch, and he passed through, closing it softly behind him. The corridor ran on, past doors similar to those behind, and led him to a curving flight of stone steps down. At the foot he turned a corner, where a torch flickered in a wall socket, and followed its light to another. Male voices this time, to his right, but out of sight. He lost himself in a labyrinth of passages, with the same mosaic floors, and it was more by chance than plan that he discovered what he was looking for: a heavy door, bound with iron, but unlocked, which led him into the back of the sanctuary itself. Here the torches were damped down, their light just flickering on the golden ornamentation of the ark, picking out the colored frescoes between the stone pillars. But it was the massive shadow of Dagon that dominated the place. The grain god stood twice the height of a man, of bronze encrusted with precious stones, a stern figure with towering headdress and flowing beard, one enormous palm uplifted over the ark, which had been cunningly sited as if in subjection to it. Samson was still looking at the ark when he heard the murmuring of a man in sleep.

Tahara had been wrong about the priests. There were two, on trestle boards between the pillars, rolled up in their bordered gowns, as if they had nodded off in the midst of conversation.

The door to the courtyard was locked, and there was no key. For a moment Samson stood undecided. The door was old and heavy, the iron hinges rough with corrosion. A disturbance of their position would waken the dead. It was then that he noticed that the feet of the bronze god stood impossibly upon smooth marble, like a man standing naturally on a pavement; there seemed to be no anchor. A closer inspection revealed a hairline crack beside one foot, that ran on all sides: a slot in the marble, whose depth he could only guess, into which a hidden tongue plunged downward beneath the floor to hold the figure upright. The second foot was the same.

If he could not remove the ark, at least he could see that it was awarded a proper respect where it was.

When he thrust his head between the twin pillars of the legs and made to straighten, he thought at first he was not going to shift it. He turned his head with difficulty toward the ark and cursed Tahara.

"*Help Samson this once, Adonai.* The woman has left me no strength."

He hooked his arms round the bronze thighs to each side and took a deep breath, softly, and felt the statue begin to move. The tongues went in deep, two spans, nearer three, and he had to change his grasp, sweating again in silence, even his breathing muted, until he had it clear at last, towering almost to the roof and swaying precariously. It was more difficult still to lower it in silence, taking the amazing weight across his bruised knees, but at last it came to rest softly as a falling leaf, face down before the ark. Then he returned the way he had come. Tahara led him to the street gate, and let him out, kissing his palm with a grave valediction in her own tongue. There was no one else to see him go.

□

He spent the following day asleep in the lodging, without telling Baasha what he had done. He expected a public uproar, but when the psalmist brought him food and drink in from the market stalls, and he asked him what news he had heard, there was nothing. He sent him to the temple, and Baasha returned to report that the gates were closed to the public, and there were men like builders going in and out with blocks and tackle, and soldiers, and some talk of a fault in the masonry. When he went up again in the early evening, without the least idea what he was looking for, the sanctuary door was open again, and the ark and the god Dagon were where they had been before.

Whatever the Philistines made of the miraculous downfall of their god during the night, it was evident that they were keeping it to themselves.

The psalmist was bewildered. It was unlike Samson to fall into inertia. He said, pacing the room with his uneven hunchback's tread, "Not even your shepherd friends could steal the ark from this place. Why do we delay?"

"I have a thing to do." Samson told him. And then: "If we cannot take the ark, the Philistines must return it of themselves."

Baasha balked at this unlikely suggestion. "Why should they do that? You have seen the show they make of it."

A good question. Samson looked up into the eaves. "Maybe Yahweh will soften their hearts; the way he did with that Pharaoh, so he let Moses go with his people out of Egypt."

And he added privately to himself, *with a little help from his servant Samson.* If you cannot be his eagle, be his ass. To Baasha he said aloud, "I shall need your help."

□

The prince Raphah was asleep in his palace when the sounds of commotion reached his ears, orchestrating an evil dream where smoke poured over the terrace from a blood-red sky, and the people ran panicking into the streets. He awoke wet with sweat and groaned with relief; but the uproar continued, and he shook the girl beside him in a nervous rage, aggravated because he could not remember her name and she was slow to waken. He dispatched her to inquire the cause of the disturbance, and dragging on his night cloak, limped across to the parapet, his face as gray as his standing hair. The shouting seemed to come from his left, but he could see nothing over the rooftops; only the lights moving and darting in the streets below like fireflies, accompanied by the barking of dogs, and then the running feet of the city patrol.

There had been rioting before, but not at night. He paced the terrace until the girl returned. "Well?"

She was a pretty child, fair-skinned and slender as a reed; and swaying like a reed too, in her fluster. But her eyes over her veil were calm. It was over, she told him: a crowd of men had come up from the taverns full of wine demanding to see the Hebrew god, and wanted to batter the gate down when the priests refused them admittance. It was all noise and wind; when the captain of the patrol arrived with soldiers there was only a brief scuffle, and they were persuaded without much difficulty to return in the morning. There were not even any arrests made.

This last piece of news pleased Raphah not at all, since his own peace had been disturbed; but it was true, the street sounds had, when he listened again, died away, and he retired to bed again with the girl, contenting himself with first passing an order to the guard commander through one of the sentries that the palace doors were to be barred until morning, and no one was to pass in or out for any reason whatsoever. It was because of this order that he did not hear until long after sun-up of the other, and much more spectacular event of the night: the second fall of Dagon in the temple before the Hebrew god.

This time there was no concealing it. The head and both hands were broken clean off in the fall, and the massive bronze trunk so wedged between the posts of the door that it could be opened from neither inside nor out. Dagon had not merely fallen down: it was as if some supernatural force had hurled the bronze god across the width of the sanctuary.

During the morning the crowds began to gather at the palace, a great number of women among them, which made the task of the soldiers more difficult. They could have filled the Court of Petitioners two and three times over, so that when Raphah came down, expecting the usual half-dozen complainants and witnesses and saw the numbers, he feared some sort of uprising and ordered the court cleared, as a result of which he came close to having a genuine riot on his hands. It was averted by the quick-wittedness of the guard commander, who persuaded the prince to grant an audience to one spokesman; and by Raphah's hasty promise to summon a full meeting of Seren to Ashdod.

When they arrived they went one by one to the temple to view the shattered remains of the god before repairing to the palace, but none could offer an explanation to contradict that on the lips of every man and woman in the city. The story of the previous fall of Dagon before the Hebrew ark had leaked out, inevitably, and feelings ran high against the priests. Not only had the awful omen been ignored, but also the warning of the plague deaths, which had noticeably increased since the ark came to Ashdod. Raphah found himself cast in the unenviable role of Pharoah Rameses who defied the Hebrew god in Egypt.

The temple priests were called to the council, but they could add nothing to what was already known, except that there had been a disturbance at the temple gate, which was why the priest-custodians were absent from the sanctuary—mercifully, or they would surely be dead—and heard nothing for the din outside; and that one of the temple prostitutes was discovered gagged and tied to her bed with her own binding straps, by a man known only by the name of Ichabod, whom she had displeased, or of a sadistic turn of mind, for the unfortunate girl had not been found until the morning.

Only Athol of Gaza, finding nothing miraculous in any of these things, put forward the suggestion that craftsmen should be sent for to repair the statue and replace it.

If he had suggested defecating in the sanctuary the priests could not have been more thoroughly appalled. It was not usual for them to stand up against the princes, but Athol's reputation as a heretic lent them the courage of indignation. They were adamant, and unanimous. Not only must Dagon's image not be made good; no man must lay hand on it, on peril of death. What the gods themselves had cast down, let no man restore. They could expect no more omens. The next fall would be the fall of the city itself.

It was, after all, the priests' business, and glancing round the circle of faces Athol found himself as usual alone. Raphah was wavering between horror at the priests' warning, and relief that it must be heeded. Now surely they must send the ark back whence it came.

"Never," Athol said. He was pale with anger, leaning

forward in his chair to point a finger of accusation. "You, Lord Raphah, were not at the battle. Many good men were lost. The ark was not taken lightly; it shall not be lightly surrendered." He straightened to address them all. "So long as we have their god, the Hebrews are tamed. *Must I remind you that I am still Lord of Battles?"*

They hesitated, looking to Raphah, but it was the youngest of the Seren, Saph of Ashkelon, who asked slyly, "Will you battle against *gods?"*

Athol turned on him swiftly. "I have battled against *this* god; and won."

There was a good deal of unease at this, and a stirring and scraping of chairs. Fortunately the priests had left.

"You may be Lord of Battles," Raphah said at last, "but you are not Lord of Ashdod. It is not your city that is filled with dead of the plague, and threatened with thunderbolts!"

Athol raised his eyebrows. "Very well. If you are afraid of thunderbolts, let us have the ark down to Gaza, for I am not. But it shall not go back to the Habiru."

There was guarded assent, until Saph reminded them in his idle way that Gaza, like his own Ashkelon, was nearly as badly afflicted with the plague as Ashdod itself; it was rife all along the coast. Nevertheless, the compromise was accepted in principle, and it was decided by a vote of four to one that the ark be transferred under strong escort away from the coast, to the most inland city–Gath.

The one vote of dissent came, naturally, from Maoch of Gath; but Maoch was a slow-thinking man, unable to devise a reason for objecting, and unwilling to appear a coward, even to himself.

Afterward, in the privacy of the guest chamber allotted to him, it occurred to Athol that *Ichabod* was a Hebrew-sounding name; and that if the massing of the priests and guards at the street gate insured that no one came in, it might nevertheless have been very possible for a man to have passed through them and gone *out.* And if that man had come from the chamber of one of the temple prostitutes, it would have been prudent to bind and gag her, so that with luck there would be no alarm until the morning, when the city gates of Ashdod would be open, and anyone could leave unhindered. He moved in thought from the couch where he had been lying, and called for Ptullis.

From the Egyptian's face, he knew at once that he had been expecting the summons. Ptullis also had visited the temple. He said, with a wry twist to his mouth that was the nearest he ever came to a smile, "This man haunts you like a dead lover, my Lord. You see him everywhere."

"You saw the statue, Ptullis? The last time it fell they say it took half the garrison to lift it back. Is there another man alive who could uproot it, and throw it down with such force as to dismember it?"

"If it was a man."

"Ah." Athol studied his old tutor's face, whose thoughts he could sometimes read; not now. He said, "You too, old sage? You think it was their god?"

"Who can say, when a chock of wood is consumed with a great flame, whether it is the wood that burns, or the fire?"

"You are too subtle for me, Ptullis; speak plainly."

"Plainly the Hebrew was here; but whether he overthrew the idol by himself, I could not say."

"I knew it!" Athol cried, leaping up. "You have been keeping it from me, you rogue. How can you be sure?"

Ptullis explained that he had spoken to the prostitute Tahara, whom they had found tied; and because he asked questions the priests had not asked, and spoke to her in her own tongue, he had elicited a detailed description of the man. She knew him by the other name; but undoubtedly it was Samson. "But she insists that he left her before the riot, when the gate was still open."

Athol, not to be balked of the satisfaction of knowing he had been right all along, was inclined to dismiss this last statement. It must have been an ordeal for the poor girl–to be crucified throughout all the hours of the night; perhaps she was confused as to the hour he had left her. There was one sure way of finding out. He said briskly, "We will put her to the torture to clear her mind; a few turns on the wheel should do it."

The Egyptian shook his head with disapproval of such impetuousness. "The priests will never permit it. Besides, there is no need. She was certainly lying."

"You are sure of it?"

"She is a simple girl, and a poor liar; yes I am sure."

Athol still hesitated. "But, why should she lie?"

"After all the years of my teaching, does Athol still look for a man's logic in the things a woman will do?"

□

After some reflection Athol decided to keep the information to himself, and warned Ptullis to do the same. Let the priests take the blame, and make their offerings and their blood sacrifices to atone for Dagon's fall. He had no mind to provide Raphah with yet another excuse to criticize the military security, by admitting that Samson had slipped through the network of patrols especially set to watch for him. Nor did he wish to enhance further the dangerous legend of the man himself.

There was another reason also. If Samson thought himself undetected, there was always the chance he would come again; if not to Ashdod, then to Ashkelon, or Gaza. His fondness for the fleshpots of the coastal towns was well known, and especially his liking for the women to be found there. And this time, Athol would be ready for him.

□

Miriam did not at first recognize him, her attention being drawn only to his superior height and standing among the merchants. She was attracted by a youthful curl of whiskers over a broad brown cheek; then disconcerted by the direct gaze of black eyes lifted blatantly in her direction. Only secondarily did she take in the drab cloak of the nomad, loosely enfolding his head against the morning chill, that was in humble contrast to the rainbow stripes and brocades crowding the treasury yard. Nevertheless the traders made way for him as he strode through them to the wall of the house, and looked up at the parapet where she stood.

"Woman! Go call your master."

Her gratification at this form of address struggled with indignation at being mistaken for a servant. Her own cloak was old, and had been passed on to her; but it was of the prized white wool from lambs kept apart and unsoiled from birth. She drew it close to make herself taller, and corrected him coldly.

"Sir, this is the house of my sister."

He looked puzzled; then turned and to her alarm started coming up the outside steps two and three at a time. But then his hood fell back, and she saw the mass of hair tied in a headband, and rushed to his arms like a child.

"Samson!"

He found himself looking down on the top of her head, the pale line where the silky black hair was drawn aside into two loosely woven plaits, soft as the white wool they rested on. He said, "You must be Miri"; and held her at arm's length, thinking how unlike her sisters she was, lacking Athaliah's fragile beauty, Esther's dark sensuousness; yet neither face had in his memory the animation of Miriam's. "You are quite grown up; I should not have known you."

"And you are grown down."

"Down?"

"I always thought of you as a giant." Miriam skipped about him. "You are big, but you're not a giant. How handsome you are, Samson! Isn't it dangerous for you to come here? The Philistines have put out a great reward for your capture."

"Have they?" He sat on the parapet watching her with affection. It seemed a lifetime since he had dwelt in this house, and carried his bed up here to the rooftop on summer nights. Nothing had changed. From the quality as well as the number of merchants in the forecourt, he judged that Amalek's trading had flourished. A thought came to him, and he asked her: "Why did you say this was your sister's house?"

A shadow crossed her face. "My father died; the year after you left and went down to Gath."

Despite himself, Samson was moved. It was difficult to believe that anyone had loved Amalek; but clearly Miriam had. She accepted his embrace with a new restraint, her small shape taut under the wool. He said simply, "I am sorry."

"You could not have known." She turned her face aside. "It happened suddenly: an accident; he fell."

Abruptly, changing subject and tone, she led him toward the steps saying conversationally, "Mama and Athaliah have taken a villa in Ashkelon, and live there now. They always wanted to . . ." She lifted her eyes in innocence and said, "They will find Athaliah a fine husband there, don't you think? They took four or five of the servants. They wanted me to go with them, but I prefer to stay here with Esther."

"So who is in charge now?"

"Why, Sheshai of course; as always."

It was the last name in the world he expected to hear in Amalek's house–or Esther's. *"Sheshai?* Here?"

"No; he has gone to Gaza for some days. To meet some caravan from Egypt, I think. Why?"

Samson did not tell her why. He might have guessed that Sheshai would have somehow escaped the holocaust at Timnath. That he would be so brazen as to return to Amalek, whose daughter he had rejected to marry another, setting aside the three-year contract and every sworn obligation, was beyond belief.

It was Esther who provided an explanation of sorts. She was unchanged, though wearing the darker garments of the matron, which suited her: a long gown of rich blue, worn under a little sleeveless jacket of deep crimson, with heavy bracelets of precious iron on wrists and ankles, as befitting the wife of a wealthy broker. She greeted him coolly, without evident surprise, and sent Miriam into the house to have a meal made ready for the guest. When they were alone she said, "You came for Athaliah."

"I need a reason to come here now?"

She fetched him wine in a silver goblet, which he recognized as one of those kept for strangers. "She has gone to the coast."

"So Miriam told me."

His indifference touched her like a nettle. She glanced round, wary of Miriam's return, and sharply back. "You dare to come back for her–after walking out, leaving us with no word; and then wedding another woman!"

She meant the Timnite, Niobe. He opened his mouth to say it was not he who wedded Niobe, and said instead, "You know she is dead."

"And that you were responsible for her death."

He was growing inured to surprises today. Anger lent Esther a dignity he remembered her as lacking; or perhaps it was her new status as wife to Sheshai. He asked, "Did Sheshai tell you that?"

"I do not blame you for running away," Esther said, struggling to be reasonable; "only for leaving your wife and father-in-law to burn in their own house."

"What else did Sheshai tell you?"

Her reply was checked by Miriam's return, the child badgering him with questions of everything he had done since he left them that day. There was no need to tell her much; merely to elaborate on the already exaggerated stories she had heard from traveling merchants and peddlers was enough. The jackals in the Philistine corn had grown to hundreds; the Philistines he had fought and slain single-handed at Lehi a thousand at least. He made Miriam laugh by telling her of the time Baasha had taken him for a ghost; of the bats in the cave that slept hanging upside down like washing put out to dry; and of the hide-and-seek games he had played with the Philistines in and out of the hills. Even Esther smiled at this, visibly relaxing her hostility when she saw that he kept the talk away from Timnath. Samson looked to see if there was any sign of pregnancy, but with her fulness it was hard to tell. Esther was a maternal creature, and would improve with childbearing. Her wariness was her way of protecting Miriam, just as her outburst of anger had sprung, he suspected, from a defense of the absent Athaliah. When he left them she embraced him, as if anxious that her previous outspokenness should not be the cause of his leaving.

He went down to the bachelor house to renew old acquaintances and passed the noon hour of rest drinking ale with the men there. Once they had recovered from the surprise of seeing him walk openly among them, they took a daring pride in making him welcome. Jaala sat at Samson's side, showing off their old friendship like a robe of honor. From them Samson learned that Amalek had fallen and died–some said from the fall, others, from a fit of cholor–in the course of a noisy quarrel with Sheshai. It was manifest everywhere that the household had been altogether happier since. Samson was still in the bachelor house when word came from Esther that a body of Philistines was approaching, and he left as he had come, avoiding the road.

It was true that he had come for Athaliah, driven by a familiar restlessness unassuaged by casual encounters with the hill women since last he had had Tahara; and not finding Athaliah had decided already to visit the coast again. And since Sheshai was in Gaza, that is where he went.

He traveled the byways, avoiding the Philistine roads as was now his habit, so that it was three days before he came upon the first of the verdant gardens for which Gaza was famous; another hour brought him within sight of the city walls, walking in shade through its leafy villages where he fell in with a family heading the same way: father, mother and four children, the youngest heavy on the woman's hip. They were Jebusites, the man a tanner, having come all the way down from Jerusalem by easy stages, to show the little ones the Great Sea. It seemed a strange distance: Japho would have been the obvious choice; even Ashkelon much nearer. But the man told Samson they had kinsfolk in Gaza. He was a young man, scarcely bearded, yet his shoulders prematurely sloped with more than the burden of bundles he carried, for they appeared to have much of their household goods about them, and no beast to bear any of it. Samson was reminded of the old saying, *Once married, a man resembles an ass, so laden with burdens is he.* He took the child from the woman, despite her startled protest, and bore it on his shoulders, where it laughed and played with his hair. It reminded him of Lilah suddenly; except that this was a boy; but he had the same violet eyes. It struck him that the father had got into trouble in Jerusalem, more probably, and was headed for Egypt, for which Gaza was the departure point.

It had been no Hebrew hand that squared the great stone blocks of the walls of Gaza, and raised them to the height of ten men. The wall with its pagan, but undeniably beautiful, multi-colored frescoes, encircled the hill on which the city stood like the headband of a rich man's turban, so that approaching you could see only the upper houses, and the inevitable temple overtopping them all. Samson passed through the great gates with his new-found family, the child now cradled in his arms and his head bent besottedly over it; and was inside unchallenged.

He had been to Gaza before with Sheshai, and it was not difficult to find the marketplace again, mingling with the busy crowds, his cloak hooding his face. Sheshai was well enough known for him to ascertain that the Amorite was lodged up at the palace, a guest of the prince himself, no less. Samson gave a street lad the fourth part of a shekel and sent him there with a message, that his kinsman would await him in the square inside the main gates, which was the common meeting place of travelers, at sundown. The boy looked at him strangely, but ran off as he was bid. This done, Samson made his way to the poorer parts of the city, where the press of men and beasts bustled the unwary almost into the sewage drains in the center of the narrow streets, the small shops crowded together under their canopies like beans in a pod. He took a meal in one of the many khans there, wondering if Sheshai would keep the tryst. On the way to the street of the prostitutes he decided that the sheer impudence of the summons, delivered to Athol's palace, would bring him. However many kinds of an evil man Sheshai was, he was no coward.

The woman was, surprisingly, Hebrew, and this at first disgusted him; but her story of a husband who had put her away with a bill of divorcement on finding her no virgin, of rejection by her own kinfolk and subsequent wanderings, made her an outcast like himself. Having neither wealth nor looks, and being of a naturally loving nature, she had turned to the profession for which she was most suited. Hearing the hill dialect softly spoken made him think of Zorah with a nostalgia he had not known he harbored, and for a moment he almost loved her. At least there was less risk of betrayal here.

They were coupling when the door opened, and she rushed to cover her face. Samson turned his head and saw Sheshai there in the doorway.

There was neither fear nor surprise in Sheshai's face; only the same malevolent humor, on seeing Samson's predicament. He tossed the woman half a shekel, telling her to fetch wine from the market, and she hastened to attire herself, not looking at him, though she clearly knew him. He wore a plain brown cloak, but when he stood aside to let her pass it fell open, exposing the richly brocaded, silken shirt beneath. Samson pulled his own tunic on anyhow, struggling off-balance with a murderous irritation. It was like the day they first met: the Amorite arrogant from the height of his lordly mule looking down amusedly on the barbarian peasant, alone and unarmed save for his ridiculous little dagger and at the peasant's mercy, had he known it. Had he brought soldiers with him this time? There was no sound beyond the door. If there were soldiers, they were not close enough to save him. Samson said, "I ought to kill you here and now."

Sheshai looked startled. "Because of Niobe?" He relaxed, leaning his long frame back against the door. "But I took her for your sake, *Kinsman*–you must know it! You rejected her in front of all *her* kin: a terrible insult to these people, an affront answerable only in blood. Her brothers would have had the whole Philistine army on your tail, if I hadn't offered myself in your stead!"

"After I had run away," Samson prompted, reaching for his headband; and had the satisfaction of seeing Sheshai caught, even momentarily, in his own web.

"Ah . . . You have seen Esther." Sheshai's tongue flickered over his lips, as if tasting this disagreeable piece of information before swallowing it with no more than a grimace of distaste. "Ah, well . . . She was upset, because of the burning. I wasn't going to tell her; but she had the story from one of the wives of the men who were with us at Timnath. . . . She got it muddled, as usual: you know Esther! She still persists in asking me about it, but I've told her as little as possible . . . obviously!"

"Aye, obviously you did not tell her you had gone through a form of marriage with another woman."

"To save a friend!" Sheshai cried. "Why else should I do such a thing?" He came beside Samson at the window and put his arm persuasively about his shoulders in his old manner. "Niobe was nothing to me."

The Hebrew prostitute was crossing the street with a tall jar on her head, approaching the house. Sheshai's arm stiffened. "You never *told* Esther?"

"I had no chance to tell her anything."

"But you won't tell her," Sheshai insisted. "Swear me your oath."

Samson shrugged himself loose. "Why should I?"

"Because I came here to save you again."

Sheshai spoke quickly, to be done before the woman came in to them. "I had your message, but it was madness to meet in the square–it is swarming with Athol's men! You were recognized in the khan; but they were too late. They know you are in the city; they don't know where. I had Beelzebub's own job finding you myself. You must get out of Gaza before the gates are shut tonight. By morning they will have the trap set: they haven't had time yet."

Samson considered this warily. "Is there no other way in or out?"

"None. The side gates are kept sealed; it's Athol's new policy since that business at Ashdod. That is why they are confident, and making no search. But I must go back before they miss me."

"How do I know you will not betray me yourself?"

Sheshai's mask of wounded innocence slipped into a merchant's grin. "A bargain," he said. "An oath for an oath. Your silence with Esther is worth more to me than any reward Athol can offer."

He was gone, and the woman came in and stopped, looking for him. Samson had his sandals on, and took up his cloak.

"He could not wait," he told her. "You will have to share the wine with your next customer; I must go myself." And he saluted her gravely: "Shalom!"

"Shalom," she said. "But you cannot leave the city, if you're thinking of it. They have closed the gates; I don't know why. It is not nearly dark yet. Something is up."

So he took off his cloak and sat, and drank the wine with her, and took her to bed again. Presently she fell asleep, breathing softly, and he lay beside her until midnight trying to remember the city gates, and the manner of their construction.

When he came to them, following the house walls down the darkest side of the square, they were more massive than he had thought: two doors of solid timber reinforced with studs and bands of iron, closed to the center and locked in place with a great beam that lodged in the massive posts on either side.

The square was deserted, lit only by two torches set in brackets to each side of the gates, and a broad street of light from the sentry house, which when he passed it revealed five or six of the Philistines, their helmets laid aside, seated on benches round a low table. They appeared to be playing with dice, the murmur of their voices rising and falling with each throw. Samson searched about and found a little ladder, used to reach the torches, and in a moment both were down, and ground out smoldering underfoot. This done, it should have been a simple matter to raise the beam; but it resisted his efforts; and after a moment he saw why. Both ends were secured in position by heavy chains, bound around and locked to the posts. Lacking the keys, the gates, rising grimly to the great height of the stonework which cupped it lovingly as a man's hands the face of his beloved, could be no more opened from within than without. Which explained the lack of vigilance on the part of the sentries. Compared with the gates of Gaza, Ashdod's brass Dagon was a sheaf of straw.

The enormity of his own folly struck him like a hammer blow. He stood a moment numb, his head pressed against the unyielding timber, beyond which lay the safety of darkness and the hills of the Shephelah.

"Adonai . . ."

How could a man find words to expiate his own vanity? All Gaza was a prison house, with the princeling Athol sitting like a spider in the center of the web. What gods backed the Philistine, that each time he raised his hand against Yahweh he triumphed?

It was on this thought that Samson lost his temper.

In the dead silence of the night, the splintering clangor shook the city like an earthquake, and fetched the sentries tumbling out of the guardhouse choking in sudden dust, staring through it in panic-stricken disbelief at the gaping hole where the gates had been. All that remained was the broken-off stumps of the posts, and the scattered blocks of masonry torn down from the arch. Nothing was visible in the blackness beyond; but a creaking and the sound of a muffled oath gave ample indication of where the gates were going.

The last Samson heard from Gaza was a growing murmur as the streets filled and the shrill voice of the guard commander ordering his men out in pursuit. But no one came after him.

He carried the gates through the night like a roof on his head, with frequent rests, and by morning had reached his goal: the hill above Hebron. He chose it because it was the highest point in the vicinity, and would be seen by Athol all the way across the plain from the city. And because Hebron marked the border of the Shephelah.

It was a happy thought: that Athol's gates should mark the entry to Samson's domain.

11

THE ARK REMAINED SEVEN MONTHS in Philistia. The Gathites kept it well away from their temple, not caring to risk another confrontation, in a chamber of the prison house in which Samson had met Samuel, where it lay harmlessly through the winter months. But with the first buds of spring, the Egyptian sickness came to Gath for the first time, together with a plague of mice for good measure; and when Maoch himself was stricken with the dreaded hemorrhoids the golden casket was dispatched north again, this time to Ekron. There were two reasons for the choice: first Ekron was nearest to Shiloh, where the ark came from, which might be thought to placate the Hebrew god in some measure (this was the priests' advice); and secondly it was the smallest and least important of the cities of the Philistine League, and therefore easily outvoted by the others, even with Maoch absent. Being again somewhat inland from the sea coast, on the edge of the Shephelah, and farthest north, Ekron had so far escaped the worst of the plague.

When the death toll rose alarmingly, Abimelech of Ekron found himself with a riot on his hands.

He told the hastily summoned council of the Seren:

"The priests are saying we have brought the ark here to kill them off, and the people with them."

"That is treason," Athol said.

"Not yet. They have appealed to me." Abimelech snorted. "And if it comes to treason, what will you do? Send in soldiers *and lose me my throne?* If they will go, that is. Soldiers are no more immune to the plague than the people."

It was true: there had been many deaths in the barracks. Athol least of all could afford to risk disaffection in the army. There were few left like himself, who ridiculed the idea that the ark had anything to do with the plague. He pointed out that Gaza had had the plague worse than any of them, and the ark had never been there. "Must we bow to this superstition?"

Abimelech was not the only one to cross his fingers for protection against divine wrath. He said belligerently, "Will you tell my people that their husbands and wives, their sons and daughters have died of superstition?"

"Very well." Athol rose to end the debate. "Let the priests declare publicly that the Hebrew god is mightier than Dagon. Then we will let the ark go."

He was confident that not even the most timid of the priests would go that far. In this, however, he underestimated them. The priests sacrificed a heifer, a sheep and two goats, and when their diviners had examined their entrails, pronounced that if the ark were sent back to Israel, it should not be sent empty, but with a trespass offering–in case the Hebrew god was still offended–of five golden mice, and five golden hemorrhoids, one for each of the cities of Philistia. The decision, whether or not to return the ark at all, was one from which they skillfully absolved themselves by decreeing that a new cart should be made, to which should be harnessed two milch kine that had never been put to the yoke, with their calves, and set upon the highway outside the city walls; the calves to be then removed into the city. If the kine took the cart, unled, up the road into the Vale of Sorek, then it would be a sign that the Hebrew god had brought the plague to them.

"But if not, then we shall know that it was not his hand that smote us; it was a chance that happened to us."

No cow in milk will leave its calf behind and set off in the opposite direction with no goad to drive it; but these did. Even Athol was impressed.

□

From the hilltop above Zorah, Samson watched the procession with growing amazement. The whole valley was white with standing corn, and he could not at first make out what it was that approached. From the bright colors he took it for a rich caravan, on its way up to Jerusalem, and was debating whether to call men up to intercept it, at once unwilling to take them from their necessary work at the harvest below, and reluctant to forgo the toll regularly claimed to sustain his growing band of irregulars. It was only when the bright sunlight caught the gold of the ark, and he saw the cart untended, that he recognized it; and saw the line of chariots and footsoldiers following at a distance, the red and white feathers of the Philistines.

Others had seen it too. Across the valley in the wheatfields below Beth-shemesh they left their reaping and began to run toward the road leaving reckless tracks through the standing corn and shouting excitedly; mostly Danites from Eshtaol and Zorah who had gone down to help bring the harvest in. It was all Samson could do to stop himself from rushing down to join them. Exultation seized him, there alone on the hilltop, and he felt his spirits soar, looking down on the beautiful valley as if he saw the world for the first time, like Adam. Anyone watching might have supposed he suffered a fit: a brawny wild-haired giant dancing a mad jig of triumph by himself in the sun. *Praise be to Yahweh of Israel!*

From the hilltop, he watched them break up the new cart on a flat stone on one of the lower terraces below Beth-shemesh, and set it afire, and slaughter the patient kine for an offering. Uzziel was there. There appeared to be some sort of altercation among a group of Canaanites, some of whom began to jeer, no doubt recalling that the ark had been lost by their neighbors; but the presence of the Philistine lords with their retinue at a little distance muted the outburst. When it was all over, the ark was borne into the shelter of the town. The last Samson saw of the Philistines were the red and white feathers and their pennons above the corn, returning on the road toward Timnath and the coast.

□

Much later, it was learned that the Egyptian sickness had followed the ark to Beth-shemesh, taking some seventy of its inhabitants to the grave, including without exception those who had mocked its return, and the ark was sent on its way again up the valley well beyond Zorah, north to the wooded highlands of Kirjath-jearim, on the borders of Benjamin. According to Uzziel, the Philistines had made it a condition of the ark's return that it should not again be fetched up against them, and having accepted their peace offerings–the golden mice and hemorrhoids–Uzziel himself had sworn the oath for them all. No one criticized him for it. No sanctuary was built in Kirjath-jearim, and no annual festival held there.

□

In after years it seemed to Samson that the return of the ark was the last ripple before long stagnation, enlivened only by border raids into Philistine territory, and the ransom of caravans passing through the Shephelah. On one such raid one of his men was recognized, or betrayed, as coming from one of the villages between Gath and Bethlehem; and the next day Philistine soldiers went there and hanged his wife and four children; but no further action was taken. When Samson went down there with a band thirty strong, he found the villagers sullen, but apathetic; evidently accepting the justice of retribution under the new rule. His appeal for men to join him was answered with gestures of protest and disbelief: they too had families, and were known. There was nothing to be done, but from that day Samson kept only the bachelors with him in the hills.

Many left in consequence as they married and returned to their homes and were gradually replaced by a new generation Manoah would scarce have recognized: young men eager to share in Samson's famous exploits for the glory of it and a share of the spoils, but as like to swear by Astarte as Yahweh and making their sacrifices in the high groves to keep on the safe side of whatever god dwelt in the place. He remonstrated with them; and then let them be. A leader who used jackals to fight with could not be choosy of men. They fought, at least.

□

Before he left the village Samson first bad farewell to his mother, and then climbed the familiar hill and sat on the top watching the last of the daylight drain away down the valley, the dark shapes of the villages, their lights already shuttered away. It was time for the evening prayer and he did not know what to say, except what he had always said, the words on the lips of every Hebrew at this hour: *Shema Israel . . .*

Hear, O Israel: there is no Lord but Yahweh, and you shall love Yahweh your God with the love of your whole heart. . . .

Their eyes were shuttered like the village lights; their ears stopped. *If I were Yahweh I'd not be bothered with them.* And he thought he'd not be bothered with Samson, either.

It was like the first time he ever left Zorah, walking into the night aimlessly with nowhere special to go; except that this time he had no need to steal his meat; any door was open to his knocking; none who would not, from friendliness or fear, no matter which, on seeing who it was, run to and fro to prepare a meal.

He found himself in Timnath; and by back paths to Jason's vineyards.

He had been back many times. The burned-out shell of the house had been partially rebuilt, perhaps to house some of the workers, for the vines were still tended; they still produced the best grapes in the region, though for whom he had not thought to inquire. Tamam's grave was so overgrown it was hard to find. They found him there and brought him wine in a skin, for he was well known, and warned him of a new Philistine garrison at Eltekeh, between Timnath and Ekron. When they had left it occurred to him to wonder if there might be one among them bold or greedy enough to inform the new garrison that Samson was here. He came close to wishing it. But no one came, and after a while the wine deprived him of even the pleasurable anticipation of a bloody and violent death. Wine is a great enlivener of men in company together; but melancholy drunk alone. Nearly all the blossom was gone from the vines, the near grapes swelling already, pressed tight as babies' buttocks; it lacked a month or two to the harvest. *Do not be afraid to pray for the impossible* Uzziel had once told him, in the toothless ravings of old age, and Samson lay face down on Tamam's grave and prayed for her return to him out of it.

□

He awoke with no memory, but a sensation of being watched that brought him to instant alertness. It was, as near as he could judge, approaching dawn: the sky roseate through a mist of rising dew that was already beginning to shroud the garden in its unearthly veils. He lay where he had slumped drunken, drenched and stiff, not moving at all but weighing the odds and husbanding the small advantage of surprise if they had not seen him waken. A solitary stone, the size of a watermelon, became visible in the half light. It lay just beyond his grasp, half hidden in undergrowth and not there by chance.

Like the jawbone at Lehi.

He flung himself on it, and something flew past his traveling legs and thudded into the mound; and then he was afoot, the great stone plucked up like a pebble in his hand ready to scatter a garden full of Philistines: and stood amazed at its emptiness.

But for the javelin, slantingly embedded among grasses still flattened with the imprint of his body, he might have been alone.

From the angle, the javelin had come from somewhere among the misty ruins of the outbuildings, and he stuffed tunic into girdle and raced across the intervening ground, vaulting a broken wall, the rock still in his hand, zigzagging between shadowy masonry and through a ragged doorway in time to see a figure halfway to the house: a youth running madly, but hindered by his cloak, which flapped about his knees and threatened to bring him down even before Samson caught him. He fell spreadeagled on his face with only the grunt of his breath driven out of his body, the Danite's left hand on his shoulderblade, the right uplifted with the stone to dash out his brains.

Only curiosity delayed the blow. It occurred to Samson, breathing heavily from the exertion after the night's drinking, to have a look at his would-be-murderer before dispatching him; and he shifted his grip to find a shoulder through the heavy cloak and flipped him over like a stranded fish, mouthing helplessly, and cuffed the hood clear of the face.

Afterwards, he would swear by the living God that his heart stopped at that moment: the angel of death came close as his shadow, whose chill breath lifted the hair at the back of his neck; looking over his shoulder at the dreadfully familiar blaze of the violet eyes, the so-well-remembered misty black hair of her who lay at his feet.

The recollected blasphemy of a drunken prayer came cartwheeling through his head with the assault of a nightmare. For a moment he swayed, with the cruel fear that he was still dreaming.

She gasped, "Are you going to kill me?"

He dropped the rock with a groan. Tamam, had she lived, would be past her middle years; older than himself. This one could have been the maid who scolded him over the milking of Manoah's goats; even the voice which he had thought never to hear again. He averted his head in agony, seeing the way he had come after her, the ruins clearly defined now in the spreading light; half-tempted to rush back beyond them to the grave mound again; *willing* it to be open and empty. *"Who are you?"*

"Delilah, daughter of Lahmi."

She said it defiantly; and seeing he had abandoned the idea of braining her, sat up painfully, feeling herself for bruises while she regained her breath. Even in daylight the illusion was not wholly banished. She had Tamam's violet eyes, and a look of her, but not the peasant's casual sexuality: she took hold of his arm uninvited to get to her feet, but her grip was impersonal, and for all her dishevelment, she held herself like a woman of breeding. Beneath the oversized man's cloak was that soft blue which can be dyed only into the finest linen. He could neither look at her, nor look away again. Her name meant nothing to him. She held one small sandal in her hand, searching about for its fellow, and the thought came to him that she must be stronger than she looked, to send the javelin so deep in the earth. It made him sweat, that only a span had separated him from the humiliation of death at the hands of a woman.

"Why did you try to kill me?"

"Because none of the men would do it."

He had forgotten that toss of her dark head when she was angered. The pain was like a blade in his chest, and he lowered his eyelids to endure it; the scornful curl of her mouth saying *you are slow and stupid, and think of nothing but your silly sheep and your wrestling games.*

"The men are all frightened of you," she said. "They think you are some kind of ifrit."

"They are my friends."

"The Philistines are not your friends, and they wouldn't come either. As soon as I heard you were here I ran all the way to Eltekeh, and they said they had too few men, and couldn't leave the garrison without orders."

She had a slight, Philistine lilt in her speaking when aroused; for the voice was not the same; but she was no Philistine. From her coloring Canaanite; even Hebrew, maybe. Not finding the second sandal, she threw the first petulantly away in the grass, and he heard her grumble, "It would have been different if Hanno had been there."

"Hanno!" The last Samson had seen of the Philistine captain had been a pile of armor and limbs at Lehi. "What have you to do with Hanno?"

The morning sun crossed her face as she turned; and held it in clear cold light, mocking him.

"You don't remember me, Samson."

He wished he had killed her before seeing her face. It was certain he had never set eyes on her before; the likeness was too uncanny to be missed. He hated her for not being Tamam, and for her childish riddles.

"I'll remember you next time. Aye, and don't think the lack of merchandise between your legs will save you."

"Next time, you may be *dead.*"

"You set small value on your own life, then. What are the Philistines offering for me? Five hundred shekels of silver? You could fetch better than that yourself on the marriage market."

"A thousand."

"Perhaps not, then."

"For your capture. Alive. There is no reward otherwise."

He had not known this. There was movement in the new part of the house, and he hesitated. If she had told the garrison, they might have sent for more men by now, and he did not want to be caught in the open. But he was determined to have some sense out of her, and seizing her wrist pulled her toward the ruins. She struggled and hung back, but finding herself unceremoniously dragged through the grass, saved her bruised feet by trotting furiously at his heels, her cloak gathered as best she could manage with her free hand. Once through the door arch he let go, and she fell back against the inside wall, panting.

Samson watched a moment through the doorway, but there was no further movement about the house. When he turned she was rubbing her wrist resentfully, but had made no move to escape.

She said, "You hurt me."

"What did you expect?"

"A gentle man," she said: "who carried me in his arms to the shade of the olive tree. And gave me to eat of a honeycomb."

He was taken aback, and lost his scowl. She was about the right age. Nothing else matched his memory of the servant's brat until Delilah, leaving her wrist at last, raised dark lashes from the violet eyes of that same child, who had innocently betrayed the secret of his riddle to Niobe and her brothers. Had she witnessed the bloody aftermath? He searched for a name: *"Lilah."*

"It is years since anyone called me that."

"You had a doll called . . ."

"Rhoda. My rose. I lost her in the fire."

Through the doorway, the new stone of the house showed raw against the blackened masonry of the old. The sunshine was raying everywhere through the vines now, the mist half-lifted giving place to the first dancing insect clouds.

Soon it would be hot. He said, "I am sorry for what happened to Niobe."

"Do not be."

But she did not explain it; only turned her head to smooth a tress from her cheek, and he saw the delicate veins in the underside of her wrist, and the marks of his fingers there. The knowledge of who she was stirred another curiosity, long dead; a disturbance of old thoughts like dry leaves in his head, to be cleared away. He asked her, "You do not still live here?" And she shook her head.

"But I have an interest in the vineyards. I come sometimes when they send to fetch the wineskins."

They had arrived the previous day, she told him; and one of the carts had cast a wheel. By the time it was mended it was too late to return before dark, so they had made do in the house. There was nothing but the cloak one of the men had given her, on the floor, and she had slept badly, being unused to such hardship, and waking early heard the men talking outside, and learned that the famous Samson was here, which no one had told her. The rest he knew.

She made herself comfortable, moving inside the ruins to the foot of the wall as she spoke, her knees folded in the cloak, her small bare feet neatly side by side, evidently prepared to wait patiently until he let her go. "Why do you look at me?"

He said, "You remind me of someone."

And then, furious with himself for such a lame answer: "God in Heaven why should I not look at you? It's not every day a man meets a murderess. A moment ago you would have spitted me on your spear like Sisera."

"I would have, but you moved so quickly. Like a snake. Who is Sisera?"

"If it was not for the reward," he said, moving backward and forward; "and neither for Niobe's sake, then why?"

"You should not have come here. It is Hanno's vineyard now. You asked me what Hanno was to me. He is my uncle."

By adoption then, if she was not lying: there could be no blood between the Philistine and this dark vixen. It would explain her *interest* in Jason's vineyard, so perhaps it was true. It would be Hanno's vineyard now. The garden was alive with birdsong, though he had not noticed it; the air already warm on his skin. He asked her, remembering, "What became of the sister, Ishba?"

"She is with me in Ashkelon."

The birdsong should have warned him: the alarm call of the blackbird that had nothing to do with the two of them hidden in the ruins. The men were already moving into position when he saw them, beside the house and beyond it, and again between the vines, the red and white conspicuous among the green. It was only because Delilah had moved further into the ruins, and he had unwittingly followed her, that he had not seen before.

When he reached the mound, she was following, watching which way he would go. It might have been Tamam picking her way through the broken walls; only the tinkle of her anklets was missing. He took the javelin out of the ground and hurled it back toward her, and she ducked out of sight.

□

It was not until the following spring that he saw her again.

With the first rains after the olive harvest came news of rioting in Benjamin, and he spent the winter months campaigning with Samuel in the border country.

Curiously, it was his mother who persuaded Samson to join Samuel after all.

Almost alone among the women, Sharah had never made a secret of her detestation of war, or accepted the inevitability of the ancient, male law that demanded an eye for an eye. Manoah's death had been personal to her, nothing to do with the national tragedy of a battle lost, or even the ceremonial mourning for a clan chieftain in Dan. There was no corner of her small world that was not empty for his going; but she had no thought of vengeance. Nevertheless, the tidings from Shiloh, and the loss of the ark, moved her to break the habit of a lifetime and place a weapon in her son's hands. It was Manoah's spear, which she had buried in a corner of the house when the Philistines began to search the villages for arms.

"You go with my blessing, Son."

Samson tested the spear's balance to hide his surprise. It was a massive thing, like a young tree; few men could have hefted it. But it had a bronze head; it would be of little use against the Philistine iron if it came to it. He said, "My father went up to Aphek to answer Samuel's call before, and died there. I don't mind dying, but I don't want to die for nothing."

"You are not afraid?"

It was the sort of small subterfuge she had once used with Manoah, but it had little effect.

"Aye, I am afraid. Why does a man fight, except he is afraid of what his enemy can do to him? It's not danger that makes cowards, but men losing the habit of living with it. The clans will not join with Samuel. I've been among them in Judah. They just look at you."

"But you are not like them! You must take your bachelors and go. The judge has called you by name."

"The judge buried a third of our army at Aphek; the priests another third and more at Shiloh. They shall not bury my young men."

"Who will help Samuel if you do not go?"

"Who will safeguard the Shephelah if we do?"

"You used to listen to me once."

It was not true, he had never listened to her; and the thought shamed him, not into looking at her, for he had been looking at her all the time, but into observing little telling things he had not noticed: the slackness of her throat and breast, as if she had somehow diminished within the former fulness of her flesh, the fleckings of age on the backs of her hands, and the retreat of her eyes. Her hair had long been white as papyrus, but he had not realized how fine it had grown. He moved to her, touching it gently, and let his arm fall about her still plump shoulders, remembering forgotten things. He said then, to please her and because he was weary of argument, "I will go up for your sake." He led his bachelors in a series of raids and ambushes that promised to spread into a full-scale renewal of the war against the Philistines. By the end of the winter, however, an uneasy truce had settled over the land, with neither side deployed in strength to invite headlong battle, each for their own reasons, and

Samson left the Benjaminites to the harassment of any threatening force and took his bachelors back to Dan, promising to return when Samuel had succeeded in rallying the tribes. It seemed a possibility, if not an immediate one.

Jason's vineyard was in blossom again, the pruners already out at the lower end, away from the house. Since Samson was last here the grass had gone and sprung up anew, sharp green underfoot, red-patched with late poppies newly opened after a dawn shower. The rebuilding of the house was nearly completed. The workmen's ladder and hod lay along a freshly plastered wall. There was no reason why Delilah should be here this particular day, except that he had prayed Adonai to send her, not seeing why he should, which is the sort of prayer that goes deservedly unanswered; but she was.

He found her in the house, in an inner room he did not remember, which must have been part of the women's quarter. She was seated cross-legged in front of a loom with her back to the doorway, absorbed in what she was doing, and for a moment he stood and watched her. Sharah's loom, like most in the villages, was a simple arrangement of two beams pegged into the ground, with the warp drawn tight between, seldom used indoors except in the winter months; this was a much more solid affair, the twin beams set firmly upright between floor and low ceiling, topped with a third like the frame of a door, already tautly screened with the long scarlet threads of the warp-strings, across which she was deftly threading a shuttle with yellow wool, pressing it down firmly with a comblike batten. Skeins of yellow, green and blue wool lay at her side. She wore a simple household shift, freshly laundered, her dark hair bound in a white band.

So he had imagined Tamam, in a house of his own in Zorah.

Turning to reach for a new strand, she saw him there and started, dropping her lashes too late to mask a pleasure as plain as his own. She turned quickly back, but he knew he was not mistaken. He let fall his cloak and came behind her, and lifted her as if she had no weight at all; and set her on her feet without releasing her, still with her back to him. This time she made no resistance; neither did she turn. "Has Samson come back for his revenge?"

Under his hands, her bare arms were still. He said truthfully, "I don't know why I came back."

"I know why."

And she leaned her head back against his breast like a contented child. She was unpredictable as rain in Ziv. Close to, there were gold spirals of almost invisible thread embroidered on her headband, of the Philistine design, appearing again at the neck of the shift which fell otherwise plain to her knees, with only a pause at the half-formed breasts. He had forgotten how young she was; though it was plain enough now. He held her gently, as he had held Miriam on the rooftop of Amalek's house. The sudden awareness of her buttocks pressing against him through the thin linen stung him like an asp. She broke away with a peal of laughter and ran to the wall, facing him with her hands pressed back against it as if trapped, though he had not moved. "If you touch me, I will call the men."

But he had had enough of her, and called them himself.

It was a womanservant who appeared, however, a spidery creature wearing her unbleached linen like a shroud, who peered in amazement for the source of the male summons. Samson sent her to fetch bread, and goat's milk if they had it; adding–since he did not know her–that if she had thought of sending for the Philistines she would do well to put it behind her, because he had a hundred men in the vineyards watching the house. She gave a startled look at her mistress, who said nothing, and vanished like the wraith she resembled.

Delilah said, "Do you always make so free of strangers' houses?"

"Aye." The prospect of a meal cheered him; he had eaten nothing since Benjamin but the scant food he carried with him. He grinned at her. "Besides, this is Hanno's house, and Hanno is no stranger to me. Where are you going?"

"You told Keturah to fetch bread. She is like to fetch nothing else, unless I order her." In the narrow doorway she asked, "Do you truly have a hundred men outside?"

"Bread will do fine," he said.

For all the time he had passed in Amalek's household, and among the looseliving people of the coast, it was still a strange thing to be alone in this quarter of the house. A woman's room, filled with her presence in the jasmine-scented air, the delicately fringed carpets, in the little rush stool too small for him, the loom itself, an intricately carved chest strewn with her trinkets, laid aside for the weaving. He had forgotten such things. He found himself picking up his cloak to tidy it, like a man who lived in a house again. Even the unwisdom of letting her go seemed unimportant.

The bread when it came was no common barley loaf, but a fine flat round of wheat such as the rich eat, served with whole pigeons in a stew of lentils. The woman Keturah brought water in a basin and a cloth, and set about washing his feet, but with such clumsy nervousness that he waved her away, and finished it himself. When he looked up she was gone again. Delilah was pouring ale from a flagon into metal goblets, watching him. She said suddenly, "How did you know I was here today?"

"I asked Adonai to send you."

"You asked–?"

"The workers in the vineyard," he said. "For the Lady Delilah. I remembered your name, you see."

She handed him a goblet and fetched one for herself, seating herself neatly on the carpet opposite him, the stew bowl between them. "Did you think of me in Benjamin?"

"Aye. Every time someone threw a spear at me." He helped himself to meat, dipping his fingers in the bowl, and paused on the thought. "You know where I have been, then?"

"All the world knows where you have been. But only I know where you are now."

Seeing her smile for the first time made him realize what it was about Tamam that had made even Manoah covet her; why Sharah spoke of her with such bitterness, and even Uzziel was deceived.

Delilah said curiously, "Are you not afraid I shall betray you?"

"Not now. There is bread and salt between us."

It made them both laugh, that Samson should claim the protection of a guest *from a woman.* Their fingers touched over the bowl, and he said, "Tell me all that happened, the day the Philistines came here and burned the house."

The laughter went out of her face. "I was little. I don't remember." She rose abruptly to replenish his goblet. "Does the beer please you? It came all the way from Assyria."

When she stooped to pour it, he closed his hand over her wrist. "You remembered *me.* And the doll you had."

"Yes."

And seeing that he would not let her go, she shrugged, and let herself be drawn down to the carpet again, beside him.

"I will try to remember."

□

They came in the forenoon, knowing perhaps that there was no work done in the vineyards at this season and the men would be away helping with the Timnath wheat harvest. There were three of them, and they came to the house door like acquaintances paying their respects, inquiring politely for the Lord Jason, with whom they had some private business. The house servants took them for Philistine merchants, for they had left their helmets in the chariots out of sight up the road with a fourth man, and wore light traveling cloaks over their body armor. Since they were from Athol's household troop in far-off Gaza, Jason himself was at first no wiser.

It was Sheshai who recognized them.

It is probable that they intended persuading Jason to accompany them on some pretext away from the house, but Sheshai, hearing voices, came out of the bridal chamber and shouted a warning. Even then, the Philistines might have taken Jason away by force or threats, warning Sheshai bluntly not to interfere; but his shout had fetched Niobe out behind him, half into a flimsy gown, and seeing her father struggling with the men below, she flew past him to his aid, screaming and clawing. It was quickly over. The daggers were out from under the cloaks, and she was struck down and silenced. After that, Jason made no further resistance, but died like the nobleman he had once been, standing his full height and facing his murderers with contempt. The servants said afterward that it took twenty-seven thrusts to dispatch him, though more likely some were inflicted after his death. For their own safety the Philistines declared themselves, showing their armor, and their leader the insignia of a Captain of chariots. Sheshai was seen to argue with them, white with fear or fury, and afterwards carried Niobe's still form back up the stairs again to their chamber, and laid her on the bed there.

Delilah had been by the laundry with the other children, and knew nothing until she heard Ishba's demented shrieks, and ran round the corner to see the house ablaze. There was much confusion, and running to and fro, but eventually they were shepherded by the house servants, mostly women, into the compound with what belongings they had managed to save–for the Philistines intended burning the outbuildings with the vines–and ordered to make their way to Timnath. Delilah was clinging to Ishba's hand, crying, she remembered, for the loss of her doll. On the road they came upon the chariots, guarded by a crippled man who stared at them, but said nothing; and then at the crossroads Phicol came on them with three more chariots, going like the wind. He took his sister, and the child he could not separate from her, into his own, sending the rest on, and so they returned to the conflagration.

When he saw it, Phicol jumped down raving like a madman, shouting for the men to fetch water, and heaping abuse on the Philistine Captain who ran across to intercept him, finally striking the man in the face. The Captain did not return the blow, but took his arm, speaking low, and presently Phicol turned aside and slumped on a broken chest, which had been pulled out of the house and abandoned, his head in his hands. Delilah heard him say with a murderous despair, *It is the Hebrew's work.* She had looked to Ishba, not understanding who the Hebrew was; and Ishba said, "Samson."

Some of the buildings were saved. They saw the smoke from the harvest fields, and the laborers came running up the terraces to assist. They were still beating out the flames when Ishba and Delilah left in one of Phicol's chariots, with just the driver and a soldier to see them safe. They went to Ashdod, and the following morning traveled south to Gaza, where Ishba was taken into the household of the third of

Jason's sons, Lahmi, and Delilah with her, to be brought up as his own daughter. The news of Phicol's death followed them there.

□

"So it was not Phicol," Samson said, "and Phicol's men, who put Jason to death."

He lay with his head in Delilah's lap, swirling the last of the Assyrian beer in his goblet, puzzling it out as best he could with the soporific effects of the meal and the ale, and the butterfly touch of her fingers on his forehead. It sounded as if Phicol had been more concerned for the buildings than his kin; and perhaps he was. With Jason dead, they would belong to him and Hanno. Samson said, "Yet Phicol threatened it. At the wedding feast; she told me herself. If not Phicol, then who?"

Her fingers worked on the knot of his headband. "Does it matter?–soldiers. Men who go where they are sent, do what they are told to do. I never heard their names."

"Sent," he said. *"Sent.* Who sent them?"

"The Lord of Battles, who else? The Prince of Gaza."

"Athol!"

He disbelieved it. Why should Athol, after all Samson had done to his Philistines, order the death–not of Samson, but of Jason? The father of his own Captains. He opened his eyes and looked at Delilah, upside down, the violet eyes concentrating on the knot, and put the question to her: "Why Jason?"

"Because he could not catch *you,* of course. It was the quickest way to put an end to the feud."

The logic of it chilled him. But it was believable, and he said wryly, "So I am blamed either way. Is that why you threw the javelin?"

"It doesn't matter now." She had the headband loose at last. "Why do you let your hair grow so long? It is almost as long as mine! Are you a holy man?"

It was a terrible question to be asked, lying with your head between a woman's thighs, and she leaning down enclosing you like an unborn child between her palms and the intimacy of her young breasts, her heart beating under the linen, and the body scent of her carrying away sensible thoughts on a tide of jasmine and musk. Samson turned and took her in his arms, not caring whether she helped or hindered him, and at first she did neither, suffering him to raise her shift and unfasten the ribbons of her drawers as if it were happening to someone else, so that he must himself lift her to be rid of them. He was prepared to force her, but there was no need. He came down on her less certainly, seeing nothing in her face but the knowledge that neither of them could deter him from his purpose, and blotted it out in the darkness of her hair with a curse for an endearment. "Hate me, then, woman, if you must."

"I do not hate you. I have loved you since I was a child."

She thrust her fingers into the thickness of his hair and took triumphant hold of two great locks to pull his mouth down to her own, her legs opening like the gates of a city to her lord; and it was as it had been at Etam, and in the fields between Zorah and Eshtaol, and behind the goats' pen, and under the stars, and every time since he had first known her.

12

PTULLIS THE EGYPTIAN was in the schoolroom when a lad came to the door with a summons from Athol, directly conveyed with none of the court civilities the Prince customarily afforded his childhood tutor and companion. Ptullis at first put his rudeness down to the lad's youth and ignorance, and went on with the astrological computations he was engaged in, not much concerned. It was one of the compensations of old age. He saw little of Athol these days, since he had become gratefully too frail to accompany him on his campaigns, and the Lord of Battles was seldom at home in Gaza. Whatever it was, it could wait until he had finished. But an unexpected sound distracted him, and when he looked up and saw the boy's face, and that there were actually tears rolling down his smooth cheeks, he dropped scrolls and pen and reaching for his staff hurried after him, punting himself down the marble corridors with all the urgency of an inshore boatman in a squall.

The boy led him directly to Athol's bedchamber, where the sight of the royal physician emerging almost at a run confirmed his worst foreboding.

"The fool wanted to bleed me," Athol's voice said. "And where's the sense in that?"

The shutters were drawn, and in the half-light his color was deathly. He was curled up on the great bed, up against one of its pillars, his knees almost to his chest, his yellow hair matted; but his voice was ironically cheerful.

"A man's meat goes in by his mouth and out at his anus, is it not so, Ptullis? And no amount of opening of veins will catch it on the way." Athol's hand weakly indicated the metal bowl on the floor beside him. "I put my fingers down my throat as you taught me to cure a surfeit of eating; though the gods know I ate little enough."

At least it wasn't the plague. Ptullis felt for the telltale swellings, under the armpits and in the groin, and there was nothing. More likely a bellyful of rotten meat; with all the abominable spices in the world passing on the trade routes through Gaza nowadays, a man hardly knew what he was eating any more.

Athol feebly pushed him off. "I didn't send for you for your Egyptian physics, but your skill in logic."

Ptullis waited for an explanation, and receiving none, asked tentatively, "Was anyone else sick?"

"Yes, one other," Athol said. "I see you begin to understand at last, old philosopher. My food taster. Who is dead." He broke off to make use of the bowl again, and wiped his mouth, adding grimly, "At least that proves his innocence."

Ptullis swayed in shock. *Poison!* It was more a use of Egypt than Philistia; especially unthinkable in Athol's own household. Yet the symptoms were so patent he was abashed at his own blindness.

"You are surprised," Athol said, flopping back. "So was I. I thought I was well loved among my own people. Was I wrong, Ptullis?"

"No, my Lord. You are much loved."

But the Egyptian allowed himself a certain dryness in the words which Athol did not miss. The white of his teeth suggested a smile, or it could have been a grimace of pain.

"You mean my fair lads: a jealous lover turned out of my bed and seeking revenge? I thought of that. But when the time comes I send them away; you know that. Out of Gaza;

they are never allowed to enter the palace again. Besides, the greed and ambition of boys outlasts their natural affections, and I provide for them well enough. Think again, old sage."

Ptullis scratched his thin nose. "You have no seed. Who would be prince of Gaza in your place?"

"My nephew. A simple soldier–you remember him; he was wounded at Aphek. He hasn't the guile for it; and I flatter myself he is too fond of me to make changes here. Nobody would gain from his accession."

It was true. Ptullis said, "Who would be Lord of Battles?"

"Ashkelon." Athol began to laugh, and doubled up again, his hands to his stomach. "I had to name somebody." He said with difficulty, "You cannot suspect . . . young Saph! No." Athol raised himself, directing Ptullis to heap bolsters behind him. The spasm seemed to have passed as quickly as it had come. "I am better now. You have been too long in Gaza, old friend, with your fusty books. Do you not know that a team of oxen would not pull Saph out of his palace these days? He is besotted with this new woman he has found–they call her a rare beauty, though with their eye kohl and their false colorings they all look the same to me. He purchased her from the temple at a ridiculous price; why I don't know, since he could have had her there for nothing. If I died now, Ptullis, this same randy young Saph would be obliged to exchange his silken bed for a soldier's tent. He has good reason to wish me a long life!"

Ptullis heard him out patiently, and nodded. "As you have said, the Lord of Battles may himself name his successor. May he not also, if he so choose, promote a man from among the Captains to lead your armies in the field in his stead?"

Athol was silent for so long, the Egyptian wondered if he had fallen asleep. But he stirred, calling for Ptullis's arm, and left the bed to direct the drawing back of the shutters, leaning on the exposed sill to stare down into the courtyard, taking deep breaths of air. Then he turned and grinned with all his former affection at Ptullis, standing there. "By the gods you are devious. Ptullis! I knew I was right to send for you. And whom, among the Captains, would Saph choose to lead the armies? Who would come forward most eagerly; whose blood runs most hot against our enemies?–*against one enemy in particular?"*

"As you truly say, Lord Athol, my days are passed in the schoolroom. I have not left the city–"

"Name him."

"Hanno," Ptullis said: "son of Jason of Timnath that was. And he has many of like mind with him."

"And Hanno is under my command, and can do nothing while I live."

The fresh air had fetched a little color back into Athol's cheeks. He walked unaided to a table, to take up a mirror and study his face in the polished metal. He straightened his hair with a serious regard. "I shall not die, Ptullis, I think." Then he put the mirror down. "We are guessing, remember. We cannot be sure Hanno is behind the poisoning."

"Your torturers will confirm it."

"I doubt it."

In this, Athol was correct. Two of the kitchen staff died on the wheel, and four–a guard and two serving men and one woman–were maimed with an ingenious variety of instruments after certainly screaming out all they knew, which amounted to nothing. Athol took no interest in any of it. The name of Hanno wrested out of burnt flesh and dislocated limbs could not have made him more sure.

The question was, what to do?

To dispose of Hanno would be an easy thing: a body floated out to sea with no need for arraignments and trials. But it was not Athol's way, and prudence reinforced a natural aversion to treachery. If Hanno had followers within the palace itself, his death would nowise lessen their enmity or render the palace safer. And after Hanno, how many more?

It was, of course, the head of Samson they were after.

To the Habiru tribesmen–even the majority who had never set eyes on him–he was a hero; not much of a hero, a local bandit chief skulking in the mountains with a handful of like-minded ruffians; but the only hero they had left. Hanno's faction imagined that they had only to rid themselves of him to be free of whatever opposition remained to their conquest of the land, never grasping Athol's master plan of pacification, never reckoning the fewness of their own numbers, or their dependence on the frail loyalties of their Canaanite acolytes; above all *never understanding that the god-ridden Habiru worshipped the dead more than the living.* Dead, the Nazirite would himself become a god, and a very dangerous one.

Could they not understand that by demanding Samson's death they risked setting a flame to the whole Hebrew nation from northern Dan to Beer-sheba in the south?

□

"Stay with me," Delilah said.

It was Samson's fourth visit, counting the time she had flung the javelin at him as the first, and the rebuilding of the house was completed, the workmen gone. The last time had been fleeting, for he had found her on the point of leaving for Ashkelon with the wine caravan, and he had used her like a whore, briefly; and she had responded like one, stifling her laughter at the thought of the men waiting puzzled below, for he was discreet in his approach and none but the maid Keturah had seen him. Since then he had been away from her only to make a brief inspection of his bachelors at Etam, seeing neither his mother nor Uzziel before returning again to the Timnath vineyard on a day when Delilah had promised to be there. The recklessness of making a tryst, which had nagged his mind all the way down the valley road, fled at the sight of her. She was clothed from neck to ankle in a long Canaanite shirt striped with the pretty pomegranate pink and white, bright as a wildflower in the green garden, her hair loose, having neither cloak nor shawl against the evening chill in her haste to greet him, her naked feet hurrying through the grasses like Eve in Eden.

She wore little ankle chains that tinkled as she ran.

She turned now in his arms with a murmur of contentment toward the fading square of the window, saying, "Stay with me," and he thought she meant until morning, but she said, "Forever."

The childlike extravagance pleased him and he chuckled, but she did not, and after a moment, tracing the silken line of her spine with an inquiring finger, he discovered that she was sulking, and ruffled her hair. "Stay *here?* In Hanno's house?"

"It is my house." Her voice was muffled and petulant. "As much as Hanno's," she said.

Even the lie only made him laugh. Whoever heard of a servant's child with a grand house, and vineyards? But he did not say it. He said more gently, "Do I not take chances enough already, coming here to you?"

"Am I not worth a little risk?"

"I'll risk my life with your Philistines. I'll not hand it to them on a platter." Samson lifted her hair and took the delicate lobe of her ear in his teeth and she squirmed, as she always did. He said, "Why are you teasing me? You know I have to be with my people."

"Your people are here: there are lots of Hebrews in Timnath; more than there are Philistines, anyway. Isn't your village just up the valley? Well, then."

He tickled the nape of her neck. "My people are not in the village, they are in the hills. How could I lead them from here?"

"If you loved me you would find a way."

"I did not say I loved you."

The effect was more startling than he had intended. Delilah turned with the speed of a trodden serpent, almost spitting in his face with a little cry of vexation, and as he opened his arms to her, thrust a hand between his thighs and gathered up his unborn children so quickly that before he knew it was no ordinary lovemaking she had the sac crushed in her fingers. *"Say it then!* Say you love me!"

The pain was excruciating. He not only said it, he bellowed it loud enough to be heard on the far side of Timnath. This appeared to satisfy her, for she let go and swung her legs over the side of the bed, leaving him to inspect the damage gingerly.

"You nearly gelded me!"

"I wish I had. I wish I had put the javelin right *through* you, when I still hated you."

She seemed to change her love and hatred like her raiment, to match her mood. It was only recently that she said she had loved him since she was a child. He reminded her now, but idly, admiring the perfect half-melon of her left breast in profile. He had soon abandoned the attempt to reconcile her many contradictions, and she was not given to explaining herself. Delilah's explanations went sideways, like crabs.

But her answer when it came, though delivered in no more friendly a tone, was a straightforward contradiction: "I said I loved you *as* a child."

It was not true; not as he remembered it; but it was something. He waited encouragingly, and she said, "That was before I learned what you did to Tamam."

Samson felt his head suddenly full of bees. Because it was of Tamam that he had been thinking, he was sure she had taken the name out of his mind. *Niobe,* she meant: what you did to Niobe. The Philistines had been quick to blame their own madness on their enemy; Sheshai too had lied—witness the story Esther had repeated; which Delilah must have heard again and again in Gaza and Ashkelon, or something like it. Yet she had remembered the episode herself, apparently, and shown a curious indifference to Niobe's fate. Perhaps Tamam, being among the servants, had meant more to the child than the daughter of the house; servants were always clannish. But it explained nothing. Samson left the bed and stood a moment at the window, fighting down an unreasonable anger. Like all house windows it faced inward toward the dark of the compound. There was lamplight in the servants' quarters, but no disturbance, though no one in the house could be so deaf as not to have heard his shout when Delilah half castrated him. The night air cooled his skin, and smelled of the sea, which was the best part of a day's journey distant. They had never spoken of Tamam. He had not even supposed that Delilah remembered her now, except that it was she who first showed him the burial place. How long had Tamam been gone by then? He turned back to the room, still angry, and saw that Delilah had put on her pomegranate shirt again and was occupied with her hair in a mirror as if he had not been there. He took the mirror from her hand and said, "Listen to me.

"I don't know how much you remember her, or what they have told you; and I don't care. Tamam and I grew up together from childhood in my father's house. I cannot even remember a time when she was not there, like the land I trod, the air I breathed. Never let me hear you say I did her any harm; I'd as soon have harmed myself."

Delilah had taken up a shawl and was trying it on her head as best she could with no mirror as if she had heard none of it. Then she said calmly, "Is that why you loved me? Because I look like her?"

The shawl was blue; but the lamplight enriched the color to a purple-red.

He said, "Who told you, you look like her?"

She looked puzzled; the way Tamam used to look when he put to her those questions children ask, which catch the mind off-balance with their irrelevance. "I don't know. Ishba, I expect."

Why must she make it sound like a lie, when it must be the truth? Who else but the sister from Jason's household would remember the Canaanite woman who labored obscurely in the laundry, not even in the house, what she looked like? Samson remembered Ishba as a simple, good-natured child; but the death of Niobe and her father had embittered her–Delilah told him this, lying amiably in his arms again, her good-humor unaccountably restored–and afterwards she had come to blame Samson more and more. It was she who had poisoned Delilah's mind against the Nazirite over the years, recalling the stories of how he had abandoned Tamam, turning her over like a market heifer to his father, who in turn had used her and tired of her, and cast her out of the tribe by herself, a woman with no kin and nowhere to go. It was a commonplace among the Habiru, to treat their women like cattle. Niobe had said that; perhaps with Samson's rejection of herself in mind, when Jason offered her in Niobe's place.

"She said many bad things about you. She says them still."

"Some of them are true," Samson told her. "I hated Manoah for what he did. I hate him still."

"Can you hate the dead?"

"Aye." Samson lifted his head from her bosom. "Why not? If you can love them, you can hate them."

And he let his head fall back, thinking it was not true: not the loving and the hating, but that they were dead. Manoah was no more dead than Abraham. Zorah was still Manoah's village, Dan his tribe, his burial place a sort of sanctuary after all, for the manner of his death had silenced those who opposed him; his recollected words had a wisdom they never had when he was alive; they formed a chain that fettered the tribe to the old generations all the more strongly for being intangible. As for Tamam, it was as if she had never left him, nor he her; she lay under him now, the answer to his impossible prayer. And he suddenly stirred again, trying to rationalize it, and asked Delilah curiously why it was important to her, what Ishba had said.

"What was Tamam to you?"

Again that little puzzled wrinkle between the violet eyes, the dark brows lifted in surprise at such a question.

Delilah said, "I thought you knew. She was my mother."

□

"I did not say there was no child," Sharah said patiently. "I said there was no *son.* You never asked me concerning a daughter."

Her tone implied that it would have been odd if he had; which in the ordinary way was no more than the truth. Everyone knew it was a man's sons who were his covenant with the eternal, the reincarnation of his seed. The birth of a female child was no great cause for concern at the best of times; and one spawned of a Canaanitish slave of no import whatever.

Sharah had never seen Samson like this. He had the deathly pallor she had seen on the faces of those defeated in battle, the day they fetched Manoah home, accentuated in Samson's case by the blackness of his curling locks. He wandered restlessly, with a sort of inward raging, as if the house were too small for him in body and spirit both. How like Manoah he was! She watched him with a fearful affection and no idea of what had upset him, certainly not the fighting in Benjamin. In his present mood it was easy to understand why the Philistines were terrified of him.

But he stopped and said almost gently, "Did she have a name, this daughter?"

"She must have," Sharah said indifferently, and closed her lips. "I don't remember."

Why had Yahweh permitted Samson unknowingly to lie with his own sister? Manoah's child!

He found himself by the old field altar, the flattened heap of rocks Manoah had raised there, so many years before in the presence of the angel, to make his sacrifice in ill-conceived thanksgiving for Sharah's pregnancy. What would Manoah have said, if he had known what he had begotten? Some of the stones had tumbled, as well they might, half-buried in the ground. The altar had never been disturbed, but it had never been used again, either. If an angel had visited Zorah since that day, he had never heard of it.

It was dusk: the brief and dangerous moment between day and dark when spirits walk abroad, and familiar things are touched with an evil magic. Easy to visualize the smoke rushing upward from the altar, and the nothing on the far side where the angel had stood.

A group of children, hurrying back to the village before dark, huddled like sheep thunderstruck by the great roaring shout, their whitened faces turned as one toward the bearlike apparition that tore at the earth, uprooting rocks like tares, roaring and shouting.

"Send him back, Adonai!"

A great stone was plucked out like a milk tooth, and smashed in half against another.

"Let him come again, as he came a second time for Manoah!"

Rocks flew through the air as if propelled by some gigantic sling.

"Let him tell *me* why I was conceived–and made Nazirite before I knew my nose from my navel!"

The earth itself seemed to rise up in heaps, scattering dust and stones.

"Forsworn to vows I could never keep–shepherd to a flock of goats–lover to a dead woman!"

The children fled.

"A dead woman who yet lives," Samson told the night. *"Whom I can have neither alive nor dead."*

There was nothing left of the altar to destroy; no easement for the massive strength of his hands. He wished Manoah were alive to see it, his precious handiwork. No stone was left standing, no vow left unbroken.

Yet there was one, and he dropped the last stone and ran through the darkness to the vineyards, falling twice before he found what he was looking for: the tall booth which served as watchtower and store for the workers' tools. The door was locked, and he stove it in. There was no lack of pruning knives, and he took one and came out of the booth into the first moonlight, that silvered the blade. He squatted on the ground, and tearing off his headband took a fistful of hair and drew it out to its length, and wrapped it round his forearm. He had set the knife edge close to his scalp when a cloud passed over the moon, and he felt the flesh crawl between his shoulder blades. It was the same as the moment when he first looked on Delilah's face and saw Tamam there: the sensation of someone standing behind him.

He turned with the knife in his hand, and the moon came out again, and there was nothing: only the shadow of the booth and the silvery vines, and a grasshopper chirring somewhere close at hand.

He stood and shook himself, but he knew he had not been mistaken; and after a moment he tossed the knife in through the black doorway and turned his face toward Etam, fastening the headband as he went.

The cave at Etam had never been a dwelling, but a place of forgathering for raids into the plain, and a safe refuge, the bachelors for the most part returning to their villages until called out again. But it also served as a storehouse for weapons and provisions, and for this reason was never left unguarded. Samson, announcing himself at the cavemouth, and answered only by the booming echo of his own voice and the leathery whirring of the bats, was more angry than alarmed to find it deserted. A solitary torch smoldering at the back of the cavern gave him light enough to make his ablutions under the twin rivulets, and open the neck of a wineskin. It was only in the morning, when he rolled out of his cloak and stood to stretch himself, that he saw the overturned grain bins and the spoiled meats. And then, making his search, the blood at the cavemouth, just inside, where the sacking was torn down.

Rage exploded in him. He ripped his tunic apart like papyrus, crashing half-naked to his knees to snap the head-band and heap the cave floor over his flying hair, rising through a cloud of dust and bat droppings to utter a thunderous curse on the mothers of the Philistines, doubled and redoubled from the echoing walls. He cursed the spies for not warning them, tramping the cave to find a spear heavy enough for his purpose; the watch for allowing them to be surprised–clearly they had been surprised–and himself for not being here; and Delilah for keeping him from Yahweh's work. By the time the echoes died away, and the twittering of the bats came through, he was at the cavemouth with the spear in his hand, pausing a moment to adjust his eyes to the sunlight; and a stone struck him on the temple, which might have killed a lesser man. He slid to his backside, blinking, and found himself looking at some thirty of his own bachelors ringing him with a forest of spears and bows.

They bore him inside the cave again, and fetched water to bathe his face and clean the mess out of his hair, and a clean tunic, and wine, which he tipped down his throat like the waterfalls of Jordan. But he had taken the full force of the slingshot, and it was some time before he understood what had occurred.

There had been no Philistines; no attack, no battle. They had kept watch faithfully as he had taught them, they swore it, with listeners on the hilltop. No body of men–not a single man alone–could have approached the cave unknown to them. But an evil spirit in the form of a bear, black as the night it came out of, and silent as only a bear or a spirit can be, had wandered into the cave, and taking fright at the clamor caused by its sudden appearance, lost the way out, and ran amuck. They had tried to head the brute off, but most of the men had been asleep, and only a single torch was burning. Two men were killed before they managed to make their way out to safety. They had pulled their dead after them, and carried each down to his village, returning at first light. When they heard the roaring, they were sure the evil spirit was still inside. The next thing, Samson had lurched out, with his torn and blackened garments and his tangled hair, looking more like a bear than the bear itself. The slinger, a stalwart youth much dismayed at his own accuracy, knelt beside Samson's recumbent form, his forehead pressed to the earth. "Forgive me, Lord."

"Oh," Samson said, giving the youth a gentle push that sent him sprawling. "Aye."

And he said, "*Lord,* is it?"

And then he said, "A bear."

And he began to laugh; slowly at first, a hiccupping chuckle that spilled the wine over his chin, and then with a growing rumble deep in his chest; those nearest fell back awkwardly, frowning and grinning; and afterward with a bursting forth of uncontrollable hilarity that infected them all, the tears rolling down Samson's broad cheeks—"A bear! Adonai—*a bear!*"—and the cavern echoing like a cattle shed to the bellowing of thirty and one fighting men and warriors, rolling about drunk with the absurdity of it.

Samson felt a warmth of affection for them. They were simple highlanders like himself, begotten of the rocky moorlands and thorny braes, rough-bred to their hard-won crops and wandering herds. Most were young, some scarcely bearded, and all more used to the mattock than the sword. In the Shephelah and up to the Benjamite hills they had shown themselves more than equal to the Philistines, few as they were; he could muster maybe a hundred, with Omar's brigands. Scarcely a meal for the chariots in the plain. How many more could Samuel call on, to leave their own tribal lands and make common cause, as the Philistine League did, under a single banner? What could they not do, if only Judah were to come up to Dan; if Ephraim and even great Manasseh came down to join with Benjamin, for a start! Others must follow.

Almost, talking of these things with his bachelors while they built a fire and prepared the morning meal, and afterward, leading half their number on a reckless expedition to track down the bear, he was persuaded that it was possible. His own mind was made up. From now on he would devote himself to Yahweh's work, as Samuel–and Uzziel–had urged him; perhaps make the journey through Judah again, to see if they were ready to come up. He had already decided never to visit Delilah again; never.

They never did find the bear. A week later, a messenger arrived from Zorah to say a strange woman was there with tidings for Samson she would tell to none else.

It was Keturah, to say that Delilah was on her deathbed with the plague, and calling for him, and he went down to Timnath the same hour.

□

She watched him from the house as he came, half-walking half-running up beside the ruins with a dreadful urgency, looking neither to left nor right; and alone, which meant he had come straightway not waiting for Keturah even; and this pleased her. Satisfied, she went inside to her bedchamber, where she arranged herself under a light silken drape before he burst in. She had yellowed her cheeks and lay with the drape drawn up to her chin and her eyes closed; but he had seen enough of the plague to doubt it, and the next moment the drape was on the floor and she was struggling furiously to fend off his exploring hands. He let her fall back on the bed and stood, breathing heavily.

"There's nothing ails you."

"You've a tender way of inquiring!" Delilah pulled her disordered robe down in outrage. Then, seeing she had given herself away, she stood, and suddenly giggled and slid her arms about his neck, on tiptoe. "Are you not glad to find me well?"

She thought he was going to kill her. From their first encounter she had always been aware of that famous strength underlying his leonine gentleness; but for all his occasional roughness, he had been more careful of her than she knew. Her first taste of the terrifying destructiveness of his anger came with a crushing embrace that lifted her clear of the ground and threatened to break her back in two. She could not breathe at all. She twisted her face aside, gasping, and he pulled her head back by the hair to look at her. If he had not let go, she would have fainted. She clung to him, sobbing for breath like a frightened child, or she would have fallen at his feet.

All he said was, "What have you got on your face?"

"Camphire."

He sat on the bed while she cleaned it off, lifting her arms with a painful stiffness by no means entirely simulated, like a victim newly released from the rack. She said reproachfully, "You gave me a fright."

"What do you suppose you gave *me?*—with your lying messages. Your woman said you were dying."

"I was afraid you wouldn't come otherwise."

He did not deny it. She moved to him, and put her hands in his. "But why? I don't understand. You love me."

He didn't deny this either. "You know why. You are my sister."

"Half sister."

He groaned. "It makes no difference, under the law. You are Manoah's child, as I am. To lie with you is to uncover the nakedness of my own father."

"*He* won't mind." Her head was in Samson's lap, her hand idly stroking his thigh. She said, "He is dead, isn't he?"

Samson stirred uneasily. It was impossible to argue with her, or to deny it when she protested that the Philistines had no such law she had ever heard of. It was true that there were Hebrews on the coast even married to their half sisters; but the coast was not Zorah, nor the Hebrews Nazirites. He told her, stroking her hair to quiet her, that he would be stoned in Dan, if it were known.

She raised her eyes at once. "Who is to know, but us?"

Later, when they were finishing the meal she had prepared and she was replenishing his cup for the fourth or fifth time, she said, "Do you never break the laws of your terrible god?"

He looked dolefully into the red of the wine, seeing his resolution dissolving in the cup. It was the third thing he could not deny. He said truthfully, "Not when I can help it."

But there were times when he could not help it; and he woke in the middle of the night in her arms on the sudden and happy thought that Sarah, Abraham's wife, had also been his half sister. The daughter of his father, but not of his mother. Manoah had never told him that; but Uzziel had, once. Not approvingly; but he had said it.

□

The latter rains failed that year, and in the second month the wheatfields on the coastal plain, already sickly, were stripped by locusts. Hanno was put in charge of the caravan sent down into Egypt to buy grain.

It was his first inkling that Athol suspected him of the poison plot.

The ration caravan was a routine command customarily given to a junior officer, and Athol's bland proclamation in Council, later published in the streets, that he was sending his most experienced Captain because of the supposed danger of attack from famine-stricken tribesmen, did nothing to ease Hanno's disquiet.

He made the best of it, leading the column himself in his distinctive personal chariot, well ahead and accompanied only by his armor-bearer, to demonstrate his contempt for the imaginary dangers; but the humiliation followed him into the emptiness of the desert. It was typical of that fox Athol to sidestep a confrontation. He had always been more politician than soldier. There had been no public word of the poison attempt; indeed, it was several days before Hanno's own spies could get word to him that it had failed. He was assured that no breath of suspicion had implicated him.

Yet Athol–or that walking skeleton of an Egyptian–had guessed.

The farther they drew away from Gaza and civilization, the deeper into the featureless desert, following the ancient trade route, the more convinced Hanno became that this . . . *shopping expedition* was Athol's scornful way of reminding him of his merchant heritage. And this after Hanno himself, and Phicol his brother, had turned their back on their father as soon as they were of military age, and allied themselves wholeheartedly with the martial League.

The ingratitude of Athol, the man's sheer disloyalty, seemed to Hanno beyond endurance.

He was a month in Egypt, marking each day's delay with fretful impatience, and it was on the return journey that he made up his mind.

The first rule of battle a soldier learned, was to seek out and destroy the enemy leaders. Without leaders, soldiers were a rabble–villagers, husbandmen, fathers, growers of crops, individual men, no more threat than single locusts. And among the Habiru, only Samson of Dan could be called a military leader at all. Hanno had promised himself revenge on the Danite a thousand times; only Athol's ridiculous insistence that he must be taken alive, and his refusal to divert enough cohorts for a proper expedition to clean up the Shephelah once and for all, had prevented it. Now Hanno had a second, and more pressing reason.

The man who took Samson would be a public hero not even the Lord of Battles could put down.

Ashkelon was the key, and it was to Saph's palace that Hanno repaired immediately on his return. He did not like Saph, but it had been necessary for his purpose to secure the favor and protection of one of the Seren, and Saph was at once one of the most powerful, and the weakest. It had not been easy, and it had required both patience and humility: qualities Hanno did not possess, and had to learn to acquire. Saph had been flattered by the inclusion of the tall young aristocrat into his circle of intimates–he had none of Athol's prejudices against trade, since he ruled over the biggest trading center in the land–and the soldier's knowledge of the diversions of back-street sexual adventures had made him a welcome companion. But Saph had little interest in military adventures, and the influence Hanno could bring to the council through him was small. Then there had been the setback of Ishba.

Hanno had fetched her up from Gaza with her maid and installed her in a small house close to the palace. Ishba had grown buxom and pretty, and it was not long before she was more in the palace than out of it. Saph for a time favored her, and under Hanno's tutelage she was well on her way to becoming princess when, as ill-luck would have it, the

Lord of Ashkelon visited her at home and promptly conceived a violent and unwelcome passion for her handmaid. And Ishba instead of offering him the girl as a gift, as any sensible woman seeking his favor would have done–the gods knew, he had no lack of such baubles in his palace!–no, Ishba must throw a fit of temperament that bid fair to upset Hanno's entire scheme, and swear she would have the girl strangled first. No doubt it had something to do with the Hebrew's rejection of her at Timnath, when she was offered in Niobe's place. It was, to be fair, the second time the wretched creature had been spurned–and the maid a peasant!

Hanno swallowed the insult to his family, but it left him with a dilemma that made planning a battle seem a simple exercise. Ironically it was Ishba herself who unwittingly turned the situation to his advantage. Hanno kept the maid out of Saph's way as much as he could by sending her down to the vineyards at Timnath; he even had the old house generously restored for her use, since she seemed to have a simple fondness for the place where she had spent her early childhood. But there was a limit to the time he himself could spend in Ashkelon, and on his return from the campaign in Benjamin he learned that Ishba had sold the maid to the priests as a temple prostitute.

In her simplicity, Ishba imagined the temple was the one place beyond even Saph's reach. What she did not know, was that Hanno's known determination to rid Philistia of the Danite had assured him of the backing of the priesthood, and gave him an influence in the temple more powerful than that of the Seren themselves. Even so, the chief priest proved adamant at first.

"She is wedded to Dagon now. Would you have us deprive our god of one of his wives?"

"Would you rather deprive the Lord Saph?" Hanno asked pointedly.

The priest shrugged. "She can attend the palace, discreetly. It can be arranged; you know that."

This was no part of Hanno's plan at all. He said, "I don't think you understand. The girl is my kinswoman, the daughter of my brother. Her coming to you was a mistake;

the deceit of a jealous woman—she was tricked into it."

"But she is not of your people!"

"My brother Lahmi adopted her," Hanno said persuasively, fighting down irritation. "Long ago, when she was a child. She is of my family, I tell you; we are very fond of her."

The priest continued to look doubtful, as well he might. "The girl said nothing of this. Your sister sold her as her own property."

"I will see the temple coffers suffer no loss."

Hanno paid in fact exactly twice what Ishba had obtained for her, which was still a small sum, and in any case it was Saph's money. Saph was delighted. The girl herself, already promoted to the comparative freedom of the temple-house, had no cause to complain at this further and double exaltation: first to be counted as Hanno's own kin, and then a favorite in the palace itself. She was after all, when you came to look at her, a pretty little thing, and shrewd with it. In no time at all she was behaving as if born to palace life; she dropped the familiar Lilah for the grander-sounding Delilah, which she said she was born with, though not even Ishba could remember it.

There was no Delilah about the palace today, however, and Hanno, brushing aside the sloppy palace guard, found Saph alone walking in the gardens, and in an uncharacteristically evil humor.

"Life's blood, Hanno, must you always dress as if you're on the battlefield?"

Hanno removed his helmet with as much grace as he could manage. "I have come this hour from Egypt."

"I know, I know." Saph showed a flicker of interest. "What price had you to pay for the corn?"

"A pim a bushel, I believe."

"You did well, then. Egyptian corn is the best there is. It will fetch a good shekel here."

A pim was two-thirds of a shekel.

Hanno said, "Our people said the rate of exchange was unfavorable. And they were not happy with the Egyptian measures, either." Then it penetrated. "You don't mean it will be sold openly here–in the marketplace?"

"Why not? We don't need it ourselves; you know that."

"*I* know it," Hanno said. "I didn't know it was common knowledge."

Saph looked ruffled. "I don't suppose it is."

"But it will be, if the grain is sold publicly. People will ask why the Lord of Battles sends his right-hand man on a fool's errand. Not for a few hundred shekels profit! If I know Athol, he will sell it at a loss."

"Why should he do that?"

"To curry favor with the Canaanites," Hanno said bitterly. "And to discredit me."

It was out now; but he had to tread carefully. He knew that he could rely on Saph only so long as the prince did not feel himself personally involved. But Saph did not seem particularly interested.

"I thought you were close to Athol."

"Too close; I know his weaknesses. He is become jealous of me, besides. I captured the Hebrew once, if you remember."

"And lost him again."

"We were betrayed," Hanno said through his teeth, and calmed himself. "He slipped through my fingers. Athol is terrified of him, and his mountain god. I am not; that is why Athol looks for a way of getting rid of me. That is why I am here. To ask a small favor."

He moved forward as he spoke and took Saph gently by the elbow, steering him out of earshot of the guards. His request was simple: appointment as captain of the palace guard. It was a post generally given to retired officers of good service, but he would put it about that he had a sickness, an old wound, and needed to rest up. Athol could not object; and it would get him away from the immediate command of the Lord of Battles, since household troops were exempt from active service. He could have some of his own men transferred to him without arousing suspicion.

"And be free to pursue your brother's murderer," Saph noted cynically; "leaving my palace unguarded half the time, I suppose."

Hanno laughed easily. "On the contrary, you will have my personal protection. And you may need it. Remember what Samson did at Ashdod. Will you do this?"

"Oh, very well. I will send a note to Athol." Saph dismissed the subject; he glanced at Hanno with troubled eyes and said, "If you will do something for me."

"You have only to name it."

"If you can," Saph continued, and pulled at his yellow robe in embarrassment. "But it's hopeless. . . . She will listen to no one. I doubt she would listen to you. But you are her—kin, you said; and you did procure her for me."

"Delilah?" Hanno said, and glanced back at the palace as if half-expecting to see her on the balcony. "Is she misbehaving?"

"If she is, it is not with me."

Hanno felt the world darken before his eyes. He knew in that moment how the gods must feel in having to do with the imbecilities of men. He said with strong disbelief: "You mean . . . ?"

"I mean she won't have me, Hanno. I have been good to her, but she's taken to turning away."

"Ah." Hanno's relief was visible. "That is just her way of leading you on; she's been trained in the temple—remember? Tie her down and flog her a bit; you'll enjoy that."

He would have enjoyed it himself. He would have enjoyed flogging the little bitch half to death. But Saph, usually quick to respond to such titillation, only shook his head in deeper dejection.

"It would do no good. It would be like . . . necrophilia. I want more of her than that."

"More of her? But she is yours—you *own* her."

"Nobody owns Delilah." Saph kicked at the ground like a spoilt boy. "She has even asked me to give her her freedom. She asked me to name my price!"

"I hope you did not. That would constitute a binding contract; even for you."

"I'm not such a fool," Saph said with some return of spirit. "I told her five thousand shekels—she is worth that to me. I tell you, I love her, Hanno."

Hanno laughed. It was an enormous sum. "Well then! Let her find the money. What is the problem?—she never will."

"The problem," Saph said, not looking at him, "is that she has another lover. I am sure of it."

It was impossible to persuade him otherwise; unlikely as it seemed. Lilah was nothing if not ambitious; where would she seek a lover to equal Saph of Ashkelon?

He was confident that Saph was wrong, and that he could prove it. He left the palace before the evening and went to Ishba's house, where he learned that Delilah was up at Timnath, and began to pursue his own inquiries.

13

IT WAS TOWARD THE END of the eighth month, after the former rains, that a boy came up from Bethlehem to Etam with the tidings that the shepherd chief Omar had been taken by the Philistines, and lay in the prison house at Ashkelon awaiting execution. It seemed that Omar had spoiled a carvan in the narrowness of the vale of Elah, coming down from Jerusalem, and had run into a border patrol on his way home.

"Damn him," Samson said. "He is too old for such tricks."

It was years since he had seen Omar, but he made preparations to leave immediately, choosing five of his bachelors and dispatching a sixth to summon Baasha to meet them in the Ashkelon marketplace the following day at noon. When he turned, the boy was still there.

"Well? Is there more?"

There was not. But it appeared the boy wanted to come with them.

Samson looked at him: a Hebrew boy, and a good-looking one, who would quicken the village girls' loins one day with his fresh complexion and curly hair. He had a way of standing square on his short legs that reminded Samson very much of himself once. The lad could not have been more than six or seven years old, but he had come all the way from Bethlehem by himself through the wilderness. He was plainly in awe of the legendary Nazirite, but not shy. Samson asked his name, and he told him, David ben Jesse.

"David, is it? So why do you want to come with us, young David?"

"Sir, Omar is my friend." The boy's gaze was steady. "I can fight." He fumbled inside his girdle and produced a shepherd's sling. "With this. I brought down a bird on the wing, once. Omar taught me."

Some of the bachelors who had overheard began to laugh, but Samson's glance silenced them. He set his hand on the boy's shoulder and steered him a little distance apart. *Adonai send me friends like this!* "You would fight for Omar?"

"For Yahweh. The Philistines are our enemies."

Samson's grip tightened. "Tell me: have you brothers?"

The curly head nodded. "I am youngest of three."

"And from Judah," Samson said. "There is hope for Judah yet." And he suddenly grinned at the boy, and swung him high on his shoulders, clutching the Danite's hair for support but no wise dismayed, and took him to show the bachelors who had not seen him yet; because if there was hope for Judah there was hope for Israel.

He told the boy, "You shall fight the Philistines, you and your brethren; but not today."

David's face fell. "But when?"

"You will know when."

It was the sort of answer Uzziel would have given, making ignorance sound like wisdom; but it was the best Samson could think of, and the thought of the boy David put him in a good humor all the next day until he arrived at Ashkelon and learned from Baasha that Omar was already dead.

There was a team of jugglers performing in the square which had collected a crowd, and Baasha was beside them with the news before they saw him.

"Keep away from the prison house." The hunchback mouthed the words without turning his head, his eyes shifting nervously in all directions. "They are expecting you. A trap."

Despite their hooded and muffled cloaks he had had no difficulty in picking out Samson, and was clearly of the opinion that others could do the same. He hissed, "The street of scent sellers," and the next moment had insinuated his small figure between two of the onlookers and was gone. One of the bachelors took a step after him, and Samson pulled him back.

The man obeyed, but reluctantly. "I don't trust him."

"Neither do I," Samson said cheerfully. "Would you follow a spider into its web?"

"What shall we do?"

"Go and find a woman." Samson joined in the cheering as one of the jugglers kept six or seven flaming torches in the air at the same time, making a wheel of fire. "There's nothing but trouble here. When you leave, go one by one. Meanwhile, amuse yourselves–it's not often you have the chance. I will see you in Etam."

He left them, and made his way to the street of the scent sellers, taking a roundabout route through side streets. He found Baasha again at the door of a tavern, and followed him inside to an upper room overlooking the bazaar. Only after a servant had brought wine in a flagon, and a meal of bread and fish–Ashkelon was famous for its fish–and Baasha had barred the door behind him, did Samson throw off his cloak. Baasha embraced him with a show of relief.

"Shalom, Samson! We are safe for the moment"–he glanced apprehensively at the door–"but you should never have come here openly."

Divested of his kaftan, the psalmist was seen to have grown noticeably fatter of late, which gave the illusion that he was somewhat less hunchback. His hair was thinner, and there were signs of good living in the fleshiness about the bridge of his nose, the fullness of his jowls; like a prosperous merchant. There was little of the village waif about him now. Samson inquired, looking at him, about the *trap:* how the Philistines could have been expecting Samson, seeing that nobody knew he was coming except his own men. And Baasha himself of course.

Baasha blinked and looked offended, reminding Samson suddenly of Sheshai, though they were in no way like. The psalmist was saying that the Philistines knew Omar had been with Samson at the massacre at Lehi; and had long memories. "They expected you would come for him: that is why they fetched him here, when Ashdod would have been nearer. Did you not suspect?"

"I never suspect anyone, it seems," Samson said still looking at him, "until it is too late."

He turned back to the window again, thinking of it, wrinkling his nose at the strong scents which had reminded him once of Tamam for no reason, when he was newly come from the hills and knew nothing much of women. The street was crowded with color, the bazaar at its busiest at this hour. Ashkelon was the main trading center for the whole coast; it was in consequence the easiest of the five cities to get in and out of. He said slowly, "If they wanted to trap me . . . why then *not* Ashdod? It is a fortress; like Gaza . . ."

"You have said it. It would have been too obvious. And besides . . ."

"Aye, besides?"

"This is Hanno's town now–you haven't forgotten Hanno? He has his own cohort quartered at the palace, under his personal command. With nobody to countermand his orders."

Meaning Athol, Samson reasoned; and he marveled as he always marveled at Baasha's inside knowledge. There was a palanquin approaching along the street, borne by four Cushites and preceded by soldiers officiously clearing a passage: from the ornamented bronze of their feathered helmets and their distinctive yellow bordered cloaks, he guessed they were from the palace guard; perhaps even Hanno's men. It was a splendid palanquin besides, much gilded, and he peered to see if it contained the Lord Saph himself: but it was a woman. He said: "But why execute poor Omar before I arrived? I might have learned of it–as you did, Baasha–and turned back. Or did they think I would come hotfoot for revenge?"

"They didn't execute him. He was drowned."

It seemed that Hanno, not trusting the prison house and Saph's jailers, had sent Omar down with a guard of his own men ostensibly to work with the other prisoners on the breakwaters, but in fact to be as far back from the city gates as possible. The guards, less happy than Hanno with this arrangement, had paid more attention to the street down which Samson must come than to their prisoner, who was after all an old man. Omar had killed one of them with an oar, and made his escape in the small boat from which he had taken it; but he was no sailor, and the boat capsized even before it was properly clear of the harbor. Omar could not swim either.

The palanquin was set down almost immediately underneath the window, and the woman descended from it. Even from this angle, she appeared among the women shopping in the street as a lily among thorns. The black silk of her hair was braided with pearls over the slender column of her neck, collared with rubies blood-red above the shimmering blues of her robe, which changed hue with the light like rippling water when she moved, turning gracefully to address one of the soldiers. She was apparently displeased. Brows and lashes, already dramatically darkened with kohl, lowered in a darker frown that brought the man's head low in a humble bow; rose-tinted lips curled from small teeth as perfect as the pearls; a gesture of dismissal revealed a small palm delicately tinted with saffron that matched the yellow-gold of her fingernails. Samson watched her, as did those about her in the bazaar, the shopkeepers running forward and fawning—for she was clearly rich as well as beautiful—but his mind was on Omar, who in all his life had been afraid of nothing on two legs or four, but like all highlanders dreaded the sea.

It was not until Baasha, following his gaze, came beside him at the window that Samson saw more in the woman than her looks and elegance. He said, knowing Baasha would have the answer, "Who is she?"

Baasha looked out, careful not to show himself. "She is the favorite of the Lord Saph. Her name is Delilah."

Samson did not move at all, and after a moment Baasha looked sideways at his face. But whatever he saw there he kept to himself, and neither of them mentioned her again.

□

Despite the drought–some of the old men said because of it–the olives ripened early that year in profusion, and in Dan the harvest was ready before the flocks had been fetched in to winter under cover. With many of the young men still away in the mountain pastures they were shorthanded, and Samson stayed to help in Zorah. Canaanites were common as flies in Dan these days and the women no longer veiled themselves when they came, except the older ones, who might have saved themselves the trouble. Eleazar was long dead and Mordecai, who as first of the elders might be expected to take charge, held no sway when Manoah's son was in the village. Samson stayed five days.

It was raining when he came to Timnath again; not much, but because he walked slowly, not knowing what to expect, and took no shelter on the way, he was soaked through before he came to the house door. Keturah opened to him and stood with no word while he fumbled with his girdle, his fingers slippery with the knot, this being her way of exhibiting disapproval of her mistress's lover. She took the sodden cloak away, struggling under the weight of it dull-faced; but Delilah, seeing him in the entrance below floundering like a beached whale, burst into laughter. She wore the white shift she had worn the day he found her weaving, with the gold thread, her dark hair unbound, flying out as she came barefoot down the stairs two and three at a time crying, "I've missed you! I've missed you!" and nothing at all like the jeweled lily of Ashkelon. The wet of his tunic darkened her shift.

It was never any use trying to keep a secret from Delilah. She read his face as a shepherd reads the sky. She had Keturah fetch a small charcoal brazier to her chamber, and by the time Samson had stripped off, and dried himself sullenly, she knew that he had seen her in the bazaar at Ashkelon, and that he was jealous; this last before Samson properly knew it himself. He had never asked her what she did when she was not with him, or how she lived in the city, supposing she was still with Ishba. He pulled the drape from her bed and wrapped it about himself, though it was warm enough with the brazier. Keturah had fetched his cloak with it to dry over the little stool, and the steam rose from it like dew in the sun. He asked Delilah, "What is he like?" And she said, "Who?" knowing who, but making him say it: "This Saph." She said, "He is moody, like you. But younger and much more handsome, as well as being a great lord." And he said between his teeth, "What is he like *in bed?*"

Delilah's thin shoulders lifted in a small shrug. She herself was half-naked, clad only in a thin shift which she had pulled down to expose one breast, seated on the bed and toying with the bud like a child which has just discovered its own genitals. "Like all men," she said indifferently: "except one."

The fall of tresses masked her face. He said, staring at her, "And which one might that be?"

"The one a woman loves, of course. Don't you know *anything?*"

Samson's fingers, which could crack a slingstone, lifted the veil of her hair as delicately as a breeze, to uncover violet eyes uplifted to his own like a bride's: a look that fetched him astride her and cleared his mind wonderfully of questions. He bore down against the flat of her hands, her averted cheek.

"Not now."

"Why not?"

"I am in flowers."

He rolled over onto the floor and sat there, not even knowing whether to believe her. It was true that he knew nothing about women. Delilah sat up; a bare leg came down beside him, and he took it into his lap. She had beautiful feet, small-boned like the rest of her, and nowhere calloused–he turned the foot and she squealed–despite her habit of going without sandals. The toenails were still lacquered a yellow-gold that sparkled, on closer inspection, like a mist of tiny stars. He told her, "I did not know you in Ashkelon at first."

And he said, "I thought you were some Philistine princess!"

"I shall be princess, if I am married to Saph."

"Aye, if."

The foot was snatched away. She rushed from the room. He heard her calling for Keturah somewhere in the house, and then there was silence.

He was asleep when she returned, his nose buried in the

scented cushions of her bed. He had been dreaming of Delilah, who in the way of dreams was sometimes Tamam, groaning in his sleep, and it was the jingle of her anklets that woke him. He lifted his head between sleeping and waking and shook himself, seeing neither Delilah nor Tamam there, but the princess of Ashkelon.

He had seen her only from above, from the tavern window, the constellation of pearls in the midnight of her hair; now it was oiled and dressed back formally, blue-black as a raven's wing across the pale lobes of her ears, from which hung the fire of rubies clasped in silver pendants. The robe was a richer blue than he remembered, and rustled heavily in its layers as she moved; the silver chains about her ankles clinked, and were still. The same jeweled collar circled her throat, and above it her face, with its supernaturally enlarged eyes, was perfect and grave as the mask of a temple goddess.

"You think Saph will not have me because I am daughter to an ignorant Hebrew?"

This apparition was Manoah's daughter. His own half-sister. The shock deprived him of words.

She said, "I will be married to him if I choose."

"I will see him dead first," Samson said, finding his tongue at last. "And you with him."

"Then you will have two Tamams. And neither will warm your bed."

The blood rushed to Samson's face. "I'll not be warmed by another man's wife!" he flung back at her. "If that's what you're thinking!"

"Don't shout at me," she said, not at all offended. She leered at him. "You would kill me first?"

"Aye, by the living God!"

He was still shouting, though he had not stood up or changed his position, when she arrived on his knees, the fluid robe settling in a pool of blue about them, into which she plunged her hands in their familiar teasing until he trapped them, as he always did. She put up a fierce struggle, wriggling like a serpent in silken coils, not with any hope of breaking free, but to shame him into releasing her. He did not. She hissed, "You are *hurting* me."

"Keep still, then."

"You are cruel."

"Am I?" He considered it, regarding her fondly. "If you were the stronger, would you not defend yourself as I do?"

She flung her head up. "If only I were!–just for a moment. So I could do what I *liked* with you."

"What would you like to do with me?"

He was intrigued enough to lose hold of one of her wrists, but only one; wrenching away she was pulled up with a jerk, no better off. Her furiously ranging eye fell on his cloak there by the brazier where Keturah had left it, over a pool of water, and the girdle trailing beside it like a dead snake. "I would tie you up," she said maliciously, "for a start."

"Much good that would do you."

"We shall see."

But he had a better idea, and shortened the space between them, though less roughly. "Tie me up in your arms, then"–he fell back on the bed, pulling her on top of him, her arms flying out to save herself–"and bind me with your legs," his muffled voice went on encouragingly: "And you shall do as you please, I promise."

She retaliated by twining her two legs round one of his with all her strength in a futile attempt to hurt him, the blue silks riding about her thighs as they lay locked together; and she giggled.

"Bindweed," she said.

"A vine. A young and supple vine."

"And an old one. Gnarled and stiff and unyielding."

"But not past fruitfulness."

"I will *crush* your grapes with my heel."

"Rather sup their wine with your mouth."

"Let me," she begged; and he lifted his head to stare down at her, his chin on his chest, because she never asked leave of him for anything she did. And she said, "Let me tie you up."

She was in earnest; he saw that she had decided it was important to her. He saw too that there would be no joy of her until she had her way, and not so much let her go as eased his hold on her, and she slipped from him. He closed his eyes, shrugging off a misgiving, and from the rush of silks, the flurry of ankle chains, knew she sped across the room to fetch the girdle before he could change his mind.

"Promise me you won't resist."

He looked up into a child's eyes, dark with mischief, that might have been Tamam's; yet impossible to imagine Tamam in silks, with the dignity of pearls and rubies. But Delilah was barefoot under her finery, and held the girdle like a skipping rope, sliding it through her fingers with all the intentness of a child at play. *"Promise,"* the child said.

"What am I promised in return?"

"Oh." She frowned, making a loop in the girdle. "I will let you tie *me,* if you like." And she added wickedly, "If you can get free."

It struck him as a poor bargain and he said so, but he allowed himself to be pulled to his feet, bringing the bed-cloth with him to cover his nakedness, seeing that she was so much dressed herself. "What's to stop me tying you anytime I've a mind to?" He offered her his hands through the open front of the makeshift cloak to be bound. "Tell me that."

"What would Samson like me to promise?" She was suddenly behind him. She slipped the cloth from his shoulders and coaxed his bare arms behind his back. The cloth fell on the floor.

He turned his head. "Leave Saph alone."

He crossed his wrists and felt her finger them and then uncross them, as if uncertainly; and after a moment's hesitation place them back to back. The coarse prickle of the girdle rope slid across his skin. "You mind about Saph," she said. "Do you?"

"Aye. You are my sister and the daughter of my father; as much a child of Yahweh as myself. It's not fitting you should be the toy of an uncircumcised Philistine."

He had the satisfaction of knowing, from the way the rope was jerked spitefully tight, that he had scored.

"I am no man's plaything," she said evenly. "As you shall learn." She was binding the rope round his hands a second time, no whit slackening it. "Not Saph's"—a third time—"not Samson's." A fourth time, for good measure. He began to think she would never be satisfied.

"I saw him once," Samson remembered. "A moony youth, soft as a cow pat."

"A gentle man," she said indistinctly, low down. She seemed to be tightening a knot with her teeth. "And rich. You have seen what Saph gives me . . . A place at the palace, and robes of honor." She straightened with a jangle of ornaments. "Precious stones, and slaves for myself, and esteem in the city. What do you give me?"

"Myself."

"Ha!"

Now she was frapping the girdle end between his wrists, drawing it over and under and over again, as if she was at her loom, meshing the cross cords tauter with determined little tugs. It began to be painful, as much from the unnatural position of his arms, twisted inward, as from the bite of the cord itself.

A worse torture was her nearness, and not being able to see her face. Once or twice she pressed against him for leverage–or devilment, he could not tell which; the effect was the same, the silkiness of her garments no accidental reminder of his own nakedness; he was sure of it now. There is no shame in nakedness between lovers; but he did not feel like a lover, more like a prisoner taken in battle. For a prisoner to be stripped before he is bound is the ultimate disgrace: she must know it. Her scent was all over him. He began to be seriously afraid of making a fool of himself, willing her to hurry so that he could have her, bound or free, not much caring which; she was not in flowers. She stood beside him at last, still holding the unused length of the rope, but loosely. Her voice was small and sad.

"Do you love me, Samson of Dan?"

"I'd not be standing here like a stud bull else."

"Shall I be your heifer?"

The softness of her little breasts caressed him through their silks, tautening as she rose on tiptoe to slide an arm affectionately round his neck. His bound hands pressed between her thighs and he turned thankfully to kiss her, thinking she had finished, and she slipped the rope over his head and down between his shoulder blades–all her weight on it–before he knew his mistake.

"A bull should have a halter," she said.

The rope cut across his throat half choking him, and he was obliged to wrench his wrists as high as they would go to ease it. She had the rope through his wrists like a pulley and hoisted them tight, halfway up his back. His elbows stood out like jug handles.

Then she bound his thumbs together, and his little fingers.

"Do you truly love me?" She was panting a little.

"You want me to say no," he said. "So you can strangle me altogether. Where did you learn such tricks?"

"In the temple house, in Ashkelon. Did you not know your sister was a temple prostitute? Before Saph sent for me."

"I thought you lived with Ishba." He had no idea whether to believe her.

Delilah explained: "She wanted to make love to me all the time. I went to the temple priests to get away from her. Can you free yourself? Try."

Samson wriggled his fingers obligingly.

She said smugly, "It's no use trying to find the knots. I have put them all on the inside, out of reach. In the temple we learned *everything*. That is why I am such a good lover."

"Because you learned to tie knots."

"Because I learned how to please men."

"Is this how you please them?"

"It is one way. There are plenty of men who would pay me handsomely to do this to them."

"Aye," Samson said. "Well, don't expect *me* to pay you."

She laughed. "Oh, you will pay! When I've finished with you."

But she had used up all the girdle, and there was nothing to tie his legs with. She surveyed his patient, trussed back with a moment's irritation, as if it was his fault, and plucked at the taut halter like an evil lyrestring until he was moved to protest.

"Are you trying to torture me?"

"I will torture you if I like."

But she stopped. In any case, it had little effect; he had somehow made rigid the great muscles of his neck, and the rope made no impression at all. She thrust her hands through the urn handles instead and Samson, discerning her intention, moved hastily away: an evasion she thwarted by clinging fast and letting herself be carried with him. When her searching hands found his child more than half grown to manhood he stopped with a groan, and she said triumphantly in his ear, "You see! You are no different from those other men."

She would not let go, and he dared not move. He said between his teeth, "I am flesh and blood like other men, if that's what you mean."

"But they say Samson is a god. Or at least an ifrit."

"Samson is flattered, then. The Canaanitish gods are mighty in copulation from what I've heard; and ifrits are famous for it. Let us see if Samson can live up to his reputation."

"You should not tease a simple girl. I think it is true you are a god." Delilah seemed to tire of her game. She moved away from him and straightened her robe, and her ornaments. "No man could have done the things you have done." She stood before him, almost tall in her new and serious dignity: the princess of Ashkelon rebuking a humble soldier.

"I should kneel before you," she said: "if you are a god. But I think you shall kneel to me instead."

"Watch you don't go too far," he warned her.

"Kneel."

"Why do you want to humble me? Am I not humble enough already?"

"You don't know what humble *means!*" she cried. She pointed to the floor. "Kneel."

He shook his head, not thinking she could make him this time; but she did, drawing him down to his knees by that part of him which was most vulnerable and his greatest weakness; he having no hands to prevent her.

After that she was worse than the black girl Tahara, because more spiteful, teasing him without mercy, first beside the bed and then on it, sitting on his pinioned arms, loosening his hair to spread it and exploring the scar on his face, and every part of him, goading him to free himself if he could. The tickling was the worst part; he had to grind his teeth to endure it. It was many hours before she allowed him release from his agony, and then none from his bonds.

They both slept as they lay. Samson, waking first with a pressing need to urinate, opened his mouth to speak her name and thought better of it. He eased himself sideways from under her, he thought without waking her, and staggered to his feet, glancing back to see if she stirred. He shook himself awake, and bending forward snapped the rope about his neck with a grunt. There was still no movement from the bed. He burst his wrists and fingers apart gratefully, flexing his numbed hands, and finding his cloak carried it–since he no longer had a girdle–slung over his shoulder to the doorway.

Her voice said, "You tricked me all along. I knew you had. What is the secret of your strength?"

"No secret." He went back and kissed her amiably. "You were very clever but the rope was old. Anyone could have snapped it. If it had been new I'd never have got loose."

He made his way quietly out of the house, not to disturb the servants, and back to Zorah, pausing only to relieve his aching bladder.

□

The old priest-hermit died that night.

He departed as he had arrived, alone and without fuss, for he died in his sleep with none beside him. The resulting lamentation in Zorah would have surprised him, for he had long outlived his allotted span–and he would have said his usefulness–and had never taken much interest in the village. Yet not even Manoah's death had called forth such a noise of public grief.

A chieftain may be replaced; but Uzziel's presence, remote as he kept himself, lent status to Zorah; and who would send another Levite priest to a humble village?

Warning of a Philistine force gathering in the vale gave Samson a reason for absenting himself. His instinct was to return to Timnath, but reason told him that was where the Philistines would gather, as they had before, and making a sensible decision for once he withdrew instead into the hills.

The first crocuses were already appearing in the uplands, and the hyacinth, encouraged by the former rains. Presently the tulips would follow, the pink and purple cyclamen, iris and the scarlet anemone. It was the season for neither ploughing nor reaping, but the in-between of mending equipment and thinking about the planting of new trees, when men had time on their hands.

It was no doubt that thought which prompted yet another message from the prophet Samuel, this time calling for representatives of the tribes to make their way to him at Mizpeh–*as many as may be spared*–for an unheard-of festival of repentance and atonement. Samson dismissed the messenger with the reply that he would hinder no man of his from going, who wished to go.

Even to his own ears it was no answer. Unless he went with them none of them would go; not even if he ordered them.

"Speak to them, Adonai. I know you are angry. Take them from me–as many as you like."

And he said uneasily, sitting on the hilltop above the cave and watching the stars come out like unblinking eyes: "You know if I go up they will all follow me. And if Dan is seen to go up to Mizpeh, might not Judah and Ephraim follow our lead? Well, I don't say they will; but they might. Then little Samuel will have his multitude. And isn't that just what the Philistines want?–an excuse to destroy the last chance of an army in Israel. So long as we remain scattered they can never overcome us. Nobody can mop up raindrops, except they are gathered in one place. The hills are ours–we've always come back to the hills. Let them keep their seacoast and turbulent waters that drowned Omar, their trading and merchandise, their fleshpots and pestilence!"

It was a fine speech: but the many eyes of heaven which could surely have twinkled approval, were unblinking, and he ripped off his headband and threw it down between his feet in disgust. "How can I go before them to the holy man, *knowing Delilah is my sister?*"

The answer was plain as if Adonai had spoken aloud.

□

It was the second time he had forsworn Delilah, and it would be the last. Once the decision was made he had an overpowering sense of lightness and clarity, like a man who has lost his way in the night, and the sun comes up and shows him where he is, and everything familiar and safe. But it was still dark on the hilltop, and he stumbled twice and a third time fell headlong in his haste to tell someone. It was too much to keep to himself. There was only one person in the world he could tell, and that was Uzziel, and he was more than halfway to Zorah before he remembered that Uzziel was dead; and by then it was too late to think of somewhere else to go.

He was afraid they would have taken down the hermit's tent; but it was still there above the olive grove as it had been for as long as he could remember, the black square against the lightening east. He drew aside the tent flap–it was closed, though Uzziel never closed it–and ducked as he always had to, half expecting to hear the dry, brittle whisper of his name in greeting; but the voice when it came was both deeper and less sure.

"Samson?"

His ear caught the muffled clink and rasp of metal and he vacated the square of the doorway in the same moment, entering the tent with the deadly comic, sideways dance of a mongoose, still facing the sound. The flap fell back, sealing the darkness in. There was a faint body-odor, teasingly familiar, but he could not place it: not Uzziel's. The parchment smell was gone, and he guessed they had scoured the place clean the first chance they had. He said aloud, but softly, "A dagger won't help you." He began to circle the tent wall. There was no sound but a small wind against the tentskins, and the cicadas outside. "Or is it a sword?"

"A dagger. I wasn't sure if it was you."

Again the metallic clink.

"I've put it away now."

"How many of you are there?"

"Ah. . . Let us say, two. The friend of Samson, and the servant of Gaza."

"Which speaks?"

"Both. Don't you know my voice?"

It was Sheshai, and the knowledge did nothing to reassure him. He followed the tent wall round until he was satisfied that they were alone. The Amorite's voice had come from a low level, close to the earth floor, and from the slight rustling he made–turning cautiously no doubt to make out where Samson was–it sounded as if he had made himself comfortable with a blanket or cloak; as if he had been there for some time. There was nothing else in the tent. Samson said, "What are you doing here?" and heard Sheshai sit up with the remark that hill people did not always take so kindly to strangers as they used to at Amalek's house.

There was no mistaking those slyly mocking tones.

"When I found this tent miraculously deserted, and not overlooked, I judged it prudent to wait here rather than chance your Hebrew hospitality."

"You were waiting for me."

"Yes."

"In the dark."

"They didn't think to leave a lamp. Besides, I told you: I didn't want your wild villagers to know I was here."

"With a dagger."

Sheshai's sigh acknowledged the joke.

"With a message from the Lord Athol. I always carry a dagger. You know that. Would you have me at the mercy of the first ruffian to take a fancy to my shirt?"

"You came here alone?"

"To the village, yes," Sheshai's voice said.

And then he said, "There are two score of Athol's best men waiting in the valley."

Samson had forgotten the report of Philistines in Sorek. The count had been a score and ten, not two score; but there had been no mention of the Amorite among them. A thought came to him.

"How did you know I would be here?"

"I have a friend in Zorah. Besides yourself, that is!"

Sheshai was facing the invisible entrance to the tent, and there was just room to move behind him, between his back and the tent wall without touching either. Samson took his head almost affectionately in the crook if his arm.

"You are lying. No one knew I was coming here. I didn't know myself an hour ago."

After the first, violent reaction, Sheshai was rigidly still.

He said between his teeth, "He said you would come to pay your respects to your holy man . . . when the wake and the wailing was done. Have a care, Samson—*you are choking me.*"

The body-odor was stronger now.

"Give me a reason why I should not," Samson said brutally in his ear. "I could break your back for the day you left me for dead in Gath. I could lift your head off your shoulders for the trick you played me in Timnath . . . it was the wine trading and the vineyards you were after, wasn't it: not Niobe." (Sheshai had on a hairy shepherd's cloak, which meant he had come privily, and it must be a blanket he sat on, though no longer comfortably. His backbone was arched over Samson's knee within a half-span of snapping). "Or I might do it for Esther's sake, whom you betrayed and ran back to when your other game was spoiled . . . aye, and put the blame for that on me!" (The dagger was sheathed in Sheshai's waistband, though Sheshai had the sense to keep his fingers well clear of it. Samson relieved him of the weapon all the same with his free hand, and threw it away in the darkness. It rattled on the floor.) "Or for Amalek," Samson went on, recalling it: "who for all his meanness was good to me. Did you murder him? Esther never suspected, did she?"

"Kill me then," Sheshai said in a strangled voice. "And you are a dead man. You are in greater danger than you know."

"Because of your Philistines waiting in the valley? I could tell you every time one of them goes to a tree to piss. I have but to give the signal and none of them leaves Sorek alive."

"No, *no!*" Sheshai writhed with helpless frustration. "Athol sent them for your *protection!*—to escort you safe down to Gaza. If you fell into the hands of Ashdod or Ashkelon, not even Athol could answer for your safety. The men will come no closer unless you come out freely to them. With me. Alone, the two of us."

This was likely true. Not even Hanno would attempt to take Samson out of Zorah with thirty men, after what happened at Lehi. Samson hesitated. "Why should I accompany you to Gaza?"

"To redeem the pledge you made to Athol in Gath. In exchange for the life of your mad prophet. You said—"

"I know what I said. It was before they burned my wife."

Sheshai said in desperation, struggling to keep his voice from rising, *"Listen to me.* Athol has given his word: he will show you to his people—not as a prisoner, as an honored ally. He will give you a robe of honor, and have you proclaimed governor of Dan. Under his protection naturally."

"Naturally," Samson echoed. "Why would he do that, after what I have done to him?"

"To save your people. And his. To make an end to the spilling of blood."

Samson was silent, a massive block of darkness, and Sheshai, stretching his neck to get his breath, cried out: "Do you hear what I'm saying?"

"I hear you," Samson said. "It sounds more like Sheshai the schemer than the Philistine Lord of Battles."

"That's because you don't know him! Athol is not one of your petty clan chieftains!—he fights to end war, not for revenge or spoils. He admires you, your strength. He spared your life in Gath when you slew his driver. You publicly humiliated him in Gaza itself . . . it took five yoke of oxen to return the gates to the city . . . he was not even angry. He wants to see Canaan one land, undivided. But the war drags on, your prophet is at his rabble-rousing again and it cannot be allowed to continue. One way or another it must end, or Athol himself could be overthrown by Hanno's wolves. Then your people would be annihilated."

Samson considered this.

"So he needs Samson to prop up his throne: an ally, since he can't catch me any other way. So says the friend of Athol. What says the friend of Samson?"

"I told you: you are in danger of your life."

"It seems to me the only danger is in listening to you. I'm safe enough where I am."

"You are not. The Philistines have laid a trap for you. Here in the vale; and you are walking into it. You are betrayed and not by me; by another."

Samson began to laugh. "You mean the hunchback, Baasha."

"I mean Delilah," Sheshai said. "She is in league with them."

For a moment Samson was glad of the dark. Not that he believed Sheshai, who was more full of tricks than a troop of jugglers; but the shock of hearing her name, so soon after he had resolved never to see her again, flooded him with an unwelcome tenderness so demoralizing he almost let Sheshai go. He had forgotten the Amorite knew her. He had still been at Jason's house when they burned it; he must have encountered Delilah often with Jason's kinfolk afterwards, if her story was true. If Delilah had truly been a prostitute in the temple house, as she insisted she had, it was more than likely Sheshai had known her there too.

He did let him go then.

Sheshai moved away, straightening painfully. From the sound, he spat; making a necessity of the insult. When he spoke his voice was blank with malice. "Why else would they set her up in the fine stone house at Timnath?–a servant's chit, a half-caste with nothing to her name but a way with men and a pretty face to go with it. Whoever heard of such a thing in all Canaan? A young and beddable woman alone, with her vineyards and household and no husband? As subtle as a bitch in heat."

Adonai, let me kill him. Now, before he says anything else.

"You are a legend on the coast," Sheshai said. He had recovered some of his composure, drawing aside the tent flap and looking out coolly, his lean shape silhouetted against the raying east. "They think you walk on the mountains up here with your head in the clouds, conversing with your terrible god. They frighten their children saying *Samson will come for you* if they misbehave. But to me you have always been a fool, never knowing who your friends are. You could have been overseer in Amalek's household; even son-in-law, if you'd learned to mend your ways. . . .

He turned back and said, "I didn't kill him. But Esther was persuaded of it. I have left her; she grew mistrustful and shrewish, I couldn't stand that, not for all the treasures in Amalek's stores. You could have had Jason's vineyards yourself for the asking, if you'd not been so stiffnecked. Now

I offer you the governorship of Dan, maybe a seat in the Council of the League, even: the one chance to save your people from extinction."

Samson did not answer, and Sheshai said, preparing to leave and holding the flap open for light while he located his dagger, "What shall I tell them in Gaza?"

"Tell them what you like. But tell Hanno that if he and his friends try to use Delilah as Athol uses you, I may not be so gentle the next time I meet him."

"Use her?"

If Sheshai's surprise was feigned, it was well done.

"You don't know her, if you think that. She uses *them.* She went to them herself. . . . Shall I tell you something of this sweet maid of yours? Shall I tell you of the two men who are dead because of her?–one a good friend of mine. A third ruined, a man of noble family? All women are dangerous and pretty ones are the worst; but Delilah is like no other. When she was still a child–"

He broke off choking in the stuff of his own cloak, gathered violently in one of Samson's huge fists and thrust upward with such force that he was propelled out of the tent, his feet clear of the ground. His arms flailed in panic. Samson said, "You are afraid she will get the reward instead of you–is that it?" and threw him sprawling, and walked into the tent again. After a moment he returned with the blanket, a fringed green affair of soft wool such as rich men have on their asses, which he hurled into Sheshai's face as he struggled to his feet.

"You are one friend I can do without."

Sheshai's face twisted in fury and alarm. He looked thinner, more ravaged, but still handsome. He gathered the blanket up with what dignity he could and set off up the hill, where the path overran the crest before it began its descent to the valley. Nevertheless he had the last word, as he always did, turning his sharp profile for one malevolent glance over his shoulder.

"Ask her who killed Niobe."

And then he was gone. Samson never saw him again.

□

On the day the Philistine council of war met in Ashkelon there was a spectacular thunderstorm, the worst that the younger ones at least–Saph and Achish–could ever remember: the unnatural dark of noon intermittently white with rain, the gods battling in the sky with an almighty collision of chariots that shook the foundations of the city. Nine ships went down that day, and fires were started in three places within the city walls. Since the god of the Hebrews was a mountain god, much associated with the elements, it was the worst possible omen.

Achish was newly Ser of Gath, since his father Maoch perished of the plague; this was his first council, and he was doubly nervous by reason of the secret knowledge he hugged to himself like the mother of a suckling. Gath was known for the stature of its men–the famous breeding ground of giants–and Achish was already as high and broad as his father had been, and like Maoch would run to fat. His size made him feel conspicuous, and he sat low in his chair for fear that he would be called upon to speak, knowing his stammer would betray him. But how he would surprise them all!–with their brisk military talk of cohorts and columns, of flying chariot reserves and the disposition of footsoldiers, of weaponry and supplies, and the calculated *expenditure* of men; when the only expenditure necessary, had they but known it, was in silver shekels. The essential part of Achish's plan however was its secrecy, and he had given his oath on it in the name of Dagon himself.

The aged Raphah, with his snowy hair and choleric explosions of criticism, had at first seemed to dominate the council. His theme, delivered in a rising diatribe of repetition, insistent as the recurring drumbeat at a wake, was–mistakes. It was a mistake to believe that because the Canaanites, Amorites and the rest had settled down peacefully under Philistine law, recognizing the benefits of a strong and stable society, the Hebrews would do the same–which ignored their arrogant claim to all the land down to the very coast, which their fanatics believed their god had given them by divine right! A mistake to show mercy as it had been shown at Ebenezer, and again at Shiloh, when the Philistine cohorts were held back like hunting dogs on the leash, instead of being loosed on the miserable survivors, to track them down in the hills and eat up every last one; this in the mistaken belief that clemency wins friends. The result was known from many spies: the Habiru tribes, having learned nothing, were gathering yet again on their northeast frontier, increasing in numbers daily and breathing the wild oaths of a holy war. A mistake above all to hold back now, when every day made a Philistine victory more costly and less certain. Raphah's shaking fist crashed down on the arm of his stool, startling them all. There could be only one rule in Canaan.

But it was Athol, coolly dismissing these truths as self-evident and proceeding with a calm reappraisal of the threat in terms of logistics, who took control of the meeting. He had used his office as Lord of Battles to break precedent, and had come dressed in a simple soldier's tunic which made their yellow finery look frivolous. They had all heard the outline of his plans for the northern campaign and–he glanced about him with a confidence not even Raphah could broach –approved them. He himself had no doubt but that they would secure victory, and at the least cost: a highly trained army against a rabble of ill-armed highlanders. Provided their own flanks were secure. Provided, that was, Judah and the south remained in alliance, or at least resisted the call to arms that was even now being spread through their villages by the spies of the Hebrew fanatic Samuel.

"At whatever cost, we must keep the Hebrews in the south apart from those in the north. Before we take the field–and I warn again those who would urge haste and recklessness–we must establish a wall between them which none may cross. And that wall is the middle tribe of Dan. Dan is little; but it is the breakwater that keeps seas apart."

But it wasn't Athol after all any more than Raphah who dominated the council, Achish realized: it was the one man on everyone's mind who was not here at all–the Hebrew Samson of Dan So long as Samson controlled the Shephelah, who came and went over the wall of Dan would be decided by him, not Athol. Any Philistine march north must have the Shephelah on its flank, and every man looking over his shoulder. Even Raphah, from his sullen silence, knew this. Achish could not repress a snigger, instantly turned to a cough behind his hand.

A thunderclap was a welcome distraction; but Athol did not miss the smaller sound. When the council dispersed at last, inconclusively as usual with plans and promises, he invited Achish to join him on the terrace. Achish found him leaning over against the balustrade, the rain lightly lashing his face and darkening the light of his hair, which he seemed to enjoy. He did not turn.

"You do not fear the storm, young Gath?"

"Ev—every man f—fears the gods, Lord Athol."

"Your father did not overmuch. He used to say he didn't like getting wet. That was when the hair had gone from the top of his head. You like to walk in the rain?"

Achish shook his head in puzzlement. He had no idea why he had been summoned.

"Yet you went into the street to meet the woman," Athol said; "and spoke with her at length before withdrawing under the archway. It must have been important. What did she have to say to you, that filled your head all through the council meeting?"

Achish was dumbstruck. He stared at the tall prince as if he was a magician. He had been positive no one had seen him. He had left the palace by a side door when the message came, wrapped in a cloak borrowed from one of the servants, a cook. Nothing could have given him away—unless it was his cursed size! He stammered, "I—I am—sw—sworn to secrecy. . . ."

Athol's wet face eased into a smile of rare charm. "Then I will tell you, for she was recognized as well as you. She is intimate with the Hebrew Samson, who is infatuated with her. She promised she would have him delivered to you bound hand and foot, never mind how, in exchange for your oath of secrecy, and your personal bond of—how much was it?"

"Eleven hundred shekels," Achish burst out; and bit his knuckle. "How c—could you *know?*"

"Because she made the same promise to me," Athol told him. "And likely to some of the others. *All* of them, before she's finished, if I'm not mistaken. This is becoming interesting! A most ingenious woman."

Achish was still at a loss. "But why sh–should she do this?

"What a simple fellow you are, Achish: you will make a good soldier, but never a general. This way she stands to collect the reward, not once, but five times over. But keep it to yourself, or you will make fools of us all."

When the young prince had gone disconsolately off, Athol stood alone, watching the lightning play over the roofs and the far hills.

"Oh Delilah!" he said aloud: "Delilah. Now I know why I prefer the company of my young lads."

14

IN THE UNCERTAIN CALM that always followed his tempestuous fits of anger, when Adonai seemed close, and generally disapproving, it occurred to Samson that Sheshai did not invent. Like all accomplished liars he distorted and embellished, but he did not invent.

Samson had no reason to think Delilah herself had ever lied to him. On the other hand, not much reason to suppose she had told all the truth either. Delilah's truths, like her weaving, followed a pattern discernible only to herself. She was undeniably by nature more Philistine than Hebrew—half Hebrew at that. She had grown up on the coast as sister, or companion, or it might be handmaid or even slave to a Philistine, promoting herself through Philistine temple whorehouse to Philistine palace with who knew what devilment in between. It would be an act of more than mortal faith to believe her ties with the Philistines altogether severed for Samson's sake. What Sheshai had meant by *in league* with them, only Delilah could say. *Ask her,* Sheshai had told Samson.

Ask her who killed Niobe.

Which is what Samson did.

□

The rope was of the thickness of her little finger, of a fine quality, white as milk, neatly coiled as it had come new from the rope maker. She cut it with a sharp knife into two equal lengths, so that when she had done with the binding of his hands and elbows, his arms and his chest, there was still as much again left for his legs.

"There was this piece of fiery wood," she said, "if you really want to know: which fell from the roof on Rhoda, and she began to burn."

Samson winced. He sat on her bed wearing only a light tunic and her tight net of ropes, his bare legs over the edge in her lap as she knelt, busy with his feet and ankles. Delilah in contrast was naked; this being a condition he had imposed, having made the happy discovery that he could make conditions himself, and he looked down on her admiringly and thought how lucky he was after all. He had asked her, "Why must you tie me up again?" and she had answered reasonably, "Because you broke free before, of course"; and he said, "First lay aside your garments." She had made a face, but she had done as he bid her.

He had forgotten who Rhoda was. Delilah said without lifting her head, "My beloved doll; you remember. I had left her propped against the wall. I was always mislaying her. When I saw her there all melting I snatched her up and ran into the house to find someone to help me. Lift up your knees. . . . There was only Niobe upstairs on her bridal bed. I knew she was dead, I had seen dead people before. But her eyes were open and it frightened me. I thought I saw her move. I dropped the doll and ran away, and I heard someone say afterward it was what started the fire in that part of the house."

"Was it Sheshai said that?"

"It may have been." She was lacing the cord up to his thighs, marking with impish delight the rise under his tunic. "I saw Sheshai several times afterward, in Gaza. He never liked me; I think I was the only woman who ever refused him. Now help me."

She managed, with what help he could afford her, to get his latticed legs onto the bed, and rolled him onto his belly. "Did Sheshai say I had killed Niobe?"

Samson lifted his head from the cushions and turned his

face to breathe more freely. He felt her weight on the bed beside him. "Aye. Not in so many words. And he forgot to say it was an accident. Must you make it so tight?"

"Yes." She knelt back, drawing the cord with her. "What else did Sheshai tell you?"

"That you had betrayed me to the Philistines."

He felt her stillness. Then she said calmly, "Do you believe him?"

"Would I let you tie me hand and foot if I believed him?"

"You might think you could get free, like before."

But this time it did not seem possible. From the soles of his feet to his neck he lay enmeshed in the white cord, drawn as tight as she could make it: so tight indeed it was almost buried in the furrows it ploughed in his tunic, while the brown flesh of his bare arms and legs swelled between the ligatures, his elbows almost meeting behind him in a cruel white weave. Last of all she threaded the remaining leg rope up under his trussed wrists, over the trussing and down again, leaning back on her heels to winch his pinioned arms down to their full stretch, so that even the limited leverage of his forearms, which might have enabled him to roll over, was taken away. "We used to call this the Grapevine, in the temple house."

"I'll remember," Samson said. "Have you ever had it done to you?"

"Only by the other girls. We learned by practicing. I know what you are thinking!"

"So why do you need to practice on me?"

"New rope," she said, ignoring the question. "I went to a lot of trouble to get this cord. It is the strongest they make, and very expensive!" She was testing the last knot, behind the lashings at his knees. "The man said it was what the fishermen use to draw in their nets when they are full."

"Did you tell him what you wanted it for?"

Delilah laughed softly. "There! I've finished. There is something I must do. See if you can free yourself."

She left him there, and the sound of her went out of the chamber. A lock of hair had escaped from his headband, and apart from rubbing his face back and forth to get it out of his eyes, Samson made no attempt to move. From where he lay he could see the pattern on her loom, and her little stool; the corner of the room by the window shutters, and little commonplace and intimate things that were hers. The thought of how close he had come to losing her brought the sweat out on his brow; yet he knew he should not have come back. He shut his eyes, giving himself up to the punishment of cords that were beginning to burn like brands into his flesh, the growing ache and numbness of constricted limbs—willingly, if it would expiate yet another broken vow.

He knew it would do no such thing.

The bonds themselves betrayed him: as much precious as irksome because fastened on him by her own small hands, a fierce and enduring embrace to remind him of her possessiveness. Nevertheless he began to be uneasy at her absence. He had guessed her gone to relieve herself, but with the crawling passage of time became convinced that she was planning some new devilment with which to afflict him. What new tricks had she brought from the temple house?

He had still not moved when she returned. He heard the light tread of her foot and lifted his head; but she stood at the foot of the bed where he could not see her.

"You do not look like a god," she said. "Unless it be a fallen god, like the poor Dagon who lies impotently across the temple door at Ashdod. Neither an ifrit. An ifrit would have slipped out of those bonds in the twinkling of an eye."

"I told you there was no magic."

"Do you love me?"

He groaned. "Yes. Aye."

"How much do you love me?"

"Free me and I will show you."

"Tell me first. Then I will free you."

"Come where I can see you, then."

"I am here. Turn over and you will see me well enough."

"Why mock me? You know I cannot; isn't it enough?"

"Ah . . ." her voice dropped tenderly. She moved beside him, but perversely on the opposite side to that he faced. "Is this the same Samson who tore the great gates from the walls of Gaza, and carried them off like sheep hurdles?" Her smooth arms slid about his neck. and when he would have turned his head, locked her fingers lovingly in the tresses of his hair to prevent it. "How does it feel to be weak, and like another man?" He had no answer, and she drew his head back on her breast. "Delilah's lamb."

She was trembling, and ran her fingers down his bound arms and wrists with a suppressed excitement that communicated itself to him so that he could not be still under her hands, but jerked and wrestled for a means to come to her; until she pressed up under his shoulder to lift it, and the efforts of both had him over on his back; she threw herself on him, moaning and whimpering, her mouth pressed to his, her fingers scrabbling to separate the ropes across his thighs, dragging his tunic up to impale herself frantically on him with the desperation of a soldier falling on his sword. He spoke her name once, and was silenced by the gag of her tongue, and the lock of her two arms about his neck. Her hair swept his face, burying him in the dark fragrance and the musk of her body, every part, so that he had the illusion in the final atonement that they were truly as one; that the same bonds held them both inseparably.

Yet she moved as he could not, pressing herself upright with her arms astride his head, content as a suckled child, and slid aside to lie and nestle beside him. It was only then, by the rustling she made, that he realized she wore a light silken shift. She must have put it on when she left him.

"You cheated."

Delilah glanced down at herself and laughed. "You've just noticed! In this game there are no rules; so how could I cheat? You have not told me how much you love me."

"Do you not know *now,* woman?"

"I know. But a woman likes to be told. Especially now."

He could press his lips to her hair at least. "What do you want me to say? Yes I love you. I loved you before I knew what love was. I have never loved another woman."

She turned on one elbow, accusingly. "What about *her?*"

"There were never two of you." He knew it now. "Tamam gave you life and my love in the same breath–it was hers, not mine to give. I lived without it until I found you again."

"I'll not share you."

She said it so softly he scarcely heard. When he looked at her, it was as if she slept, a little satisfied smile playing about her lips. Alarmed that she really was going to sleep, he lifted his head to remind her of her promise. "You said you would untie me if I told you."

"Yes." Delilah did not open her eyes, though the smile deepened. "But I never said *when*. . . . Can you truly not get free?"

"You know the answer," he said. "But you want me to say it, like before."

"Yes. I think you are beginning to understand women."

"I'll never understand *you*. But I will say it: unless you let me go, I cannot escape."

"Have you tried?"

"Aye. I have."

From the beginning he had tried: from the day he quit Zorah and his youth, to look for a new life among the shepherds, then the Canaanites, even with the woman of Timnath, to be free of her forever; only to find her again in the upturned face of a child in a man's cloak. Again, after the birdsong warned him of the Philistine's approach through the vineyard (was it at her behest? He had never asked her); and then when he discovered that she was Manoah's daughter; yet again when he saw her in the street of Ashkelon and did not know her, the strange princess of the Philistines, favorite of Saph himself; and last when Samuel's message called him to himself, and Adonai spoke to him on the hilltop at Etam. Was there ever a man tried so hard to escape his own destiny?

"Come, I will let you go," Delilah said, with a sudden and unexpected softening. She felt for the knot behind his knees, embracing his thighs. "If you will only promise me one thing."

He said, "Aye; anything," and closed his eyes.

And she said, "Take me to wife"; and he opened his eyes again.

"If you wish it. What difference would it make? Are we not married enough? I come to you whenever I can; you know that."

"I don't mean a *sadika* marriage when the wife is visited

in her father's house only–like Niobe," Delilah said fiercely. "I mean a real marriage. I want us to live together. Always."

He bit her shoulder, and she sprang back with a cry. He said amiably, "Where? In the caves in the mountains?–you'd not care for that, Princess. In Zorah? Brother and sister? They would stone us to death."

"I hate you," she said. "Why can *you* not come live with *me?"*

He looked at her, and she said sulkily, "I know. You must be among your own people. *Damn* your people!"

She had the knife in her hand from nowhere. "I could slit your throat, and you couldn't stop me. I could cut off your eggs and your manhood."

And she said, "I could just *leave* you here to die of hunger and thirst. I could shut up the house and take the servants with me–no one would find you."

She left him with such a flurry of purpose that he strained to raise his head, in time to see her pass between the curtains of the door; she spoke to someone there–it must be Keturah–*"Go call the soldiers and tell them I have something for them."*

Samson was upright, a heaving web of ropes beside the bed.

"Vixen!"

It was like the day in the cavemouth, when the slingshot took him full in the head. The idea that Keturah had been within earshot all the time stunned his senses: it was a moment before it came to him that those Delilah called for *could be within the house itself.* He shook himself dazedly. "Help me, Adonai." From their long constriction his limbs were bloodless; he could scarcely stand.

"Help me!"

A terrible, impotent fury pounded in his head, clouding his vision, and exploded through him with a volcanic eruption that burst the ropes snapping like threads, shaken off like so many cobwebs trailing in his rush for the doorway.

Delilah was alone. Samson crashed to a halt, flinging her aside–she clung frantically to the curtain drapes–to scan the passage that ran to left and right; the empty stairs; and absurdly, the curtains themselves. There was no Keturah; nowhere that anybody could have gone in the time.

"You tricked me!"

Delilah disentangled herself from the curtains and rose nimbly, smoothing her shift with injured satisfaction.

"I told you: no rules."

But she had gone too far, and he carried her under his arm back into the bedchamber, gathering sufficient scraps of rope on the way to fasten her to the bed, face down, too angry to notice her frantic struggles, and beat her like the slave Tamam had been, who taunted the boy Samson with her *You would like to beat me yourself,* and he had never understood it until now. Delilah threshed about like a beached fish, cursing him for the peasant he was, then sobbing and pleading with a desperation more than the beating merited, which puzzled him until she abruptly and helplessly climaxed, and he fell over on his backside with laughing.

Afterward she lay curled beside him, remote and enigmatic, sliding a tress of her dark hair through pale fingers and watching him over it. He could feel her brooding resentment like an evil spell, an almost tangible malice. Outside the window the rain began to fall again. It was not the beating she resented; it was the fact that he had lied to her. He had freed himself.

□

There was a change in Zorah, something in the air he could not name. Mordecai, who had never shown Samson anything but ill-will, greeted him almost fawningly with *Shalom, son of Manoah!—upon whom be prayer and peace!* Those of the bachelors about the village, and such as he called his friends, seemed not to see him, moving away restless as kine before a storm. Even Jemuel, crossing the well path with his children trotting at his knee, who could have been expected to leave them, to run and greet him with a kiss, saluted him at a distance and went his way. Only Abigail the sister, a woman now, but still unmarried, ran and kissed his palm warmly; and she too ran off as if overcome by what she had done before he could remember who she was.

There were other changes too, when he wrenched his

thoughts away from Timnath long enough to take them in: houses that stood unaccountably empty; an absence of familiar faces; and curious glances from faces unfamiliar to him, several unmistakably Canaanite. One or two he could have sworn–*did* swear, volubly–Philistine.

"You sound just like your father," Sharah told him, pleased.

And that was it. It was as if Manoah had finally departed from the village.

"What does it mean?" he asked Sharah. "Where have they gone?"

Sharah looked tired–the smallest tasks tired her these days–but not unhappy. She laid a frail hand reassuringly on his arm. "North, to the new Dan. Do not be troubled for them, son. It was only the old ones . . . They took their families to find their kinsfolk. They were too old to face the coming changes."

Then she said, crinkling her old eyes softly, "But I want you to know that I am glad. Only I am glad, too, that Manoah is not here to see it."

"See what?" Samson said. "What changes?"

And she said, surprised, "Why, when you bring the Philistines to live among us, and make an end to war."

Sharah did not see his face. She held his one arm in the two of hers, and laid her wrinkled face along it blissfully. "Then I shall have my son back here, for good."

The only time Sharah would have her son back in Zorah for good would be when he was buried alongside Manoah; but Samson had not the stomach to tell her. Instead he went in search of the source of the rumor.

It was Baasha; he knew even before they told him. Baasha, Sheshai's friend in Zorah, who knew of the Amorite's errand, and the offer of a Philistine puppet lordship, and had come psalming his news through the villages without stopping to be sure it was accepted. Baasha was nowhere to be found; but there was no lack of those to repeat his words. There were those among his bachelors who thought it was another of Samson's tricks: to lure the Philistines into Dan and maybe persuade them to be circumcised as a condition, and fall on them while they were still sore, as Simeon and Levi did to the Hivites, and slaughter them.

Samson was obliged to knock some few of their heads together to let such idiotic thoughts out.

"Do you think the Philistines are as wooden-headed as you are?" he roared at them. "They are soldiers, warriors and men of war, who sleep with their daggers on their arms, and one eye open. Do you think you can outwit them–*you?* Once we let them into the Shephelah they will be all over us like maggots on carrion. Dan will be their serf, as Judah is their serf. Baasha told you I was going down in friendship to the Philistines, to be made some sort of prince, did he? Well, I tell you now–all of you–that the only time Samson will go openly among the Philistines will be in chains. *And they have got to catch him first.*"

There was a cheer at this, and the same day the strangers who were perhaps Philistines, and not a few of the Canaanites, vanished from Zorah.

It might have been Manoah all over again.

The thought depressed Samson hugely. Indecision fragmented every purpose that came to him. Sharah said confidently, when they were speaking of nothing more important than the mending of a shutter, "Uzziel always said we must listen to you. He said Yahweh spoke with your voice, even when you did not know it. He said in the end you would do what is right."

It seemed to Samson that he had done nothing right in his life. The rumor of his overlordship as a vassal of the Philistine League, though given the lie, nevertheless made his position here intolerable. Baasha had done his work well. Everybody knew of it.

Delilah, however, did not know.

New ropes having proved no more effective than old ropes, she was convinced he had lied to her. "You have mocked me." Her smile acknowledged a defeat; but there was a wistfulness to it that trembled between forgiveness and anger. "You believed Sheshai. You don't trust me."

Samson lifted her chin. "Don't be cross with me. Truly, Delilah, I didn't know what strength was in me. I never know. I can't explain."

The violet eyes disbelieved him. They hardened. "If you do not tell me the secret of your strength, how you can be properly bound, I will hate you."

He told her the first thing that came into his head, which was bowstrings. They were, after all, the traditional standby for binding captives taken in war–the green and supple sinews of the vine of which bowmen invariably carried two or three spare about them in hunting or battle. And seeing Delilah's unconvinced look he added, "*Seven* bowstrings," because everybody knew seven was a magic number signifying completeness, the whole truth.

He had forgotten it until he saw the bowstrings laid out in her chamber like corn on the threshing floor. Seeing that he was troubled she left them there, and ran to throw her arms round him in alarm.

"What is it?"

He asked if she had seen Baasha. She shook her head.

"Why?"

"I am going to break his neck."

"The little hunchback?"

He stared at her, waiting for her to say it: *Brave fighter! A hunchback boy!* But Baasha, though he would be hunchback always, was no longer a boy; and there was none of Tamam's ridicule in Delilah's upturned face, only concern. She said again, "Why? What has Baasha done?"

He told her: spread word through the villages that the Philistines had offered him amnesty if he would bring Dan into their League; himself to be overlord. "Who will trust me now?"

"But it isn't true!"

When she learned that it was not only true, but that Samson had spurned the offer and assaulted the messenger (he did not say it was Sheshai), Delilah turned pale.

"But *why?*"

"Why?" he echoed. Uzziel had said once that for every appetite on earth there is a satisfaction; that is to say, for hunger there is meat, for thirst wine and water. For weariness, sleep; for fullness the emptying of the bowels, and for lust, women. For justice, Yahweh himself. How then was woman made with curiosity but no understanding? "Why do you suppose I've lived like a fox in the rocks these past ten years and more, and risked the lives of my young men–aye, and lost not a few?"

"Why, because they made you outlaw; for what you did to them, and no wonder. Now they have forgiven you."

The audacity of it took his breath. He gave up, and reached for her again, and she moved away.

"Delilah. *Do you think it was for my own sake?"*

"Why not? From all you've told me, everything you have ever done has been to please yourself."

"Aye, may be." He refused to be drawn or put into an ill-humor. "But I am not my own master. How can I make you understand? Things *happen* to me; not of my choosing. The breath of Yahweh blows softer on some of his children than on others; but with me it is always a gale. If your mother had stayed with us, if you had grown up among us, you would understand."

He was unsure as he said it. Would she? Had Tamam ever understood his black moods? Tamam had said Manoah was afraid of him when he was a half-grown boy, half Manoah's size and in awe of him; and there was truth in it more than she knew; more than he knew himself for years to come.

He said, "Listen!" without looking to see if she listened or not–Delilah could be deaf when she chose–thinking aloud, prowling with his thoughts to the open window. Though the window looked inward, you could see the tops of the trees over the roof, the sky's fading blue, and the outline of one dark hill, like the great ash heap of Zorah, which was not a hill at all but a cloud formation. "The first Philistine I ever saw knocked me to the ground. I went among them in friendship and they mocked me and cheated me; when I paid them back in their own measure, they burned my wife. Well, be that as it may, I can look after myself, and I paid them back for that too. But the quarrel was none of my making. So long as they stay out of the Shephelah and leave us alone, they can make their own music. But I'll not dance to their tunes."

A first star appeared, one wise eye that winked at him with the wisdom of the ages, as if to say, "Go on. Tell her." He turned, and Delilah sat on her stool, her hands in her lap and her eyes lowered. She was painting her nails.

He said, "The Land is the Lord's, Delilah, and we are

his people . . . you too, for it's your birthright as it's mine. The Egyptians could not destroy us, and neither can the Philistines, do you not see that? No man can stand up against Yahweh–so long as we keep ourselves apart, keep faith. What do we want with the Philistines? We are not traders, we have no cities, no earthly kings to oppress us, no nobles to fear and fawn to; we are a free people. We have the Land and the Law. If your young men go down among the pagans they forget the Law. And if the Philistines come among us, we shall lose the Land, as Judah lost theirs."

It sounded like Samuel. He said more cheerfully, "Besides, I am no war lord to lead an army against them for the glory of it!–I'd rather stay here and make love to you. All I have done is to show that they are men as we are; their bones can be broken and their iron bent. And they forgive me!–you say. Who will forgive me if I sell Yahweh's land for a robe of honor and a pagan dukedom?"

Delilah gave no indication that she had heard any of it.

"Well?"

She jumped to her feet. "Have you once thought of *me?*"

There was nothing he could say to pacify her. If he had accepted Athol's offer, he could have taken her down to Gaza to live with him; they could have lived there, or in Ashkelon, anywhere–in Zorah if he must. Who would throw the first stone at the governor appointed by the League, or at his lady? "You don't love me!" she stormed. "You don't *want* me! The smallest sacrifice is too much."

He moved toward her, and thinking he meant to pick her up in his arms as usual she shrank back, determined to resist him; but he walked past her and helped himself to her Assyrian ale. She left him, and was gone so long he had finished the flagon before her return, and regarded her unsteadily. She looked decidedly different. She had exchanged her pretty shift for an embroidered kaftan and traveling cloak, her sandals for jackal-leather shoes that curled delicately at the toes. And she had braided her hair close like a pearled black turban that capped her small, pale face with a royal dignity. No one, looking at her, could doubt her fitness to be wife to the governor of Dan.

Her eyes were unsmiling. "I am going to Ashkelon," she said. "To Saph. I never want to see you again."

□

Hanno was with the Philistine garrison at Eltekeh when a sleepy guard brought him word that there was a man at the gate asking for him by name. Though it was not yet light, he was already up and shaved, for he was an early riser by nature with a physical man's disregard of bodily comforts that grew more determined with the approach of middle age. The young sentry had to trot to keep up with him, hastening to lift the bar at his nod and fetch the torch down from the wall bracket. The man outside was heavily cloaked, but there was no disguising the twist to his shoulders.

"It's you." Hanno drew him inside and dismissed the guard. "What news?"

"Samson is in Timnath," Baasha said.

"I know that, you fool."

"No—" The fool lifted a heavily ringed hand in a plea to be heard out. "Not with *her.* In the town." He grinned and shuffled his feet in a gleeful dance of anticipation, keeping the best until last. "He is in the prison house."

There were seventy-nine in the garrison, not reckoning the sick, scribes and menials, and Hanno took them all. They made a ragged exodus from the town gates, marching a wavering four abreast with the stumbling quickstep of men pulled from their blankets and beset by rumors, but for once Hanno paid no attention. He led the column in his chariot, taking the reins himself, curbing the fresh horses and his burning excitement with the same ruthlessness. As for Baasha, it was the first time he had ever traveled in a chariot, and he clung miserably to the handrail, a martyr to every rut. The last thing he had expected was to return with the army. Hanno had paid him before they left, but the alarm gong had sounded, and in the resulting confusion of running men and shouted orders and counter-orders there was no time for further questions. Hanno insisted he tell him the story on the way.

It seemed that Samson had been drinking heavily in a public khan by the water gate, where he was accosted by a prostitute, well known in the place. Her hair was naturally cropped short, this being the sign of her trade, and his unusually long; a circumstance that called forth some speculative comments on the sex of each from a group of youths standing nearby. According to Samson, he *reasoned with them;* but witnesses said he simply dropped the prostitute on the floor with a roar that made the cups jump on the table, and squashing the two nearest youths under his arm like empty wineskins, bore them out through the doorway into the street, collecting a third by the hair as he went, and deposited all three into the well that gave the gate its name; the rest fled howling. He then returned to the khan, leaving the local citizens to fish them out. The watch, when they were sent for, recognized him, though they were ignorant of his name, and approached him with caution. Apparently he had done something of the sort before, and they suggested that if he was going to make a habit of drowning those who offended him, perhaps he could go to the river, or foul the water of some other town.

It might have ended with the warning for the prostitute, no stranger to drunks, had succeeded in pacifying the unruly giant, who was by this time singing a melancholy Hebrew song, more or less in tune, his head on her breast, and according to the innkeeper wetting her cloth with his tears, though it was as likely the ale from his waving flagon. But an added complication arose from the circumstance that, when his reckoning was presented for the prodigious quantities of both ale and wine he had consumed, he was unable to pay it; either because he had brought no money or, as he insisted, his scrip had been stolen. It was, however, of no consequence, because did they know who he was? He was governor of Dan and a lord of the Philistine League, and they could send the reckoning to Prince Athol in Gaza.

It was then that the keeper of the khan called on the watch to arrest him.

They had no choice. If they did not succeed in *arresting* Samson, they at least distracted him from wrecking more than the public rooms of the khan. It was the girl who eventually got Samson out of the place, and it was to her house that they followed after a prudent interval: long enough to allow him to fall into a sleep so deep as to be near a coma. They wheeled his insensible bulk to the prison house in a cart with no trouble at all.

Baasha told the story well, with many gestures and changes of voice, forgetting the discomfort of the journey and mentally beginning to transpose it into verses, already half-imagining the tune for it, which the children would chant in the villages. Despite himself Hanno listened attentively, and even smiled, distracted by the storyteller's spell. It was for this reason that the uneasy, half-formed thought that troubled him like a vaguely recollected dream, remained at the back of his mind when it should have been his foremost concern.

It was not until they had entered the town, less than an hour after leaving Eltekeh, and reined up before the squat stone prison house, and Hanno had forced through the crowd there, and seen for himself the iron bars in the window crumpled like burnt grass–half the masonry gone–that he remembered the gates of Gaza.

He turned to find Baasha gone.

A search was made for both, but it was a perfunctory business; the men were exhausted after their forced march, and apart from the labyrinthine warren of Timnath itself, the town was surrounded on three sides by vineyards that could have concealed an army, and would take another to discover it. It was a bitter and disconsolate Hanno who led the march back by easy stages to Eltekeh; but a madman who surveyed the spectacle that greeted his return. There was no need to inquire which way Samson had gone.

Whatever havoc the Nazirite had wrought in Timnath that day, it was nothing to what he had done within the walls of the unmanned garrison at Eltekeh.

□

Not even the most loyal of the bachelors, spurred on by his latest exploits and their earlier doubts dispelled, could approach Samson in his present mood. The Nazirite's only concern was watching for Hanno, squatting on the hill overlooking the valley road with a wineskin for company. Apart from a brief detour to skirt the Philistine column entering Timnath as he left it, he had made no secret of his movements; it seemed inevitable that Hanno must follow his trail back to Zorah this time.

Others shared the same thought. Despite the loyal bachelors, half Zorah and nearly all Eshtaol would have handed him over to the Philistines, like the men of Judah before, if they had dared. The Philistines would come for sure, and they were frightened.

Sharah sent a girl up to him with bread and a cake of figs, and hardened milk. But he ate none of it, though he took her hand, and thanked her, and remembered her name: Abigail.

Where was Hanno?

The sun and the wine made him dizzy; he kept seeing movement, marching men, where there was none.

"Adonai . . . What am I to do? *I love her.* How shall I live without her?"

But it was not a question. Neither was it a prayer. The prayer when it came was made in desperation and humility, his face pressed into the grasses with an intensity that must be answered.

"Only send the Philistines up the valley; I will fulfill the promise you made to Samuel, which he told me in Gath—remember? Which he told me, saying *Are you the man?*

"I will raise me a heap of Philistine bones in Sorek which shall be for all time. And when the children's children shall ask, what mean these bones?—they shall cause them to remember the stuff of which Yahweh made Israel.

"Aye; and it shall serve for a memorial to Samson the Nazirite also."

No Philistine army appeared in the Vale of Sorek that day, however; no iron chariots, no plumed columns, no river of spears: only a solitary figure too insignificant to be Hanno that made its way up the road beside the stream toward evening. It came almost to the foot of the hill where Samson sprawled with his empty wineskin before his bloodshot vision recognized Delilah. He went bounding down from rock to rock like the middle-aged goat he was to meet her.

"We never did try the bowstrings," she said.

□

She had missed him as much as he missed her, that much was plain, though she never admitted it; she walked behind him with swinging hips, flaunting herself to any who cared to look down from the hill villages–Samson's figure being unmistakable–as if she was his wife already. It was all he could do not to turn round and take her beside the public road.

She said behind him, "Are you not afraid to return this way? After what you did at Eltekeh?"

Teasing him.

He compressed his shoulder blades. "Should I be? I don't remember."

"Don't you remember *anything?*"

"Aye; you said you never wanted to see me again."

She fell silent and he said, jeering, "So what happened? Did the boy Saph not please you? They do say a taste of vintage will spoil you for new wine."

"I didn't go to Ashkelon," she said.

He walked on ten paces. "Not to Saph?"

"No."

"Where then? I saw you go!–your servants all in a flurry with the cart, and Keturah dragging her heels as if you'd newly whipped her."

"I went to Ashdod."

But she would not say why, or answer any more questions until they were past the ruins of the old outbuildings which had not been rebuilt, taking his hand as they entered the house and letting it go only to clap for the servants. She had a little banquet ready for him, as for a homecoming: lamb roasted in his honor the Hebrew way, over the wood of the vine, stuffed fish with honey and wine sauces followed by pistachio sweetmeats and honey doughnuts which made him remember Bilhah; and wine. A great deal of wine. Delilah fed him with her fingers, giggling like a child and sliding away when he reached out for her.

Afterward, in her bedchamber, there were the bowstrings. Delilah led him by the hand again and he saw the bowstrings first, nodding soberly, and only then the dark girl, who rose like an opening flower in an unfolding of multicolored shifts from the bed on which she had been reclining, with a jangle of ornaments. Samson steadied himself in the doorway and peered at her in surprise.

"Tahara!"

"Ichabod," she said and grinned, as only a black girl can grin, showing the little gate between her teeth. The last time Samson had seen Tahara it was stretched on her Egyptian bed like fabric on a loom, strung between the lions' heads and ringed tailposts by four pretty red leashes from her coffers, her mouth crammed with one of her own bright shifts and her brown eyes wide with puzzlement; because whatever she had expected him to do, it was not to put on his clothes and walk away from her.

Delilah said, "Now you know what I went to Ashdod for."

"Nobody missed me until the morning," Tahara said. She took up a pair of bowstrings, and separated them, and handed one to Delilah. "I kept waking up, and trying to turn over; I nearly went mad from wanting to scratch. And I wet myself."

"She was the best we ever had at this game," Delilah explained: "no one ever got away from Tahara. Not even you, my darling."

"When Lilah came and asked me to help her, I didn't know at first who you were."

"And then, when I learned what you had done to *her*—"

"And she told me who *Ichabod* was—"

"We made a bargain."

Tahara had removed Samson's tunic, and Delilah his undershirt, hesitating over the saq at his loins, their eyes meeting above him and giggling, and left it. They had him on his back on Delilah's bed, one to each arm, raising them tenderly above his head and apart to the corners; and he suddenly pulled back, fetching his captors sprawling over him, and sat up.

"What bargain?"

But he had been three days drinking himself in and out of misery, and not eating, and though Delilah's return had cleared his senses like the noon sun the dew, and her little banquet sobered him, there was overmuch wine with that also, and if they told him what the bargain was, he had no recollection afterward. They had no difficulty in easing him back to the familiar softness of the cushioned bed, and he was fully asleep before they had finished securing him to it. The last thing he remembered was the sound of the Egyptian girl's voice, naturally husky, but pitched so low it was almost a whisper. Tahara was familiar with the incidental use of bowstrings. She was demonstrating to Delilah how their pliancy, when fresh and green as these were, made tight knotting possible; how their stretchiness frustrated strain, resistance only shrinking the knots in on themselves.

"The more he struggles, the tighter it will get."

He was to verify this in a sort of phantasmagoric dream of the night that was full of the scent of jasmine and musk, and the fox-smell of sweat, much of it his own; of soft moanings and mountings like tender leeches, and the sudden unendurable cruelty of love bites endured because, in the way of dreamers, he was powerless to move; his saq gone, his nakedness exposed and vulnerable as the seashore to the sea, abandoning himself to the exquisite invasions that explored him like the first fingers of an incoming breaker, the ebb and flow of liquid flesh carrying him out to a sea of tortured ecstasy through the surge of breathing tides into an oceanic whirlpool that choked and drowned him.

Waking exhausted, he tried to lift his head and choked again. An instinctive attempt to reach for his throat produced fires of pain through his outstretched limbs and almost no movement at all. The room was in semidarkness; there was no lamp lit, but a brazier somewhere over toward the door curtains made a glow that left half the room in deep shadow. As he had done to Tahara at Ashdod, so they had done to him: spreadeagled him. Except that–no doubt to make good use of the *seven* bowstrings he had unthinkingly specified–his arms were made doubly fast with a ligature above each elbow, pinning it down. He counted them by feel: one bowstring for each wrist–two; one for each elbow

–four; two at his ankles–six. The seventh must be what choked his neck. He could not make out what it was tied *to:* the upright of Delilah's loom perhaps. His stirring made the bed creak, and there was an answering jangle in the room behind his head.

"Lie still."

It was Tahara. He heard the approaching sound of her ornaments, the swish of her skirts, and the brazier picked up their brightness; but her face was the color of the dark, invisible. She stood beside him.

"No matter how strong you are, you will only hurt yourself."

"My left leg itches," he said. "Just above the knee."

"Good."

He saw the white of her teeth. Then it vanished. It was a moment before he saw she was pulling her shift over her head. He watched as a second shift followed, and an undergarment: the last, for the colors were gone, leaving only a darker shape among the shadows. "Will you not scratch it for me?"

The white of her grin again, and she shook her head.

"Free one of my hands, then. I can't do anything with just one hand."

"Can you not! I saw what you did to the Dagon in our temple."

Splayed out, he took up all the bed. There was no way she could come down beside him without putting her weight on an arm and a leg at least. The sudden pressure sharply intensified the pull on his wrist and ankle, and he winced. She saw it, and laughed; but she took some of the weight on her elbow. "You are luckier than I was, Ichabod. You have me to keep you company, at least. And I haven't gagged you, though Lilah told me to."

"Won't Delilah–" he said, and broke off with a groan because of what she was doing to him with her left hand.

"Delilah said I could do what I liked with you, so long as I kept you here. You are weak after last night; I mean to see you stay weak."

He said between his teeth: "Is this her idea?"

"No"–Tahara leaned down to kiss his mouth, prising his teeth apart with her strong tongue. "Mine," she said indistinctly. "I think she thought I would whip you, or make you suffer in some way, as you made me suffer. Tit for tat."

And she added reasonably, "It is fair."

To Samson, clinging to a mental precipice, it was monstrous. There was a cruelty in Delilah's games–on both sides; he was not blameless–just as in Tamam's teasing and his own deception, promising what he could not give her; but an innocence also. There was nothing innocent about Tahara.

"*Wait,*" he said; with such urgency that Tahara obeyed. "You mean, she doesn't *care*?"

"If you ask that, you don't know her."

It was what Sheshai had said.

"Of course she doesn't care," Tahara said, looking at him almost with pity. "Delilah always gets what she wants: haven't you discovered?–it doesn't matter what the cost, or who pays it. If it was my price for helping her . . ." Tahara shrugged.

"And what *does* she want?"

"You," Tahara told him. "For husband. She really loves you. And if the only way is to deliver you bound to the Philistines . . . since you will not go freely of your own accord. It has to be the coast, doesn't it? That was what she said. You will not have her for wife anywhere else."

There was no need to ask where Delilah had gone.

□

The neglected brazier had almost burned itself out before Delilah returned, sweeping aside the curtains to stand triumphant in the doorway, swaying a little with her exertions.

"The Philistines are here, Samson! I have you this time, my lover."

Because of the dimness it was not for some moments that she saw the still figure lashed helplessly to the bed was Tahara.

15

"MARRY HER," Samuel said.

He stood on the low hill before Ebenezer, overlooking the coastal highway up which the Philistine column had come against Ephraim so many years before, and drove his staff emphatically in among the grass tufts. Samuel was a great man for emphasis. "You are obsessed with the woman; it is a sickness in your blood. Nothing else will cure you. So marry her!"

He had brought Samson up here ignoring the scorching heat to show him the place where his father had died; but it was obvious the Danite was incapable of thinking of anything but the woman Delilah, even when he seemed to listen. A dog barking in the village was the only answer Samuel had. Ebenezer had been sacked and burned by Athol's cohorts, but bricks and masonry are not easily destroyed by fire, and poor men are by nature practical. The new village was made of the old, and not a bowshot from it.

"Fill her with children," Samuel said callously, offhand. His staff poked the soil. "Content her with sucklings, and come join us at Mizpeh. Yahweh has need of you, and you're no use to God or man as you are now."

Samson stirred at his feet, and removed the grass stalk

he had been chewing gloomily to ask if Yahweh had spoken to Samuel and said this, that Samson should marry Delilah, who was his half-sister and the daughter of his father; no whit amazed at the scornful rejoinder: *"Never ask of Yahweh what you can answer yourself.* In the least she is a daughter of Israel; not of the uncircumcised like the Timnite Niobe!"

So he had not asked him. Which was a pity, because Yahweh could have told him Delilah did not consider herself a daughter of Israel. The only feeling she harbored in her pretty bosom for Israel was a bottomless hatred. Besides, this was no time to speak of marriage, when she was still furious with him over the loom.

He had smashed it beyond repair. Not that he was to blame. He had told her–because she had never ceased plaguing him since the business with Tahara–that the secret of his strength lay in his hair: meaning righteousness, which was a sort of bad joke against himself, his unshaven head being the outward sign of his Nazirite dedication to the source of all strength and power, namely Yahweh; but she had taken him literally. It was her idea to weave the locks of his hair–the magic *seven* locks–into the warp of her loom for all the world like lambswool, pressing it down with her batten and fastening it with the pin. She was not entirely sober herself when she suggested it. No doubt the proximity of the bed to the loom gave her the idea. The head of the bed was up against the standing loom, and he himself was asleep when she did it, after their usual play. She shook him awake with the unlikely news that the Philistines were on the stairs, and he carried the beam halfway to the door with him, bringing a considerable part of the ceiling down. It took them the rest of the night to disentangle the mess, disabled by the comic absurdity of it. It was only in the morning light, when she saw the extent of the ruin of her precious loom, that her mood changed to fury. There was no reasoning with her, and on an impulse he had gone to find Samuel after all.

Chewing the bitter grass stalk now, and surveying the hillside down to Philistine Aphek, he knew it had been a mistake. To Samuel every road led to Yahweh. Samson had thought the prophet's charisma was his singlemindedness; but he was devious. What obstacles he could not overcome, he was ready to circumvent with compromise. In this he was very like Athol. From his ultimate goal he never deviated. Samuel bore the mark of Yahweh as surely as Cain ever did. If the love of God was a torch, as Uzziel was fond of saying, to light a man's way through the dark of the world, then Samuel's was a conflagration that reduced lesser loves to sparks, to be trampled in his ruthless passage. *Marry her.*

Manoah had fallen somewhere on these slopes, and Samson could imagine his father rushing forward with the same unreasonable confidence to his death. It was ironical that Manoah, to whom the Law was more than life, should have gone to such pains to deny his son Tamam; while Samuel, who had inherited the priestly staff of Eli himself, thought the woman of so little importance.

He wondered if Samuel loved Yahweh half as much as he loved Delilah.

Adonai!–forgive me.

Samuel was looking at him.

"Did you speak?"

"No," Samson said.

But there was a sort of truth in it that troubled him all the way back to Dan. He wished he could have asked Uzziel. Does the spark not come out of the fire? Is love divisible?

□

"You mean me and Tamam," Delilah said.

She was washing his hair, as Tamam had done so many times, making him lie back across her folded knees. He had never enjoyed it as a child, and did not now, but she insisted; just as she insisted he kept his beard shaven, which he was inclined to neglect, and made him clean his fingernails. He grumbled that she wanted him to look like a Philistine, and she laughed jeeringly.

"No fear of that! You might look more handsome, though, if you cut your hair."

"Aye," he said, and swore, because she had let the oil run into his eyes. "Because I couldn't look less so. Samuel thinks I should marry you."

"Samuel is right. Whoever Samuel is. I will marry you if you will trim your locks."

He wiped his eyes on the hem of her shift. "You know I

cannot. Any more than I can marry you and live among your fancy friends."

"Because of being a *Nazirite?*" She snatched the cloth away. "All those silly vows someone else made for you!"

"It's one I made myself. Have you done?"

"Yes."

Samson lifted his head and shook it like a dog, soaking her. She retreated with a little scream.

"It makes you look . . . conspicuous." She considered him without his headband. "It makes you look different."

"I am different."

"*Is* your hair the secret?"

"First you say it's conspicuous; then you say it's a secret."

Delilah stayed out of range, her violet eyes thoughtfully upon him, looking like Tamam at her chores, the house slave: her hair damply close about her small defiant face, the wetness of her shift clinging provocatively to her shape, both of them knowing it aroused him if anything more than her nakedness. He said, "Why are you looking at me like that?" and she said, "Like what."

He was as good as living with her now, for he spent more of his days and nights at Timnath than at Etam or Zorah. Nor was his presence any longer a secret, since he lent a powerful hand in the rebuilding of the laborers' quarters, and helped them in with the grape harvest, carousing with the men afterward. Hanno must have known. Yet still there was no move against him from Eltekeh or Ashdod; no alarm of the Philistines save the false alarms with which Delilah never tired of teasing him, in her fruitless attempts to prove the ever more varied and ingenious bonds she contrived to put on him, in place of the one bond she could not.

The whore's trick of tying was as much a part of her love play as her childlike craving for affection, one mood of many as varied as her dressing and undressing, the provocative tinkle of her ankle chains (which she knew reminded him of Tamam), riding him like a camel, kissing his feet like a king, the tremblings in the quiet of the night when he pleased her, her way of turning her back when he did not; her rages with inanimate things disobedient to her—a spluttering lamp, a missing slipper, a knot that would not stay fast—but most of all the unpredictable shifts of mood from depravity to innocence. His rapid arms, grasping at a nest of vipers, would close on the stillness of a trusting child, whose submission filled him with shame at his own excesses. Then he would feel himself in truth the uncouth hill peasant she sometimes named him, reminding him of the place that awaited her at Saph's court, until his temper broke and he left her. Sometimes she let him go without a word; and as often came running after to throw herself at his feet and beg his forgiveness, swearing on as many gods as she could name that she could not live without him. Again, he would if she wearied him take the rope and put it to his own use; once merely knotting it about the narrowness of her waist with one end fast to the head of her bed, the other to the foot, beyond the utmost reach of her fingers. She could no more slip her girdle than a dog its leash, but hurled every cushion at him until the bed was empty of everything but herself. She hated herself to be tied; but with another of her many contradictions would afflict and provoke him until he imprisoned her wrists in one hand over her head, arching herself to meet him with lips parted in a sigh of contentment.

Their life together was circumscribed by the house and its vineyards, for they could go in each other's company neither up the valley into Dan, nor down it to the coast; not even into Timnath itself. But in Jason's vineyard every man was his spy now; none would betray him, not even Keturah. It was the happiest time of his life. It seemed to him, seeing nothing but his mirror-image in those violet eyes, predestined from the day Tamam entered his life: the impossible prayer which Yahweh, to whom all things were possible, had answered after all, crowning his life with loving when all about him filled theirs with hate, from Hanno to Samuel. He cared for none of them. Yahweh had taken Tamam from him, and Yahweh had restored her to him, which was a mystery no one could understand, not even himself; unless it was Uzziel. Eden itself could have been scarcely larger than these vineyards, nor any more green and beautiful to look on, with the woman's hand soft in his palm. Delilah's present contentment doubled his own. He asked if she was happy, though there was no need.

"Now I am."

"Now?"

"You have told me the truth," she said. "It is your hair, isn't it. After all." And she touched it lightly.

"What is?"

"I don't know. The secret. The part of you I cannot have."

He had found a mole on her thigh. "Have you not enough of me already?"

"I'll never have enough of you."

But she laughed, and he came to believe that she accepted their relationship as he did—to no man does Adonai give everything he wants—and had finally put the thought of a lawful marriage, openly witnessed, from her.

In this, he was wrong.

□

He was absent from her three days, and on the fourth she was not at the house to meet him, returning in the following forenoon, so it made five days. They quarreled, because he was drinking too much, or else he drank too much by reason of the quarrel. Delilah wept, and he comforted her, and fell asleep toward evening with his head in her lap, as he had sometimes done as a boy in Zorah, when he went to help her mind the goats, or at the edge of a group of women gossiping at the well in the noon heat, who paid him no attention because he was still a boy and in his mother's care. Tamam was stroking his hair absently, sometimes with a little tug of private affection, talking to a friend over his head; and Baasha the little hunchback lad was there with his first lute, peering down at him curiously to know if he slept or not.

"Samson! Samson—wake up!"

Delilah's voice was far away; and then suddenly close; his head was still in her lap, cushioned in the hollow of her thighs. He lay across her bed, while she sat at the edge, shaking him by the shoulders. His arms were tightly bound, though he had no recollection of her binding them.

"The Philistines are upon you!"

His waking grin faded when he saw the pallor of her face; and heaving himself up, a movement at the door curtains. The lamp was turned up; there was no mistaking it, no breath of wind at the window. He still did not believe her until he swung his legs to the floor and his foot slipped on what lay scattered there, and he felt for the first time the cool lightness of his shaven head.

Adonai!

It carpeted the floor beside the bed, an incredible mass of overlapping clumps and tresses like black pelts, the lamplight picking out the gray; the same hair Sharah had combed out and oiled lovingly on her knee, and Tamam had casually washed and dried on a squirming boy; which marked him as Yahweh's all his life when nothing else did. Samson the Nazirite!

It was as if Adonai had departed from him.

A terrible sickness assailed him in the pit of his stomach bringing up the bile of rage and despair. He doubled himself vigorously against the constraining ropes, sucking in breath to expand his chest as before, flexing the iron of his biceps, twisting his wrists and arms, and then more confidently exploding all his strength outward in one almighty heave that must destroy his bonds like an eagle in a cobweb.

The ropes held.

He saw, for a fleeting moment, the nervous triumph in Delilah's face, her lips caught in her small, perfect teeth. And then the room was full of men.

□

Baasha stood aside on the stairway until the last of them had gone by him, then hurried on down and out at the front of the house, where the barber waited for him under the fig tree. There was little moon, and Baasha did not see him until the man coughed; then he almost ran with his peculiar, lurching gait, and drew the barber out by the arm, half-dragging him toward the road.

"I don't understand," the man was saying: "who were all those men? Where are we going?"

He was an old man, nearly as hunched as Baasha himself, and rickety with it, much hampered by his barber's satchel and his staff, which kept getting entangled with his cloak.

"Home," Baasha told him, without slackening their pace. "Libnah, isn't it?"

"Tonight?"

The barber's mouth was agape with fright. Libnah was four or five hours away–more in the dark; who in his right mind would risk such a journey by night and alone? He had planned a night's sojourn in Timnath, returning in daylight he explained, out of breath and dragging back; but Baasha's grip on his arm was unrelenting. The old man protested further: he lived outside the city gates, in a household whose doors would certainly be barred at this hour. He implored his captor to give him his recompense and let him go. "I shaved the Hebrew's head clean, as you said. I did my job."

Baasha stopped. He caught the barber as he stumbled. "Who said he was a Hebrew?"

"I . . . recognized him. I was called to shave him once before: just his beard, that is; it was at Amalek's house. I would have trimmed his hair, but he would not suffer it. It was the one they call Samson, wasn't it."

"It was," Baasha agreed.

And he stood there, cursing to himself the ill-fortune that sent him this one man, who knew Samson and recognized him; who did not know Baasha but would certainly recognize him again, and would describe him with no hesitation at all, and make public with the garrulous mouth of all barbers that which Baasha had gone to considerable trouble to keep secret. He might have summoned any one of a dozen barbers from Timnath, when Delilah gave him his instructions; but he had sent farther afield from a private caution; and hit upon the only barber in the world who had shaved Samson before, and recognized him. How long would it be before word got back to Zorah, and Samson's bachelors?

"I will pay you now," he said.

And he put his hand inside the front of his kaftan, as if reaching for his purse, and slid the dagger into his palm. "Come here then, old man. Don't you want to count it?"

"No, no! I trust you."

The barber was an old man, not as clear-headed as he had been once, and confused by the night's happenings; but he was no simpleton. In his profession he had encountered every manner of man, and had observed them all, close to.

He had not trusted Baasha from the moment he met him. Even to his failing eyesight it was obvious that whatever it was the hunchback held it was no purse. Fright gave him strength. Baasha's striking arm met the razor's upward-scything edge. The second slash of the razor, swiped with the force of panic, was across the bridge of his fleshy nose, doing little damage but bringing much pain, so that Baasha dropped the dagger, which was fatal. The third cut severed the great cord of his throat and silenced the shriek which was the last sound Baasha ever uttered. Before he left, the barber took the dagger from the ground beside the dead man, and from the corpse a purse, which was in the waistband, and contained his fee seven times over. The clink of the metal alarmed him, and he crouched to muffle the sound.

□

To Delilah, the ring of shekel on shekel after shekel was a peal of victory, a triumphant carillon endlessly proclaiming her own cleverness. They had left the silver in five leathern bags, one from each of the five Seren, eleven hundred to a bag–five thousand five hundred shekels in all. She had tipped just one of the bags out on the carpet, and it made a great heap half as high as her knee. She knelt, and worked her fingers in among the cold metal, and tossed it recklessly upward, giggling at the clattering silver shower it made, spectacular in the lamplight, like tumbling stars; and in the same moment felt herself observed and stiffened in fright. But it was only Keturah.

"He called for you, mistress. Before they led him away, he called for you."

Delilah turned her shoulder. "Cursed me, more like!" She began to balance shekel on shekel, like a child's blocks. "I fought him, Keturah, strong as he is: him, and his magic, and his terrible old mountain god–and I won. *I won.*" She jumped up, tossing her head away from the servant's unsmiling face in a whirl of tresses. "Go fetch the best wine: Jason's vintage. And two goblets, Keturah–you shall celebrate with me!"

"Better I should fetch meat; you have eaten nothing all day. You are pale as dawn, and no wonder."

"Oh, Keturah! Don't fuss." Delilah added a careful story to her silver tower. "This is meat enough for me. Aye, and drink." (Why must she say *Aye,* even sounding like him?) "It is a heap of silver for one man, is it not?"

"Enough to bury him, for sure. It is blood money."

Delilah scattered the shekels furiously. "You dare to criticize me? Now look what you've made me do: I must start counting all over again. I thought you hated him."

"I am only your handmaid," Keturah said dourly, neither admitting nor denying it. "But I would never sleep easy again if I sent to his death a man who loved me like that."

"What man ever loved *you,* you barren old stick!"

Delilah reached up and pinched the old woman's cheek with playful spite; and put her arms round her gaunt shoulders.

"Besides, he is not to *die,* silly. I am to follow him to Gaza, and be married to him there. It is all arranged."

Keturah's mouth fell agape. "Is it true? I did not know."

"No more does he. It was the only way I could get him away from his people and his god."

For a moment Keturah looked almost happy. Then her face fell. "But my Lord Saph. He . . ."

"Yes, he *owns* me. Just as I own you, Keturah; though he paid a deal more for me, and had the worse bargain. I have arranged for that too."

And she told the handmaid what she must do: first help her count out five hundred of the shekels and set them aside. Then to divide the five thousand into the bags again, packed tight with their drawstrings, and load them on a cart, and cover them with wineskins; and have the men ready to take them down in the morning to Ashdod, as it were to the market as usual. Keturah was to accompany them, and herself deliver the bags into the hands of the prince Saph and none other, saying this was the sum agreed, for which the lady Delilah purchased her freedom.

"And see it is sealed, and witnessed. But first the wine!"

Delilah did not tell her the best part of it: that eleven hundred of the shekels came from Saph himself.

□

To Sharah it was an evil reincarnation, a nightmarish reappearance of one long dead, whom of all people she had been most exercised to forget–the Baal-child Tamam, Manoah's first gift to her along with her loom and the first jewelry he ever gave her, the rare and precious iron trinkets; the little slave with violet eyes who was nursemaid to her firstborn son, and afterward mistress to her husband; coming to her then as she came now, with the pitying arrogance of youth, flaunting her new-found plumage, the lord's favorite among women, and challenging the aging Sharah to deny it. Barren again after the one God-given birth, Sharah had sent her maid to Manoah's bed half out of a kindness to the girl, thinking he might use her the more kindly for it; not suspecting that his previous severity contained an inner ferment, like the crust of a loaf baked too quickly: an unthinkable fermentation of lust that probably even Manoah himself was not aware of: but Tamam was aware.

"He loves me," Delilah said. "We are to be married in Gaza, but I think we shall not live there. We shall return and make this our city. It is a poor place, but we shall change all that. Zorah-Eshtaol shall be the sixth city of the Philistine League; not to be compared to Ashkelon or Gaza, but with Samson as prince it will grow; you'll see."

Sharah lifted unwilling eyes to consider her, this young woman who looked so like Tamam, with her loose hair and knowing ways. She stood defiant in the old doorway, as Tamam had, one slim hand against the post as if to steady the inner excitement that animated her features, but slender in her light cloak: Tamam had been heavy with child.

Sharah was by nature gentle and unresentful. The bitterness that assailed her when Tamam became pregnant–almost immediately, and seemingly without effort–was unfamiliar and quickly turned to self-reproach. It could only be for Manoah's sake that Yahweh had favored her; and it was after all the purpose of the liaison. What more natural than that Manoah should take her for second wife, for the sake of the sons he confidently expected her to bear him. She was a simple girl, of a backward nomad tribe, and such an honor went to her head; one should not expect gratitude from the young. But even the calamitous birth of a female child did not humble Tamam. She continued to play queen to the villagers, who hated her. They would hate this one more.

Sharah said slowly, "You took my husband from me. Now you have taken my son also."

"You are confused, old woman. Your husband was my father. For what you did to my mother I will take not only your son but your villages and your tribe—and your god!"

It was not what she had come to Zorah to say. She had come to tell a backward and persecuted people that their troubles were over; a mother that her son was safe and would return heaped with honors, bringing all the advantages of civilization and peace to the hills. She felt no particular enmity for this old crone, with her walnut face and snowy hair, whom Tamam had in all probability tried to poison off, as they said. But in place of gratitude, they had received her with contempt, looking askance at her unveiled face, her unbound hair. It was known by now that Samson had gone down to Gaza—though not the manner of his going—and there were those in the village who spat at her feet as she passed. Sharah herself had not risen to greet her, and though she said little, by her look made Delilah feel like a servant.

The next time she came to Zorah, the old witch would bend her knee with the rest.

She had arranged a tryst with Baasha in the village; but he was nowhere to be found, and receiving no answers to her questions, Delilah returned down the valley as she had come, alone. A small group, composed mostly of children, trailed at a distance after her. When she came beside the stream, from their higher situation they began to pelt her with stones. She was struck on the arm and thigh, and snatched up her skirts to run, shaking with anger and for the first time fright. She half-turned her head to shout an imprecation and a considerable rock, which might otherwise have passed harmlessly, took her full on the temple. For one blinding instant she soared to embrace Shemesh in a wheeling sky; the next plunged through the earth in a black abyss, knowing nothing but the lingering sweet smell of the oleanders, and the salt taste of her own blood.

□

The first face she saw was Saph's, though she did not know it.

There were other faces, not all of them human; but one surely Keturah, though so distorted with weeping it was hard to be sure, for she had never seen Keturah weep, and could not imagine why she should weep now. The horned Baal had come and gone many times, beckoning her with Sheshai's wolfish grin and one casual finger that reached for her clit, so that she shrank back whimpering. And Baal's consort Astarte, the cold star looking down on her with disdain, whose face was the face of a young Sharah. Hanno's voice she identified, and the recurring songs of Baasha, some of them bawdy in the extreme, so that she didn't know whether to laugh or scold. Tamam, regarding her gravely through her own violet eyes; and Samson watching them both with nothing but love and his terrifyingly misplaced faith in humanity; or it might have been Adonai. And then the prince of Ashkelon again.

"She knows me," Saph said. "You can tell by the way she looks."

It was true. A grown-up likeness, the pretty bloom of his youth blighted with experience and a certain sadness that made him more attractive to her than he had ever been: but beyond doubt Saph. She became uneasily conscious of the male scent of the pillows under her head, the familiar carpets and hangings of the royal bedchamber; the noble pillars, and the light that streamed in through the palace windows; and raised her head weakly in protest. "Saph. You have tricked me."

"No."

He said it again, *"No;"* it might have been days later—she had no sense of time. The faces had come and gone again, ever-changing in a phantom caravan; through the palace windows she identified the Plough, that led her eye to the north star, somewhere out over the sea, for there was no land directly north of Ashkelon. Saph said, "You are my guest here; no more." He seemed anxious not to excite her, and spoke soothingly, as to a child, which was unlike the Saph she remembered. "You took a great risk, entrusting so great a sum to your maid. She might have run off and bought herself a handsome portion in Egypt, or Assyria!"

It was a small joke, she understood; but it brought back her memory. She heard Saph say reassuringly, "But you were right, dear one. She came straight to me, and would not budge until I called for the scribe and wrote out your bill of emancipation. You have been a free woman ever since. Ask Keturah."

"Ever since . . ." Delilah said. *"Dear god, how long is Ever Since?"* She struggled to sit up. "What day–what *month* is it?"

Saph was silent and it was Keturah, appearing at his shoulder, mercifully unchanged from her shroudlike clothes, who told her. "The fourth month. Since two days past."

Delilah's hand flew to her mouth.

It had been at the end of the eleventh month, which Samson called *Tebet,* that she had delivered him to the Philistines. The knuckle between her teeth was fleshless, her wrist, her arm almost skeletal in their thinness, the skin yellow and scaly as a snake's. She flung herself from the bed and could not stand unaided; the women restrained her without difficulty. She clutched at Keturah's arm, her eyes begging the maid, but Saph dismissed them all, and it was from him that she learned what had passed, so far as he was able to tell her.

She had been discovered, apparently dead, lying in Jason's vineyard; which at first puzzled her, until she reasoned that the Danites who stoned her must have supposed her dead also, and made haste to remove the evidence of their crime from the vicinity of their villages. What more natural than that they should have carried her corpse home, where no blame could be traced to themselves? No doubt they considered Samson's wrath too. When her own servants saw that she was alive–if barely–they bore her down to Ashkelon, not knowing that she had purchased her freedom from the Lord Saph. Keturah had not yet returned, and because of the vast store of shekels involved, none had been told. Delilah had been under the care of the palace physician ever since: a gifted and patient man, an Egyptian, who had coaxed her back from the lip of the grave a dozen times. He had spent night after night forgoing sleep to watch over her.

But it was Saph's devotion that most moved her. He made no mention of her unfaithfulness, of the trick she had played on him; not even of the humiliation he must have suffered. It was clear he adored her still. It was written on his face for anyone to read there; and it was this that made her afraid. But even when she asked him the question she had been biting back and dared not ask, and must–"What of Samson?"–he betrayed none of the jealousy and resentment she had dreaded.

"He is in Gaza still. I have not seen him. But they say he is well, and a great favorite among Athol's townspeople. His arrival caused something of a stir!"

"He . . ." Delilah made herself say it. "He has not been here? To see me?"

"Dear Delilah." Saph's tone was gentle. "He has been very busy. He has had much to do. You should not blame him in the least. . . . It was your doing after all, remember."

He took her fingers. "You wish to see him?–of course you do. And I know he would want nothing more than to see you. In ten day's time they are having their harvest festival in Gaza. It was a little surprise I was saving for you. They are making it a feast in Samson's honor. Do you think you will be well enough to make the journey down there with me?–all the Seren are going."

"Yes!" she cried. "Oh, yes." And then: "You are good to me, Saph. I don't know why. After what I have done."

He said simply, "I love you."

"Yet you know it is Samson I will marry."

"It is your choice." Saph was quiet for a moment, studying the veins in her thin hand. Then he lifted his eyes and said, "You are free to decide. It is some time since you have seen your famous Hebrew. If you still want him when you meet again . . . then you have my blessing." And he smiled.

Even now, she could not bring herself to trust Saph entirely. She said cautiously, feeling her way, "You mean–do you not–if he still wants me?"

Saph liftea his shoulders. "Why should he not?"

A dozen reasons came to her mind at once: none of them known to Saph. Not her illness: people became thin and discolored when they were ill, even gaunt and yellow; but they recovered. If you loved someone it didn't matter. It was not until Saph had left her, and she was alone, and raised a hand idly to scratch a familiar irritation on her temple, and felt the irregularity there, that the fear returned. There was no mirror in the room. She remembered there had been three, one especially her own, the metal polished on the one side, inlaid with precious stones the other, and the length of the handle. All had been removed. Her trembling fingers traced the scar tissue, where the rock had struck, running up from the corner of her eye into the hairline. There was a ewer of water in the room, and a basin, and she poured water into the basin and carried it shakily and set it down on the flagstones, and fetched a lamp and held it over the basin, peering down. The water would not settle, nor the lamp throw its light where she wanted it, and she fretted with impatience; but at last it was right. Even then the image was far from clear. Nevertheless it told her what she wanted to know. The scar was of no great breadth, nor the discoloring of the flesh too marked; but it drew the corner of her one eye upwards above the level of the other, destroying the balance of her features and giving her a crazy, lopsided look. She shrieked, and shouted for Keturah, but it was Saph who came through the doorway, running. "What is it? Delilah–"

She stamped her foot. "Where is Keturah?"

"What is the matter? Asleep I should think. Do you know what hour it is?"

"I want a mirror."

"You should not be up–"

"I want a mirror."

He fetched her own at once. It was in the sandalwood chest on top of her house clothes, where she had tossed it when she left him. The disfigurement was no better and no worse than it had been in the basin. She looked at Saph and his expression had not changed. It did not change when the tears began to roll down her cheeks.

"I am a freak."

"Not to me."

"But to Samson. Is that what you mean? Is–*this* why he hasn't been to visit me? Is it?" She was shivering as if from an ague. *"Does he know?"*

"No."

"You want me to go to Gaza with you to confront him with it? You think he will be dismayed and disgusted."

"I think no such thing," Saph said calmly. "I leave in

the morning. If you are coming with us, you must sleep now."

She allowed herself to be led back to the great canopied bed, and made comfortable with cushions and her own silken coverlets. She said, "I shall not come with you."

"You need sleep, all the same."

She would have slept if she could. In the vast and darkened chamber–for Saph had turned down the lamp on leaving–her thoughts were more to be feared than her face. The thought of meeting Samson face to face at the festival, with the eyes of all Philistia upon them, made her double up under the silks in spasm of physical pain. Of all the festivals, that of Dagon god of grain, and the earth Baals, was the gaiest and the happiest. It was a peasant festival, and they behaved like peasants, but arrayed themselves like princes and princesses every one; even the plainest girls were beautiful for the harvest. How could Saph, if he had any remnant of feeling for her, expose her to such public humiliation? Let Samson come to *her*–first, and in private. Perhaps Saph did not love her at all. Had she not rejected him?–*him,* Ser of Ashkelon and a prince of the League of Princes. Except that, being a man, he might want her the more for it. Might be so sure that Samson would turn from her now, and reject *her.* Could he really believe that? How could a pampered and bloodless creature like Saph understand the love that bound Samson and Delilah? What had Samson said of him?–soft as a cow pat. If Saph deceived himself that Samson would abandon her for her scarred face, then it was time Saph was taught a lesson.

She would show him. She would show them all.

□

Even the sea breezes, which could usually be counted on to make a journey along the coast tolerable, wee absent today. Within the airless palanquin Delilah fanned herself listlessly, envying Saph who had gone on ahead in the cool of the morning to take part in the ritual offerings and sacrifices. These had, she knew, to be performed by the Seren themselves this day, with their priests in attendance. When she had first attended herself, as a temple novice, she had been shocked and thrilled at so much letting of blood: the frantic flapping of wings, the squeals and lowings, the rolling white of the beasts' eyes; then the solemn smearing of the blood on the horns of the earth Baals, at the feet of the great brass god, on the foreheads of the men, everywhere. But one sacrifice is very like another, and she was glad enough now to escape the tedium of their endless repetitions. After the Seren came the royal sons and kin, then the court officials, the captains of the armies and other dignitaries down to the tax gatherers and lesser fry, followed by the people themselves, each bringing a tithe of grain or whatever they produced, the firstborn of their flocks and herds, goat or sheep or ox. In effect, it was a tax, since the grain went to the state granaries, and wholly burnt sacrifices were rare, most of the meat being kept back. In return the people–or as many as could fight their way into the temple courtyards–were treated by the palace to a feast the like of which they were not likely to see from one year to the next, and license to misbehave with no official hindrance whatsoever. It was a busy time for the temple girls.

Like most state functions, the harvest festival was held in each of the five cities of the League in turn. It was in Gaza this year, she knew, because Samson was in Gaza. And Samson had been taken to Gaza, by arrangement with Athol, to keep him out of Hanno's hands until such time as the proclamation could be made. To this extent, everything was going to plan.

Delilah was uneasy, nevertheless. The heat and the swaying of the palanquin brought on a renewal of her sickness indistinguishable from foreboding. What had kept Samson so long in Gaza? The idea of another woman rose briefly in her mind, and was mentally trampled. Why had the proclamation of his appointment to the governorship of Dan been so long delayed? The happy thought came to her, that he had waited until she herself was sufficiently recovered to join him; and then she remembered that Saph had said Samson did not know she was sick. But he must have known where she was; every Hebrew was his spy, and many besides; Baasha could have told him; Baasha would tell anything for a price. So why no word from Samson, no message? Had Saph been lying? Was Samson *dead?* She began to feel hysterical.

The nearer they approached Gaza, the more crowded the road became, whole families coming down from their villages on all sides in their finery like flocks of brightly colored birds coming down to roost, to be swept along onward with the throng. The four Cushites, as anxious as any not to miss the least part of the festivities, took advantage of the wasted little frame they bore in the palanquin to drive their way through at a smart trot. The escorting soldiers, nothing loath, kept pace easily. Only the servants had difficulty in keeping up. Keturah, out of breath, saw the curtains plucked and parted, and the wreckage of that once-lovely face mercifully veiled, the uneven eyes, made more grotesque by their violet shadows, searching the crowd for her.

"Mistress!"

"Am I such a fright, Keturah?–that even you look on me with pity."

"I don't know about pity." Keturah stumbled, and put a hand on the palanquin, and one of the soldiers threw a glance at her. "If ever I learned about pity, my lady, it was not from you." And she added a little more kindly, "You should not draw your hair to one side. Let it down a little in front, as I showed. Just until it heals."

"It is too hot," Delilah grumbled. "And it will never heal. Is it far now?"

"Not far. We are approaching the gardens. It will be cooler there. Rest now, Delilah. I must join the others."

"Stay and talk to me."

"The Lord Saph has forbidden it."

This made Delilah furious, Keturah being her servant, not Saph's. "Why? What is it? What secret are you all keeping from me?" Her voice rose. *"Tell me."*

"No secret, Lady." Keturah hesitated nervously. "It was the physician. He said you were not to be excited."

"I will be a hundred times more excited if you do not stay and tell me all you know."

This was manifestly true, and alarmed, Keturah compromised, persuading Delilah to let the curtains fall back with only a small gap, while she herself kept her face to the front, so that the soldiers if they noticed would not feel obliged to make a report.

But for all that, she had little news to fill the missing months. She had not seen Samson, but they spoke of him often, and she had heard them say he remained in Gaza for his own safety, not only for fear of the many Philistines clamoring for his head, but also because it was uncertain how his own villages would receive him, after his defection. There had been unrest up and down the Shephelah at first, and blood spilled on the borders; but without Samson the raids lacked determination, and many failed. The long silence puzzled everybody. Two or three of Samson's bachelors had appeared at Gaza, bulging with concealed weapons, evidently with some idea of fetching him back. They were recognized at the gates and turned back, but strangely not harmed. The attempt on Delilah's life was kept from Samson, lest he saw Philistine treachery there, after the affair of Niobe; besides, they took her to be dying. Later, when they learned from Delilah herself–for she had said many things in her delirium–that the Zorahites were to blame, Saph was in a rage to send Hanno out to deal with them. But they were Samson's own kin, and there was a dilemma. In the end they agreed to let Samson deal with them himself, on his return.

And he would, Delilah thought with satisfaction. And she would watch him do it.

Baasha was dead. From the way Keturah mentioned it, it was plain she thought Delilah responsible. But they were entering in at the great gates–the same that Samson had carried from the wall, unbelievably, looking at them–and further conversation was impossible. Delilah began to tremble uncontrollably. She drew the curtains shut and did not turn her head again until they had climbed the hill to the temple, slowing for the throng, the clamor of the street pressing in on her, and were inside the comparative quiet of the courtyard; and they set the palanquin down.

"You have come," Saph said.

Beyond his taut face she saw the reason for the quiet: four of the temple girls were coming to the end of the famous Dance of the Four Seasons, which is performed with no music but the tinsel whispering of tambourines, their streamer ribbons interweaving in complicated patterns of color that made her dizzy. In the violent sunlight, the dancing shadows had more substance than the dancers themselves. It was a moment before she recognized that Autumn was Tahara. The center was kept clear, affording ample room for the palanquin to return as it had come without disturbing the dance; the rest of the court was packed like a sheep pen before the shearing. The cloisters underneath the houses of the prostitutes on both sides were tiered with trestles, so that they appeared to be crammed with faces piled horridly one of top of another, like a melon harvest, many twisting toward the newest arrival to see who she was behind the veil. These, like the royal party within the columned arches before her, colorful as a bazaar, had at least shade; the rest, overcrowding the flat roof that extended back over the sanctuary, seemed heedless of the sun, jostling silently for a better view. They swam in her vision like the faces of her dreams; and then she passed beneath, following the yellow of Saph's flowing robe to a cushioned stool. His arm supported her. After a little he held a cup to her lips, awkwardly because of the veil, until she lifted her hand to a corner of the gauze and removed it altogether. There was a sudden falling away of conversation, the sharp scrape of a chair; but she did not lift her eyes, and presently it was resumed.

She was afraid of the wine; but Saph with characteristic thoughtfulness had watered it, and it was only cool and refreshing. Samson would have spat it out in disgust. She turned her head then deliberately to look for him, and met the startled gaze of the young Achish of Gath who crimsoned, his bulk shrinking inside his silks; beyond him Hanno in profile, leaning across to talk to a jeweled woman Delilah did not recognize. In the brilliant extravagance of their state robes it was hard to recognize anyone. She had difficulty in focusing, besides. They were spaced along the laden trestles, facing the court; from the scattered platters and depleted dishes, the feasting was far advanced. More than a few were lolling with a surfeit already. The nodding snowfall of Raphah's head gave him away, and on her other hand she managed to identify Abimelech of Ekron. All the Seren with their innumerable kin seemed to be here but Samson, who would have stood out in any gathering, was not. Saph was watching her closely. She said, "Where is he?"

"Athol? Of course, you couldn't know. In the palace. He is under house arrest."

She had not noticed Athol's absence. She said impatiently, "Samson."

"Presently."

He touched her arm reassuringly and turned to answer one of the priests, who had paused in passing to bend with some message. A roar of applause all about them drowned what was said. The dancers had gone, and in the yard two huge men were wrestling in the sun, their glistening bodies naked but for their saqs.

The significance of what Saph had said penetrated her clouded mind. She looked for Hanno again, with a sudden, sick urgency. His face was toward her now and he nodded, acknowledging her presence without expression, and looked away. He was placed exactly in the center of the royal party, in the seat of honor where Athol should have been. And behind his seat, what she had certainly seen before, but had not taken in, a javelin, that stood tall, thrust into the ground with a yellow pennant drooping limply from its shaft.

The flag of the Lord of Battles.

When she signaled for the wine-bearer Saph protested, but seeing her face, filled her cup himself. It was not diluted this time, and though it made her head spin, it eased the knot in her stomach. Saph was asking if she wished to leave, and she told him, "No." The music was loud now; there was singing, much of it from the roof overhead, an animal noise like kine lowing, not much in tune. One of the Seren–she could not make out which–had slid under the trestles, and servants gathered like bees to lift him back to his seat. A man, a priest, stood in the court alone, the sun shining on his bald head, making some sort of speech. She saw two priests; and by closing an eye, one.

"Our god has delivered Samson into our hands: our enemy and the destroyer of our country, who slew many of our people. Rejoice to Dagon! Rejoice!"

She asked Saph, her head against his shoulder, "What does he say?" and he told her, "Samson is coming now."

The next moment the court was suddenly cleared and

empty; to a rising fanfare of trumpets the far gates drew apart and opened. The cheering was deafening, and Delilah put her hands to her ears. People everywhere were rising, banging their hands on trestles with a roar of applause. Saph's hand, under her arm, brought her to her feet with the rest. There were soldiers, their headplumes stiff and upright, their body armor glinting, spears advancing in line like a moving fence. It was only when they had come well forward, and parted marching left and right that she saw Samson in their midst.

16

THERE WAS A BOY with him, a young slave who led him forward by the hand, the way you sometimes see the children of the poor lead their aged, and this puzzled her, for there was nothing infirm about Samson's massive figure. His simple tunic, at odds with the flamboyance on every side, only emphasized the treelike girth of his bare arms and legs. Only his head was bowed, displaying the new growth of hair, a curly black cap, which made him look like a boy himself. The soldiers wheeled and withdrew, leaving the uneven pair alone, facing the royal tables. Hanno was on his feet in a sudden silence.

"Samson of Dan!"

He lifted his head.

Delilah felt the ground tilt beneath her. She had Saph's hand under her arm still and had turned her unveiled face toward Samson like an exposed nerve, to be sure he saw her. Only Saph prevented her from falling.

"Is it you, Hanno?" Samson called. "Still ploughing with my heifer."

Few present could have understood the meaning; but the taunting tone, and the rush of blood to Hanno's face started a swell of uncertain laughter and cheering among the crowd in anticipation of some sport. Hanno's reply, if he made one, was lost in the surge of those behind to see what would happen next. Twice Delilah was nearly knocked down. Hysteria lent her a strength to fight and claw a demented path through the human wolf-pack, the grinning faces thrust close to her own, clutching her veil against the regurgitated wine fumes, fighting off hands that tore at her garments, and then abruptly gave way; and she was through the narrowness of the sanctuary door, in the dark and alone.

Hanno found her there much later, widening the door to illuminate the small heap on the flagstones at the feet of Dagon, retching with sobs like a whipped child.

He regarded her without compassion. "Saph is looking everywhere for you. You have led us quite a dance, have you not."

She did not answer, and he said, "Now it is Samson who dances for us. . . . Can't you hear them applauding? And you are not even watching."

"No one told me."

He had to stoop to catch the words above the commotion outside.

"That he is blind? It is ironical, is it not? He will never see what they have done to your pretty face. You are lucky."

Delilah lifted her head then. This time the words were clear. "As Dagon is my witness, I will kill you, Hanno."

He took a pace back at such vehemence; and laughed. "Why me? It was your friend Athol who had him blinded, not I."

"You are lying. He was under Athol's protection. He was to be made governor of Dan."

"So he was. We all know about your little scheme, Delilah. You were very clever. You played upon one man's greed, another's vanity, the lust of a third; on ambition and self-love and vindictiveness–all the things you understood and knew about. But you didn't understand integrity, and never allowed for it. Perhaps it's a man's word. Not even the gods can bestow honors on a man except he consents to receive them, and your Hebrew refused. They kept him in chains in the prison here, turning the wheel that grinds the corn like the stiffnecked ox he is, until he came to his senses;

but he never did. You cannot help admiring a man like that, however stupid. There was a council of the Seren called to decide on the manner of his death; I'd have voted for an honorable death myself, though the gods know I owe him no favors! But in the meantime that bastard Athol had his eyes put out. It cost Athol his office, and he may be exiled yet."

Delilah was sitting cross-legged, her face a crooked mask of pain. She said slowly, "What did the council decide to do with Samson."

"Nothing. There was no decision; no meeting." Hanno turned at a sudden increase in the noise outside. "You know the law . . . or perhaps you do not. A blind man is under the protection of the gods, and may not be harmed. When they have finished their sport with Samson he will be released."

In the doorway, he said, "He is all yours now, Delilah. You will make a pretty pair."

He was long gone before she stirred. He had let the door swing to, and the sanctuary's darkness was almost total, a dark womb that sheltered her for a little from the inescapable grief of being alive. It meant that the door was well made. The old man Jason had told her that once—he had seemed old to her then: a door made by a craftsman will close of itself if unhindered. A door in the house had closed on her foot, a heavy door, and she had wept; and Jason chanced to be passing. It was one of the few occasions he ever spoke to her directly; the day before she led Samson to Tamam's grave.

Without his eyes, he was no danger to the Philistines or anyone else. The Hebrews too, she was sure, had the same law, that none should harm a blind man. Perhaps it embraced the maimed also, like herself. She had returned all but a handful of shekels; without Saph's favor she had nothing. Hanno had no further use for her; he would never permit her to return to the house at Timnath. *You will make a pretty pair*—the contemptuous dismissal was final.

Not pretty: a blind giant and a disfigured woman, to excite only derision or pity, like the beggars in the streets of Gaza or Ashkelon, beseeching alms. Yet they lived.

She lifted her eyes slowly to the height of the god towering above her, the head lost in the dimness, and threw her head forward and spat. The spittle ran down one bronze leg.

"You think Delilah is beaten," she hissed, and jumped to her feet. "But she is not!"

Even beggars lived.

And loved one another.

□

The soft living with Delilah had put flesh on Samson, as had Bilhah's overfeeding once before; the prison fodder and inhuman labor had stripped it off again. He was as hard and fit as he had ever been. The burning warmth of the sun on his shoulders, after his long incarceration, felt as if he had come into the presence of Adonai again. He was free of fetters for the first time in months, and rubbed his wrists for the pleasure of it. They had sent for him from the prison house to make sport for them. What he knew, and they did not, was that his former strength had returned. Standing there in the warmth of Yahweh's favor, he was sure of it.

If they wanted sport, they should have it.

He had already performed the shepherds' dance, the crowd at first roaring and stamping their feet, waiting for him to stumble; but he was nimble and sure; the better so when the musicians took up the unfamiliar rhythms on drum and cymbals. It was the slave boy, opposite Samson and aping him comically, who was clumsy. Finding himself unexpectedly the object of derision, the boy ran behind Samson and tripped him, and was rewarded with howls of approval, no whit abated when Samson caught him by the ankle and swung him thrice around his head before setting him tenderly back to earth, whereupon he immediately fell on his face. This was better than bear-baiting.

The temple dancers were better still. At a signal from between the pillars where Hanno sat in the shade, a dozen of them flowed into the court on a tide of music, rushing on Samson from the four quarters to whirl away again at the last moment, their bright streamers brushing his empty face and slipping through his outstretched fingers. Amid the darting, butterfly figures, Samson revolved oafishly, clutching the air in short and futile rushes. Men and women stood to shout encouragement.

"Let's see you catch one!"

"Come on Samson–pin them down!"

"Tie their tails together!"

"You don't need eyes–sniff them out!"

The dancers themselves, emboldened by their success, joined in.

"Catch me then, Hebrew!"

"Ho thirsty one–let me refresh you!"

"Here I am–here–here"

"Come grind my corn!"

One girl, slower than the rest, he did catch, his fingers locked on her arm. In the uproar she pressed against him, as if to twist free. "It is Tahara. Delilah is here." He made a display of struggling to hold her, remembering her smell. "You can help me, Tahara. Quickly–the temple at Ashkelon: is this the same?" She whispered, "The same; bigger." He said, "But built the same–the side houses, the sanctuary?" "Yes." He loosed his hold and stumbled a few steps blindly after her, adding his voice to the disappointment of the crowd.

After that they tied a lion skin on him, the head lolling fiercely above his own, and a handful of Hanno's captains, dressed as hunters, pursued him about the court with blunted staves for spears. Several onlookers left the shelter of the cloisters to run and join in the fun; more followed, most of them too drunk to threaten him with more than words; but the staves were hard, and not all to be avoided. Samson caught the ends of several and pulled the attackers off balance, but he was careful not to harm them, not to show his strength. He roared realistically, all the louder when a buffet penetrated his whirling arms. The sweat ran down inside the skin, already noisome, and he slowed with a show of exhaustion. It ended when someone threw a net over him. They brought him to the ground, still growling, and dragged him to Hanno in a tumult of cheering that echoed from the walls, through which one word became audible, repeated to a slow, surging pulse of *More, more, more.*

Hanno lifted his hand. "We have had enough of this buffoon. Release him and give him something to drink. And let us see something more amusing."

Delilah, squeezing between a portly Philistine and the

cool of a pillar, intercepted the slave boy and took the cup from his hand. She had found a common robe among the many discarded for the heat, and was veiled again. The boy did not know her, and was disposed to argue, but she pulled the veil aside and he stepped back startled. Samson sat in the sun to one side, and she squatted to put the cup into his hand. He seized it gratefully, rolling the first mouthful round his tongue to spit it out between them. Two Nubians were carrying a burning brazier into the open court, followed by a strutting young man who looked like an Egyptian, his thin muscular body bared to the waist, elaborately girdled over flowing golden skirts. The sweat ran freely from Samson's matted hair, into the blackened sockets that blinked and screwed up to nothing, like the sucked-in mouth of a toothless man. It coursed in furrows through the dust on his cheeks, and dripped from his chin. The familiar grin tore her heart from her body.

"Delilah?"

The Egyptian had his hand to his mouth. He threw his head back and belched forth a stream of living flame into the air. The applause gave her a moment.

"How could you know?"

"Tahara told me. But I knew you were here somewhere."

"You are hurt."

She heard herself say it. The absurdity of the remark betrayed deserts of remoteness between them. But it was true: his arms were purpled with bruising from the staves, which showed again through the fray of his torn tunic. He drank from the wine cup, and wiped his mouth with the back of his hand with satisfaction, and said, "It is not important," which was true also.

The fire eater had a sword. He held it upright, the point between his teeth. He began to slide it down his straitened throat. A fat man to their left climbed into a trestle, toppled, and fell backward into the crowd. The din was tremendous.

"You are crying."

He had still not touched her. He said, "They told me you were dead. At the hands of my own people. I never believed them."

"You must have wished me dead."

"No."

"Hated me."

"Aye," he said: "that. But I never threw a javelin at you."

"Oh, Samson! Samson!" The empty wine cup rolled in the sand as she clasped his hand and pressed it to her forehead, regardless of who saw her. There were no more tears left; only a spark of hope more terrifying than all her grief. She lifted her head fearfully. "Only say we can be together again."

He reached to find her hair, and touch it. *Adonai!* His hand fell back.

He said gently, "Who shall separate us now, one from the other?"

She became aware of external things: of men brawling on the roof; faces turned in their direction; an ache in her legs. She reached her his hand again. So much to say; but not now. "Come!"

"There is something I have to do. Send the boy to me—the lad who brought me here."

"There is no need. I will be your eyes."

Samson shook his head, smiling. "No. Wait for me beyond the gates."

She was too happy to argue. "Where shall we live?"

"Where we have always lived."

"Hanno will hardly suffer me to stay at Timnath."

"Timnath is only a place."

"I love you."

"And I you," he said; "And I you. Now go quickly."

He listened for the departing rush of her garments, seeing her in imagination hastening obediently across the sand toward the double gates, which must be before him, and a little to the right; then he remembered that she had to find the boy first. The houses of the prostitutes, male and female, were to his left and right, according to Tahara, where most of the noise came from. These would be townspeople, sheltered from the sun in the covered ways; the girls, except those who danced like Tahara, would be up at their windows with a few favored guests; they would be out later, when the gates were opened and the festival moved into the streets for activities more suited to the dark. The Philistines of any importance would be behind him, under the arched terrace where Hanno was, and on the roof above, which would afford the best view. The boy announced himself sulkily by asking what he wanted now.

"I am not bound to attend you any more. You are free to go. Why didn't you go with the funny woman?"

"What funny woman?"

"The one who sent me; who took the cup out of my hand before and brought it to you herself. I thought she belonged to you."

"Aye," Samson said; "she does." And he said, "Why was she funny?"

"Scarface. Her eyes are all crooked. Not so funny as yours, though."

She had been injured, then. Why had she not said? Did she think it would make any difference? Samson raised himself slowly, and sensed the boy move back. "Don't be afraid."

"Who is afraid of *you!*"

"Take my hand, then. Take me into the shade; I want to rest my head against a pillar–there are pillars? When did she go?"

"Just now."

They were under the roof, a sudden change in the air and voices close by; there was a step up, which there had not been at Ashkelon. Samson asked if she was still in sight, and the boy turned indifferently. "No."

Then he said, "Yes. She is there at the gates."

"Go after her. Tell her to be sure to wait outside the wall."

"Go after her yourself," the boy said.

Samson scarcely heard him. At the gates he saw her hesitate, looking back over her shoulder at him, and there was no scar; the violet eyes were clear and level, those marvelous eyes with their half-teasing, half-quizzical look he had seen a thousand thousand times. He thought she turned away, pulling the purple-red of her shawl over her head; he could not be sure.

"Do as I say," he told the boy. "For your own sake–run now."

There was no answer. Someone–a woman–gave him a

flagon with ale in it, and farther down the tables there was a burst of laughter. A man, coming out into the court, stumbled over him and swore, crushing his robes to get past, and cursed him again for sitting there in the way.

He knew then that he had judged right.

He leaned forward from the pillar against which he sat and almost at once his outstretched fingers touched another. He got to his feet, and slid his fingers up to be sure. The pillars in the temple at Ashkelon had been widely spaced, with five or six paces in between.

And then he remembered: except in the center. The central arch had been much wider, affording as it did the chief access to the sanctuary, along a walk of colored mosaics. The symmetry had been retained by pairing the two pillars to either side, which device must also serve to strengthen the wider span, the main support of the great roof.

He stood between the loadbearing pillars of the whole temple building.

Remember Samson, Adonai.

He took one in each arm, facing outward toward the court, and slid his palms down until he was half-crouching, spreading the soles of his feet on the flagstones before anyone noticed. The pillars were like rock, slippery with sweat and immovable. He heard the crack of his own joints: an uncertain laugh. The voices gathering in about him.

"It's Samson!"

"What is he doing?"

"The blind man"–a woman's voice. "He thinks he has found a lover."

"Two lovers!"

"He is mad. Take care he doesn't bite you!"

"Lord Hanno! Come and see this!"

Lord Hanno. He was a lord now.

The darkness reddened. Samson could feel his right foot begin to slip. *Strengthen me this once more, Adonai. That I may be revenged for just one of my two eyes.*

"He prays to his god!"

"He's away to the hills, Samson."

"Pray to Dagon! Maybe he will give you your eyes back."

"Let me die," Samson said, "with these Philistines."

And he threw himself forward with the last and utmost strength of his being.

It was those to the front of the roof, stretching their necks to discover the cause of so much hilarity below, who first saw the crack in the paving, which appeared immediately under their feet. Their screams stopped the music and turned every head in the court upward.

The right-hand pillar gave first. It did not break at once, being constructed of single stone blocks of massive proportions, rounded off and strongly mortared together with a mixture of sea shells and potsherds ground into tempered clay under the plaster; but it came away at the base. The capital, losing support, dropped a double span of two hands' breadth, the stone above sagging under its own weight, which the second pillar might have sustained but for the sudden increase of the multitude above, scrambling over one another in panic flight away from the subsidence.

Delilah, returning through the gates with a burning impatience for him to come to her, saw both pillars fall, one atop the other in a giant cross, burying all beneath in a thunderous disintegration whose rising dust met the fall of masonry interspersed with colored figures like rag dolls tossed from a child's crib, and swallowed them.

"Samson!"

The screaming was continuous on all sides; even if he was alive, he could never have heard her. She could not go back to him; the court was an incoming torrent of fleeing men and women, brutish with fear; she had to press back to the wall to escape being trampled. Above them the dust cleared, revealing less than half the roof still standing, massed with clinging figures which, even as she watched, unable to look away, began to tilt, spilling its human burden onto the rubble far below. The line of pillars buckled one by one, like the fingers of a slowly closing hand. Those beneath who had not yet reached the open court were too late.

She turned away, remembering to veil herself, and joined the throng making its way into the street.

□

Some two thousand Philistines, men and woman, and half as many again of their Canaanite followers, perished that day in Gaza.

Of the five Seren only two, Athol and Saph–who had left the court in his fruitless search for Delilah–were spared. The succession was hereditary, and for every son who was with his father in the temple when it fell, there was a younger son safe at home, or a cousin, and no lack of uncles to tutor them until they came of age. Replacing the Captains of chariots and footsoldiers, the majority of whom had been included in the royal party on Hanno's insistence, was less simple, and Athol spent the first day of his return to office with his scribes, drawing up a list of promotions and training schemes.

He was interrupted by a deputation from Zorah led by Jemuel ben Jethro, requesting the body of Samson. They had a long journey back and since the body must be buried before morning, this being summer, Athol agreed at once.

Saph was surprised. He had been out all day supervising the handing over of remains himself, but to their own people. He looked exhausted and depressed. "Is that wise? Will they not set up a shrine to him? Then he will always be there, to remind them."

Athol looked at him.

"What difference does it make?"

And he said, "Who is ever going to forget him now?"

□

They buried Samson in the vale between Zorah and Eshtaol, by the stream under the oleanders, alongside the grave of his father Manoah. There was no shrine, nor any need of one. Before the summer ended his name was on the lips of every man, woman and child in Israel. No Hebrew would ever look upon Philistine in the same way again. The invincible had been beaten; and could be again. No man–none–could stand against the chosen of Yahweh.

In Mizpeh, on the borderlands of Benjamin, the prophet Samuel began to prepare his call to the clan chiefs for the third time. *Gather all Israel to Mizpeh, and I Samuel will pray for you to Yahweh.*

This time, they would come.

Only Sharah and Jemuel's sister Abigail visited Samson's resting place daily, as Sharah had visited that of his father, for a twelve-month and a day after his death. They were returning from the grave together, one early morning after the rains, when the woman came down the path toward them. The first crocuses were out, and Sharah had stopped to give thanks for them, as she always did. The woman passed her without a word, and it was not until she had gone by that Sharah recognized her.

"Delilah!"

Abigail, pausing to wait for her, turned her head. "You spoke?"

"To that woman," Sharah said. She saw Abigail's face. "You saw her. You must have seen."

Abigail shook her head, concerned for her, for Sharah was an old woman now; the climb was too much for her. "Nobody comes here but us. You know that."

In Ashkelon, in the great canopied bed beside Saph, Delilah turned in her sleep, but did not waken.